John Stuart White

Recent Examination Papers for Admission to Harvard, Yale, Princeton, Sheffield Scientific School, and Columbia School of Mines

John Stuart White

Recent Examination Papers for Admission to Harvard, Yale, Princeton, Sheffield Scientific School, and Columbia School of Mines

ISBN/EAN: 9783337165178

Printed in Europe, USA, Canada, Australia, Japan

Cover: Foto ©Paul-Georg Meister /pixelio.de

More available books at **www.hansebooks.com**

RECENT
EXAMINATION PAPERS

FOR ADMISSION TO

HARVARD, YALE, PRINCETON, SHEFFIELD SCIENTIFIC SCHOOL, AND COLUMBIA SCHOOL OF MINES.

SELECTED AND EDITED FOR THE USE OF PREPARATORY SCHOOLS

JOHN S. WHITE, LL.D.,

HEAD MASTER OF BERKELEY SCHOOL, NEW YORK CITY.

BOSTON:
PUBLISHED BY GINN & COMPANY.
1888.

Entered according to Act of Congress, in the year 1888, by
JOHN S. WHITE,
in the Office of the Librarian of Congress, at Washington.

TYPOGRAPHY BY J. S. CUSHING & CO., BOSTON.

PRESSWORK BY GINN & CO., BOSTON.

PREFACE.

The work of preparing students for the three or four leading colleges of America (with the advanced requisitions made during the last three or four years) has become so complicated that it can be thoroughly done only by the expert teacher who keeps himself thoroughly informed as to the methods used in the various colleges and the peculiarities of the individual examination papers presented. As these colleges are quietly but steadily pushing on to that point where they will become universities in fact, as well as in name, the necessity for admitting young men at a greater age than formerly grows more and more apparent. Harvard College in particular, after introducing the elective system into all classes of undergraduates, has adjusted the character of its entrance examinations in such a way as to ask for *original* work and thought from the candidates for admission, not only in mathematics and physics, but in the languages. The old idea of preparation for college, that a boy must have read a stipulated number of the orations of Cicero, and just so many books of Homer and Xenophon, and be examined upon that and that only, has been entirely discarded, and to-day the candidate must be practically able to read Latin, Greek, and either French or German, *at sight;* and in geometry and algebra he finds more than one-half of the matter demanded from him put into the form of original problems or demonstrations. In other words, he must have just about as good a training, if not as good an education, in original thought and correct methods, as the entire college curriculum of fifty years ago could have given to him; and the preparatory school of to-day, or the private tutor, must be competent to carry the student to this point.

What is true of Harvard is true to a less extent of three or four other leading colleges; and while, happily, for this reason, it is no longer possible to make "cramming" for a special examination take the place of genuine training, the necessity for understanding the specific demands of the various colleges, as indicated in their examination papers, has become vastly more necessary than before. In the compilation from recent examinations which this volume presents, the aim has been to select those papers which will give to the teacher in this higher work the best understanding of what the colleges demand, and the work is intended to be used as a regular text-book during the last year or two of the preparatory course. In the case of Harvard and Yale, one full set of the papers given at the last examination has been presented, and a number of other earlier examinations, selected as practice papers, have been printed consecutively. It is a matter of regret that the faculty of Columbia College objected to the printing of the admission papers to the School of Arts.

Many an able and industrious student prepared by a teacher who is not expert, fails to do himself justice on college entrance examinations, for the simple reason that he was not taught accurately what the college would ask for and how it would present its questions. To neglect the opportunity which lies within the reach of every teacher is as culpable as it would be for the captain of a yacht to enter a race with no previous understanding of the prevailing currents and signals or the character of the course over which he is to sail.

PAPERS

OF

HARVARD UNIVERSITY.

NEW METHOD.

September, 1887.

PRESCRIBED.

ENGLISH COMPOSITION. 1.

Write a composition — with special attention to clearness of arrangement, accuracy of expression, and quality rather than quantity of matter — on one of the following subjects: —

1. The Story of Milton's Life.
2. The Story of the First Book of Paradise Lost.
3. Macaulay's Estimate of Paradise Lost.
4. An Outline of the Story of Quentin Durward.
5. The Character of King Louis XI. as represented by Scott.

PRESCRIBED.

ENGLISH COMPOSITION. 2.

SPECIMENS OF BAD ENGLISH.

[Write your number on this paper.]

Correct on this paper all the errors you discover in the following sentences — the work of candidates for admission to Harvard College: —

1. Quentin Durward as we know was escaping with Isabelle's aunt thinking it to be the girl he loved.

2. He was willing to undertake no journey or decide upon any plan until he had found out whether the stars foretold a result favorable to him.

3. I dont think he ever really trusted any one, for even if they might have saved his life he would find some fault or rather in him.

4. The Duke of Burgundy was roused to such anger that he caused the king's imprisonment, whom he thought helped the matter on.

5. He has no moral scruples about anything; and they have.

6. Instead of going up the side of the river he intended, he remained on the same side he was.

7. Very interesting is the description given by Scott of the famous men of that time, Louis and his barber, etc., — who exerted a powerful influence over the superstitious mind of Louis.

8. William thought that Louis would aid him, and, without doubt, he would have, had he not feared the Duke of Burgundy.

9. Quentin finds Isabelle, prepared for the worst, and when, having induced her to disguise herself, they endeavor to escape they find flight impossible.

10. He sent Quentin's uncle with an order to enscribe his scotish relation in the guards.

11. He was very superstitious, and before undertaking a great project he always consulted the heavens to find if the affair would be successful or not.

12. Of large frame and bulk, fierce expression and harsh voice, we seem to almost see before us this monster.

13. Galeotti, having gone to him and being about to be slain, as a last resource told the King that he read in the

stars, that he (Galeotti) would die just twenty-four hours before the death of His Majesty would take place.

14. After the old man had left Quentin and having seen his uncle, the youth, having an adventurous spirit, wandering from the inn came upon several people looking at something up a tree.

15. Quentin marries his lady love and died after a most happy life full of adventures.

ELEMENTARY GREEK.

ATTIC PROSE AT SIGHT.

You are advised not to write any part of the translation until you have read the passage through two or three times.

Divide your time equally between the translation and the questions.

[SUBJECT. — The victory of Agesilaus at Coroneia, in 394 B.C.]

TRANSLATE: —

Ἐπειδὴ δὲ ἡ μὲν νίκη σὺν Ἀγησιλάῳ ἐγένετο, τετρωμένος δ' αὐτὸς προσηνέχθη πρὸς τὴν φάλαγγα, προσελάσαντές τινες τῶν ἱππέων λέγουσιν αὐτῷ ὅτι τῶν πολεμίων ὀγδοήκοντα σὺν τοῖς ὅπλοις ὑπὸ τῷ ναῷ εἰσι,
5 καὶ ἠρώτων, τί χρὴ ποιεῖν. Ὁ δὲ καίπερ πολλὰ τραύματα ἔχων πάντοσε καὶ παντοίοις ὅπλοις ὅμως οὐκ ἐπελάθετο τοῦ θείου, ἀλλ' ἐάν τε ἀπιέναι ὅποι βούλοιντο ἐκέλευε καὶ ἀδικεῖν οὐκ εἴα, καὶ προπέμψαι ἐπέταξε τοὺς ἀμφ' αὐτὸν ἱππεῖς ἔστε ἐν τῷ ἀσφαλεῖ
10 ἐγένοντο. Ἐπεί γε μὴν ἔληξεν ἡ μάχη, παρῆν δὴ θεάσασθαι, ἔνθα συνέπεσον ἀλλήλοις, τὴν μὲν γῆν αἵματι πεφυρμένην,[1] νεκροὺς δὲ κειμένους φιλίους καὶ πολεμίους μετ' ἀλλήλων, ἀσπίδας δὲ διατεθρυμμένας,[2] δόρατα συντεθραυσμένα, ἐγχειρίδια γυμνὰ κολεῶν,[3] τὰ μὲν χα-

[1] φύρω, *soil, defile.* [2] θρύπτω, *shiver.* [3] κολεός, *sheath.*

15 μαί, τὰ δ' ἐν σώμασι, τὰ δ' ἔτι μετὰ χεῖρας. Τότε μὲν οὖν, καὶ γὰρ ἦν ἤδη ὀψέ, συνελκύσαντες τοὺς νεκροὺς εἴσω φάλαγγος ἐδειπνοποιήσαντο καὶ ἐκοιμήθησαν· πρωὶ δὲ Γῦλιν τὸν πολέμαρχον παρατάξαι τε ἐκέλευσε τὸ στράτευμα καὶ τρόπαιον ἵστασθαι, καὶ στεφανοῦσθαι
20 πάντας τῷ θεῷ καὶ τοὺς αὐλητὰς πάντας αὐλεῖν.

XEN. *Ages.* II. 13-15.

ANSWER THE FOLLOWING : —

(*a*) Decline in the plural number the nouns to which the forms ναῷ (4) and φάλαγγος (13) belong.

(*b*) In what tense, mood, and voice is τετρωμένος (1)? Analyze this form, showing how it is built up from the simple stem.

(*c*) Give the principal parts of τάσσω (14). Inflect its aorist subjunctive passive.

(*d*) Give the derivation of τρόπαιον (14), by naming the ultimate verb-stem and intermediative noun-stem from which it is formed, and give as many Greek words from the same stems, with their meanings, as you can recall.

(*e*) Account for the case of αἵματι (19) and of φάλαγγος (13).

(*f*) Account for the tense of προσελάσαντες (2) and of ἔχον (5).

(*g*) In what other mood might εἰσι (4) have been? State the principle.

(*h*) Explain the construction of ἐᾶν and ἀπιέναι (6) and of ἀδικεῖν (6).

ELEMENTARY LATIN.

I. TRANSLATE : —

At Drappes unaque Lucterius, cum legiones Caniniumque adesse cognoscerent, nec se sine certa pernicie persequente exercitu putarent provinciae fines intrare posse, nec iam liberam vagandi latrociniorumque faciendorum facultatem haberent, consistunt in agris Cadurcorum. Ibi cum Lucterius apud suos cives quondam integris rebus multum potuisset, semperque auctor novorum consiliorum magnam apud barbaros auctoritatem haberet, oppidum Uxellodunum, quod in clientela fuerat eius, natura loci egregie munitum, occupat suis et Drappetis copiis, oppidanosque sibi coniungit. Quo cum confestim C. Caninius venisset, animadverteretque omnes oppidi partes praeruptissimis saxis esse munitas, quo defendente nullo tamen armatis ascendere esset difficile, magna autem impedimenta oppidanorum videret, quae si clandestina fuga subtrahere conarentur, effugere non modo equitatum, sed ne legiones quidem possent, tripertito cohortibus divisis trina excelsissimo loco castra fecit, a quibus paullatim, quantum copiae patiebantur, vallum in oppidi circuitum ducere instituit.

Give all the participles and infinitives of *cognoscerent*.
Give the future indicative of *vagandi* and *munitum*.
Compare *libere* and *difficile*.
Decline *pernicie*.
Derivation of *impedimenta, tripertito, oppidanos*.
Construction of *persequente, faciendorum, saxis, armatis*.

II. TRANSLATE:—

Iusiurandum apud Romanos inviolate sancteque habitum servatumque est. Id et moribus legibusque multis ostenditur, et hoc, quod dicemus, ei rei non tenue argumentum esse potest. Post proelium Cannense Hannibal, Carthaginiensium imperator, ex captivis nostris electos decem Romam misit mandavitque eis pactusque est, ut, si populo Romano videretur, permutatio fieret captivorum et pro his, quos alteri plures acciperent, darent argenti pondo libram et selibram. Hoc, priusquam proficiscerentur, iusiurandum eos adegit, redituros esse in castra Poenica, si Romani captivos non permutarent.

ELEMENTARY GERMAN.

[No. I., if well translated, will be enough. A good rendering of II. will compensate in some measure for deficiencies in I.]

I. TRANSLATE: —

Es war die Gewohnheit dieses großen Königs, um 5 Uhr des Morgens aufzustehen, bisweilen sogar früher. Er frisierte sich gewöhnlich selbst und gebrauchte selten mehr als zwei Minuten dazu. Nachdem er sich angekleidet hatte, brachte ihm ein Adjutant ein Verzeichnis von allen den Personen, welche in Potsdam angekommen oder von da abgereist waren, und einen Bericht von dem, was sich in der Garnison zugetragen hatte. Wenn er diesem Offizier seine Befehle gegeben hatte, zog er sich in sein Arbeitszimmer zurück, wo er sich allein bis 7 Uhr beschäftigte. Dann ging er in ein andres Zimmer, wo er Kaffee oder Schokolade trank, und hier fand er auf dem Tisch alle die Briefe, welche aus Potsdam, Berlin oder andern Teilen seines Königreichs an ihn gerichtet waren. Ausländische Briefe wurden auf einen besondern Tisch gelegt. Nachdem er alle diese Briefe gelesen hatte, schrieb er Bemerkungen an den Rand derjenigen, welche von seinen Schreibern beantwortet werden sollten. Diejenigen, welche er selbst beantworten wollte, nahm er mit in sein Arbeitszimmer. Hier beschäftigte sich der König bis 9 Uhr mit einem seiner Geheimschreiber. Dann ging er in das vorige Zimmer zurück, wo die Schreiber ihm von dem, was sie gethan hatten, Rechenschaft gaben; worauf ihnen der König seine Befehle gab mit den Briefen, welche sie beantworten sollten. Diese Antworten wurden jedoch niemals abgeschickt, ohne vom König selbst gelesen und unterzeichnet zu sein. Um 10 Uhr begleiteten ihn die Generale, welche um seine Person waren, in sein Arbeitszimmer, wo er sich mit ihnen über die Tagesneuigkeiten, über Politik und andre Gegenstände unterhielt, und zu derselben Zeit gab er verschiednen Personen Audienz. Um 11 Uhr bestieg er sein Pferd und ritt auf die Parade, wo er sein Garderegiment musterte, und zu derselben Stunde, sagt

Voltaire, thaten die Obersten dasselbe in allen Provinzen des König=
reichs. Nachher ging er eine Zeitlang im Garten spazieren, begleitet
von seinen Generalen und der übrigen Gesellschaft, welche er einge=
laden hatte, mit ihm zu Mittag zu speisen. Um 1 Uhr setzte sich
Friedrich zu Tisch. Seine Gesellschaft bestand gewöhnlich aus den
Prinzen, den ausgezeichnetsten Offizieren und einigen berühmten
Gelehrten und Künstlern. Die Unterhaltung war immer sehr leb=
haft, und der König machte selbst die Honneurs wie ein Privatmann.
Nach Tische ging er eine Viertelstunde lang im Zimmer umher, indem
er sich mit einigen seiner Gäste unterhielt. Dann zog er sich in sein
Privatzimmer zurück, spielte die Flöte, unterzeichnete Briefe, trank
Kaffee und arbeitete bis 5 Uhr, wo sein Vorleser erschien. Von 6
bis 7 Uhr war ein Konzert, zu welchem nur Musiker zugelassen
wurden und in welchem sich der König selbst auf der Flöte hören
ließ. Wenn das Konzert vorüber war, nahm Friedrich seine Abend=
mahlzeit ein mit Voltaire, Algarotti, Maupertuis und einigen
andern geistreichen Männern, welche eingeladen worden waren. Um
12 Uhr ging der König zu Bett.

II. TRANSLATE INTO GERMAN:—

Queen Elizabeth was once making a journey in England,
and on her approaching the city of Coventry, the mayor,
with a numerous cavalcade, went out to meet her. On their
return they had to pass through a wide brook, and the mayor's
horse being thirsty, attempted several times to drink, but his
rider prevented him. The queen, observing it, said to him:
"Pray, Mr. Mayor, permit your horse to drink." — The
mayor, bowing very humbly, replied: "Madam, it would be
the height of presumption for my unworthy horse to drink
till your Majesty's royal steed has satisfied his thirst."

ELEMENTARY FRENCH.

I. Translate into English:—

Il faisait nuit noire, sans lune et sans étoile. Je venais de quitter Grenoble, et j'allais traverser Voreppe, petit village non sans quelque importance à cause du voisinage de la Grande Chartreuse, qui attire, tous les ans, à cette époque, moins de croyants que de curieux. Tout d'un coup les chevaux s'arrêtèrent, j'entendis au dehors une sourde rumeur, et les vitres de ma voiture furent frappées d'une lueur sanglante, que j'aurais prise pour celle du couchant si le soleil n'eût été depuis longtemps couché. Je mis pied à terre ; l'unique auberge du village brûlait. C'était dans ce petit hameau un remue-ménage infernal. On criait, on courait, on se heurtait. Le maître de l'hôtel, aidé de sa femme, de ses enfants et de ses valets, vidait les étables et les écuries. Les chevaux hennissaient, les bœufs mugissaient, tandis que les pourceaux, comme s'ils avaient l'instinct qu'il est dans leur destinée d'être grillés tôt ou tard, opposaient à leurs sauveurs une résistance opiniâtre, pleine de philosophie. Pendant ce temps, les notables de l'endroit, groupés sur la place, discouraient magistralement sur les causes de l'incendie, que personne ne s'occupait d'éteindre, et qui, enflammant la nuit sombre et embrasant les coteaux d'alentour, lançait au ciel avec furie ses gerbes et ses fusées d'étincelles. Vous, poète, vous auriez trouvé cela beau.—Jules Sandeau.

[A good translation of the above passage is required to pass the examination ; the following questions are added to enable candidates to make up for any slight deficiencies in the translation.]

II. Translate into English:—

(*a*) Je viens voir votre frère.
(*b*) Je viens de voir votre frère.

III. Translate into French: —

I see him. I speak to him. I speak to her. I spoke to her. I gave her your letter, and she returned it to me. I will never read it to you. My school is better than yours. He has more than a hundred books. Better late than never.

IV. Write in French a dozen lines about your native place.

HISTORY OF THE UNITED STATES.

[Take 1 and three others.]

1. Hispaniola, Fort St. George, Williamsburg, Fort Christiana, Lundy's Lane, Harper's Ferry, — where?

2. State the provisions of the Boston "Port-Bill." What was its effect?

3. What have been the principal annexations of territory made by the United States since 1800?

4. [Take any two.] The Alien and Sedition laws; the Monroe Doctrine; the Alabama Claims.

5. [Take any three.] Robert Fulton, John C. Calhoun, Samuel F. B. Morse, George H. Thomas.

Questions on the "additional reading."

6. Describe the state of society in Virginia in 1765, and contrast it with that of New England at the same time.

7. What is your impression of John Adams? of Lafayette? of John Randolph?

HISTORY OF ENGLAND.

[Take 1 and three others.]

1. Give the geographical position of Cumberland, Somerset, Worcester, Naseby, the Severn, the Tweed.

2. Mention the Danish kings of England. What was *Danelagh? Danegeld?*

3. [Take ONE.] Thomas Becket, Cardinal Wolsey.

4. [Take ONE.] The Rebellion of Wat Tyler; the Gunpowder Plot.

5. [Take TWO.] The battles of Senlac, Culloden, and Quebec. [Give dates.]

Question on the "additional reading."

6. [MACAULAY.] The English country gentleman in the 17th century.

ANCIENT HISTORY.

I.

(*a*) [Take FIVE.] The Allia, Agrigentum, Lilybaeum, Placentia, Cannae, Numantia, Massilia, — where? Mention (with dates) historical events connected with four of these places.

(*b*) [Take FIVE.] Sybaris, Delos, Phocis, Sardis, Megalopolis, Potidaea, Delium, — where? Mention (with dates) historical events connected with four of these places.

II.

[Take any two.]

1. How were the members of the Roman Senate chosen at different times?

2. The origin of the Praetorship. What were the duties of the Praetor?

3. Describe or explain any five: — pater patratus, Feriae Latinae, Curia, equites, flamines, the Licinian laws, the law of Majestas.

Questions on the "additional reading."

[Candidates who have read the books recommended for additional reading may substitute one of the following questions for one of the first three in this group.]

4. [TIGHE.] How did the practical powers of the Roman Senate differ from its theoretical powers?

5. [BEESLEY.] What can be said in defence of the lex frumentaria of Gaius Gracchus?

III.

[Take any two.]

1. Describe the Spartan constitution. What effect did this constitution have upon the people?

2. The Peace of Calias. What was the result of this peace with reference to Sparta and Thebes?

3. [Take TWO.] Miltiades, Nicias, Aeschylus.

Question on the "additional reading."

[Candidates who have read Curtius may substitute question 4 for one of the first three in this group.]

4. [CURTIUS.] The earlier and later influence of Delphi.

ALGEBRA.

One hour allowed.

[Write legibly and without crowding; give the work clearly and find all possible answers. The shortest methods are preferred.]

1. Solve the following equation, finding four values of x:—

$$(x+a)(x-b) - \frac{a^2(x+a)}{x+b} - \frac{b^2(x-b)}{x-a} = \frac{3a^2b^2}{(x-a)(x+b)}.$$

2. At 6 o'clock on a certain morning, A and B set out on their bicycles from the same place, A going north and B south, to ride until $1\frac{1}{2}$ P.M. A moved constantly northwards at the rate of 6 miles per hour. B also moved always at a fixed rate; but, after a while, he turned back to join A. Four hours after he turned, B passed the point at which A was when B turned; and, at $1\frac{1}{2}$ P.M., when he stopped, he had reduced by one-half the distance that was between them at the time of turning.

Find B's rate, the time at which he turned, the distance between A and B at that time, and the time at which B would have joined A if the ride had been continued at the same rates of speed. Find the answers for *both solutions*.

3. Find the sixth term of each of the following powers:—

$$(x-y)^7 ; \left(\frac{6a^2}{7b\sqrt{b}} - \frac{b}{\sqrt{3a}}\right)^7.$$

4. Reduce the following fraction to its lowest terms:—

$$\frac{6x^4 - 13x^3 + 3x^2 + 2x}{6x^4 - 9x^3 + 15x^2 - 27x - 9}.$$

PLANE GEOMETRY.

One hour allowed.

[In solving problems use for π the approximate value 3⅐.]

1. Prove that every point in the bisector of an angle is equally distant from the sides of the angle; and that every point not in the bisector, but within the angle, is unequally distant from the sides of the angle.

2. Prove that the tangents drawn through the vertices of a rectangle inscribed in a circle enclose a rhombus. What is the area of this rhombus if the rectangle is a square and if the radius of the circle is $4\sqrt{2}$?

3. Prove that the opposite angles of any quadrilateral inscribed in a circle are supplements of each other.

Three of the sides, taken in order, of an inscribed quadrilateral subtend arcs of 80°, 100°, and 60°, respectively; find the angles of the quadrilateral.

4. Prove that the areas of two similar triangles — and thence of any two similar polygons — are to each other as the squares of their homologous sides.

5. Upon each side of a square as a diameter is described a semi-circumference within the square. In this way four leaf-shaped figures are marked out. If the side of the square is 14 feet long, find the areas of the four "leaves."

PHYSICS (Elementary I).

[Candidates who offer alternative (1) of the New Method will take the Astronomy questions instead of Physics questions 4 and 7.]

1. A spring balance is held in a horizontal position and pulled at by two men, one at each end. The pointer indicates 100 lbs. and the balance is at rest. How great is the force exerted by each man?

2. A rod one meter long, whose weight may be neglected, has at one end a mass of 5 kilograms and at the other end a mass of 3 kilograms. How far from the larger mass must a supporting point be placed in order that the whole may be in equilibrium with the rod horizontal?

3. (a) How far can a two-horse-power engine raise 10 tons in 1 minute?

or

(b) A ball is started vertically upward with a velocity of 20 meters per second. How far above the starting-point will it be at the end of 4 seconds?

4. (a) State the velocity of sound in air at some particular temperature. Explain the difference observed between two musical notes equal in pitch and loudness.

or

(b) Give a series of numbers expressing the relative rates of vibration of the notes of the *diatonic*, or *natural*, scale. Explain the following terms relating to this scale: *fifth, fourth, third.*

5. (a) The volume of a certain quantity of gas at 20° C. is 200 cu. cm. What would be its volume at 80° C., the pressure remaining unchanged?

or

(b) State fully your reasons for regarding "radiant heat" and "radiant light" as alike in their nature. Of what substance would you make a lens or prism for handling "radiant heat"? Why? Name a substance, or preparation, which is diathermanous but not transparent.

6. Give the theory of a compound microscope, illustrating carefully by means of a diagram.

7. Describe carefully the construction and action of an induction coil.

ASTRONOMY.

1. About how many stars may be visible to the naked eye at once? What is the *altitude* and *azimuth* of a star? the *right ascension* and *declination*? When is a superior planet said to be in *conjunction* with the sun? when in *opposition*?

2. What is the zodiac? Why are the *signs of the zodiac* so called? Name them. Explain carefully why they do not coincide respectively with the *zodiacal constellations* of the same names.

ALTERNATIVE 2.

ELEMENTARY PHYSICS.

1. Describe fully, but concisely, some experiment in mechanics in which you have spent not less than one and a half hours of laboratory work.

2. If a carriage wheel be resting upright upon the ground, and be prevented from slipping at the bottom, how great a force applied directly downward at the end of the horizontal diameter will just neutralize a force of 50 pounds applied horizontally at the centre of the wheel, both forces being in the same plane?

3. A rod one meter long, whose weight may be neglected, has at one end a mass of 5 kilograms, and at the other end a mass of .3 kilograms. How far from the larger mass must a supporting point be placed in order that the whole may be in equilibrium with the rod horizontal?

4. Define carefully the *dyne* and *erg* or the *poundal* and *foot-poundal.*

5. Describe carefully the process of boiling, showing how it differs from ordinary evaporation.

6. Define the *principal focus* of a lens.

The rays which come to a lens directly from the sun are called *parallel rays*. Does this imply that each ray is practically parallel to all the others? If not, what does it mean?

7. Describe carefully some form of galvanometer that you have used.

ADVANCED GREEK.

[Do either A or B, but not both. Allow one hour for the translation and one hour for the questions.]

A.—HOMER.

I. TRANSLATE:—

[SUBJECT.—Odysseus answers the taunts of Euryalus.]

Τὸν δ' ἄρ' ὑπόδρα ἰδὼν προσέφη πολύμητις 'Οδυσσεύς·
"ξεῖν', οὐ καλὸν ἔειπες· ἀτασθάλῳ[1] ἀνδρὶ ἔοικας. 166
οὕτως οὐ πάντεσσι θεοὶ χαρίεντα διδοῦσιν
ἀνδράσιν, οὔτε φυὴν οὔτ' ἂρ φρένας οὔτ' ἀγορητύν.
ἄλλος μὲν γάρ τ' εἶδος ἀκιδνότερος[2] πέλει ἀνήρ,
ἀλλὰ θεὸς μορφὴν ἔπεσι στέφει, οἱ δέ τ' ἐς αὐτὸν 170
τερπόμενοι λεύσσουσιν·[3] ὁ δ' ἀσφαλέως ἀγορεύει
αἰδοῖ μειλιχίῃ, μετὰ δὲ πρέπει ἀγρομένοισιν,
ἐρχόμενον δ' ἀνὰ ἄστυ θεὸν ὣς εἰσορόωσιν.
ἄλλος δ' αὖ εἶδος μὲν ἀλίγκιος[4] ἀθανάτοισιν,
ἀλλ' οὔ οἱ χάρις ἀμφιπεριστέφεται ἐπέεσσιν, 175
ὡς καὶ σοὶ εἶδος μὲν ἀριπρεπές, οὐδέ κεν ἄλλως
οὐδὲ θεὸς τεύξειε, νόον δ' ἀποφώλιός[5] ἐσσι.
ὤρινάς μοι θυμὸν ἐνὶ στήθεσσι φίλοισιν
εἰπὼν οὐ κατὰ κόσμον· ἐγὼ δ' οὐ νῆις[6] ἀέθλων,
ὡς σύ γε μυθεῖαι, ἀλλ' ἐν πρώτοισιν ὀίω 180

[1] *presumptuous.* [2] ἀκιδνός, *feeble.* [3] *look.* [4] *like.* [5] *foolish.* [6] Negative prefix νη- and root ἰδ (ἴδμεναι).

ἔμμεναι, ὄφρ' ἥβῃ τε πεποίθεα χερσί τ' ἐμῇσι.
νῦν δ' ἔχομαι κακότητι καὶ ἄλγεσι· πολλὰ γὰρ ἔτλην,
ἀνδρῶν τε πτολέμους ἀλεγεινά τε κύματα πείρων.
ἀλλὰ καὶ ὣς κακὰ πολλὰ παθὼν πειρήσομ' ἀέθλων·
θυμοδακὴς γὰρ μῦθος· ἐπώτρυνας δέ με εἰπών." 185

Hom. *Odys.* VIII. 165–185.

II. ANSWER THE FOLLOWING :—

(a) Give the Attic equivalents of the following forms: τὸν (165); πάντεσσι (167); ἀέθλων (179); ἐμῇσι (181). Give the Homeric form of the genitive singular of πτολέμους (183).

(b) Give the Attic equivalents of the following forms: κεν (176); ἔσσι (177); μυθεῖαι (180); ἔμμεναι (181). Explain the assimilation in εἰσορόωσιν (173).

(c) Name the parts (with their meanings) of which the following words are compounded: πολύμητις (165); ἀριπρεπὲς (176); θυμοδακὴς (185).

(d) Point out the case of tmesis in 172.

(e) Account for the case of οἱ (175) and for the mood and tense of τεύξειε (177).

(f) State the difference in the use of the participles τερπόμενοι (171) and παθών (184).

(g) Write out verses 165, 166, dividing them into feet, and marking the caesural pause in each verse.

(h) In what particular do these two caesural pauses differ from one another? Account for the quantity of the last syllable of the fourth foot in verse 166.

B.—HOMER AND HERODOTUS.

I. TRANSLATE :—

[SUBJECT.— Circe finds Odysseus mourning for his companions who had been changed into swine.]

Κίρκη δ' ὡς ἐνόησεν ἔμ' ἥμενον οὐδ' ἐπὶ σίτῳ 375

χεῖρας ἰάλλοντα,[1] κρατερὸν δέ με πένθος ἔχοντα,
ἄγχι παρισταμένη ἔπεα πρερόεντα προσηύδα·
"Τίφθ' οὕτως, Ὀδυσεῦ, κατ' ἄρ' ἕζεαι ἶσος ἀναύδῳ,[2]
θυμὸν ἔδων,[3] βρώμης[4] δ' οὐχ ἅπτεαι οὐδὲ ποτῆτος;
ἦ τινά που δόλον ἄλλον ὀΐεαι· οὐδέ τί σε χρὴ   380
δειδίμεν· ἤδη γάρ τοι ἀπώμοσα καρτερὸν ὅρκον."
Ὣς ἔφατ', αὐτὰρ ἐγώ μιν ἀμειβόμενος προσέειπον·
"ὦ Κίρκη, τίς γάρ κεν ἀνὴρ, ὃς ἐναίσιμος[5] εἴη,
πρὶν τλαίη πάσσασθαι[6] ἐδητύος ἠδέ ποτῆτος,
πρὶν λύσασθ' ἑτάρους καὶ ἐν ὀφθαλμοῖσιν ἰδέσθαι;   385
Hom. Odys. X. 375–385.

[1] ἰάλλω, cf. *mitto*.   [2] cf. προσηύδα (377).   [3] Literally "*eating*."   [4] *food*.
[5] *right-minded*.   [6] cf. *pascor*.

II. ANSWER THE FOLLOWING:—

(a) Give the Attic equivalents of the following forms: ἔπεα (377); μιν (382); ὀφθαλμοῖσιν (385). Give the Homeric form of the genitive singular of σίτῳ (375).

(b) Give the Attic equivalents of the following forms: ὀΐεαι (380); δειδίμεν (381); προσέειπον (382). What principle is illustrated by the forms κρατερὸν (376) and καρτερὸν (381).

(c) Write out verse 385, dividing it into feet, and marking the caesural pause.

(d) In what particular does this caesural pause differ from the one in the preceding verse? Account for the quantity of the second syllable of the third foot in verse 385.

III. TRANSLATE:—

[The signet, which Polycrates had thrown away, is found in the belly of a fish.]

Πέμπτῃ δὲ ἢ ἕκτῃ ἡμέρῃ ἀπὸ τούτων τάδε οἱ συνήνεικε[1] γενέσθαι· ἀνὴρ ἁλιεὺς[2] λαβὼν ἰχθῦν μέγαν τε καὶ καλόν, ἠξίου μιν Πολυκράτεϊ δῶρον δοθῆναι· φέρων

δὴ ἐπὶ τὰς θύρας Πολυκράτεϊ ἔφη ἐθέλειν ἐλθεῖν ἐς
5 ὄψιν· χωρήσαντος³ δέ οἱ τούτου, ἔλεγε διδοὺς τὸν
ἰχθῦν· "ὦ βασιλεῦ, ἐγὼ τόνδε ἑλὼν οὐκ ἐδικαίωσα
φέρειν ἐς ἀγορὴν, καίπερ γε ἐὼν ἀποχειροβίωτος· ἀλλά
μοι ἐδόκεε σεῦ τε εἶναι ἄξιος καὶ τῆς σῆς ἀρχῆς· σοὶ δή
μιν φέρων δίδωμι." ὁ δὲ ἡσθεὶς τοῖσι ἔπεσι ἀμείβεται
10 τοῖσδε· "κάρτα⁴ τε εὖ ἐποίησας καὶ χάρες διπλέη τῶν
τε λόγων καὶ τοῦ δώρου· καί σε ἐπὶ δεῖπνον καλέομεν."
ὁ μὲν δὴ ἁλιεὺς μέγα ποιεύμενος ταῦτα ἤϊε ἐς τὰ οἰκία·
τὸν δὲ ἰχθῦν τάμνοντες οἱ θεράποντες⁵ εὑρίσκουσι ἐν
τῇ νηδύϊ αὐτοῦ ἐνεοῦσαν τὴν Πολυκράτεος σφρηγῖδα.

HEROD. III. 42.

¹ συμφέρω, happen.   ² fisherman.   ³ χωρέω, literally "make room for."
⁴ very.   ⁵ servants.

(e) Name the parts (with their meanings) of the following compounds: Πολυκράτεϊ (3); ἀποχειροβίοτος (7).

(f) Give the Attic equivalents of the following forms: ἀγορήν (7); ἐδόκεε (8); ἤϊε (12).

(g) Account for the case of τούτου (5) and of τευ (8).

(h) Explain the use of the participles ἐών (7) and ἐνεοῦσαν (14).

ADVANCED LATIN.

I. TRANSLATE:—

Qua re hoc maius est vestrum in nos promeritum, quod non multitudini propinquorum, sed nobismet ipsis nos reddidistis. Sed quem ad modum propinqui, quos ego parare non potui, mihi ad deprecandam calamitatem meam non adfuerunt, sic, illud, quod mea virtus praestare debuit, auditores, auctores hortatoresque ad me restituendum ita multi fuerunt, ut longe superiores omnes hac dignitate copiaque superarem. Numquam de P. Popilio, clarissimo atque fortissimo viro, numquam de Q. Metello, nobilissimo et constantissimo cive, numquam de C. Mario, custode civitatis atque imperii vestri, in senatu mentio facta est. Tribuniciis superiores illi rogationibus, nulla auctoritate senatus sunt restituti. Marius vero non modo non a senatu, sed etiam oppresso senatu est restitutus, nec rerum gestarum memoria in reditu C. Marii, sed exercitus atque arma valuerunt. At de me ut valeret, semper senatus flagitavit: ut aliquando perficeretur, cum primum licuit, frequentia atque auctoritate perfecit. Nullus in eorum reditu motus municipiorum et coloniarum factus est: at me in patriam ter suis decretis Italia cuncta revocavit. Illi, inimicis interfectis, magna civium caede facta, reducti sunt: ego iis, a quibus eiectus sum, provincias obtinentibus, inimico hoc, optimo viro et mitissimo, altero consule referente reductus sum: cum is inimicus, qui ad meam perniciem vocem suam communibus hostibus praebuisset, spiritu dumtaxat viveret, re quidem infra omnes mortuos amandatus esset.

Explain construction of *hoc*, *mihi*, *dignitate*.

Compare the constructions of *rogationibus*, and *a senatu*.

Explain mood and tense of *valeret*, *perficeretur*.

Give all the participles, with their meaning, of *reddidistis*, *deprecandam*, *gestarum*, *perfecit*.

What is meant by *auctoritate senatus;* by *tribuniciis rogationibus?*

Compare the meaning of *inimicis interfectis* with that of *communibus hostibus*. Who was Marius, and how did his restitution differ from Cicero's?

II. TRANSLATE:—

[Aristaeus in trouble visits his mother, the water nymph Cyrene, asking of her relief, and is referred to the sea god Proteus.]

Postquam est in thalami pendentia pumice tecta
Perventum, et nati fletus cognovit inanis

Cyrene, manibus liquidos dant ordine fontis
Germanae, tonsisque ferunt mantelia villis ;
Pars epulis onerant mensas, et plena reponunt
Pocula ; Panchaeis adolescunt ignibus arae ;
Et mater, Cape Maeonii carchesia Bacchi :
Oceano libemus, ait, Simul, ipsa precatur
Oceanumque patrem rerum Nymphasque sorores,
Centum quae silvas, centum quae flumina servant.
Ter liquido ardentem perfudit nectare Vestam,
Ter flamma ad summum tecti subiecta reluxit.
Omine quo firmans animum sic incipit ipsa :
 Est in Carpathio Neptuni gurgite vates
Caeruleus Proteus, magnum qui piscibus aequor
Et iuncto bipedum curru metitur equorum.
Hic nunc Emathiae portus patriamque revisit
Pallenen : hunc et Nymphae veneramur et ipse
Grandaevus Nereus ; novit namque omnia vates,
Quae sint, quae fuerint, quae mox ventura trahantur.
Quippe ita Neptuno visum est, inmania cuius
Armenta et turpis pascit sub gurgite phocas.[1]

Mark the metre, with caesura, of the 6th and 8th verses.

[1] Phocas, *sea-calves, seals.*

ADVANCED GREEK.
GREEK COMPOSITION.

When the mother of Cyrus was about to return home to her husband, Astyages asked her to leave Cyrus in Media.[1] But Mandane replied that, though[2] she wished to gratify her father in everything, she still thought it hard to leave her son behind if he did not wish[3] to stay. Upon this his grandfather said to Cyrus : " If you stay with me, my boy, you shall, in the first place,[4] be allowed access[5] to me whenever you please; and, besides, you shall use my horses while you stay here, and have as many as you wish to carry with you when you return to your father." And when he was asked whether he wanted to go home or to stay with his grandfather, he quickly answered that he thought it was better for him to stay and learn to ride,[6] in order that he might become[7] the best of his grandfather's horsemen, and so be able to be an ally[8] of the Medes if they should need him.

[1] *among the Medes.* [2] μέν. [3] participle. [4] πρῶτον μέν. [5] εἰσιέναι. [6] ἱππεύω. [7] participle. [8] συμμαχέω.

ADVANCED LATIN COMPOSITION.

TRANSLATE INTO LATIN:—

In a naval battle which Eumenes, king of Pergamum, fought against King Prusias of Pontus, Hannibal, who was in exile at the court of Prusias, conquered the much larger numbers of the enemy by the following stratagem. He ordered a large number of poisonous snakes to be got together in earthen jars and placed upon the ships of Prusias, and, when the battle began, he directed the ships to attack only the ship of King Eumenes and merely defend themselves from the others. In order to show his men on which ship Eumenes was sailing, he sent a messenger with a letter among the enemy's ships to ask for King Eumenes as if to propose peace. When the king opened the letter, after the messenger had gone off, he found nothing in it but gibes against himself. He began the fight however at once, although he wondered what the letter could mean. Then his ship was attacked by all the hostile ships and compelled to flee, and the other Pergamenean vessels, at first surprised by the earthen jars thrown upon them, presently fled in dismay, when they found their ships filled with snakes.

ADVANCED GERMAN.

I. Write, in German, two pages on one of the following subjects: —

(a) Why does Tellheim consider himself unworthy of Minna von Barnhelm's hand?

(b) The scene in „Wilhelm Tell" in which Tell shoots the apple from his son's head.

(c) Any scene from „Hermann und Dorothea."

(d) The gray man in „Peter Schlemihl."

II. Man übersetze: —

"It is coming, Maggie!" Tom said, in a deep hoarse voice, losing the oars, and clasping her.

The next instant the boat was no longer seen upon the water, and the huge mass was hurrying on in hideous triumph.

But soon the keel of the boat reappeared — a black speck on the golden water.

The boat reappeared, but brother and sister had gone down in an embrace never to be parted; living through again in one supreme moment the days when they had clasped their little hands in love, and roamed the daisied fields together.

III. Translate: —

(a) Nein, ich brauch' es auch nicht einmal zu hören. Es versteht sich von selbst. Sie könnten eines so häßlichen Streiches fähig sein, daß Sie mich nun nicht wollten? Wissen Sie, daß ich auf Zeit meines Lebens beschimpft wäre? Meine Landsmänninnen würden mit Fingern auf mich weisen. — „Das ist sie," würde es heißen, „das ist das Fräulein von Barnhelm, die sich einbildete, weil sie reich sei, den wackern Tellheim zu bekommen: als ob die wackern Männer für Geld zu haben wären!" So würde es heißen; denn meine Landsmänninnen sind alle neidisch auf mich).

(b) So rannten die Bauern und ihre Weiber unter einander.

Die Anna aber sah nicht rechts noch links, erwiderte auch die Grüße
kaum mit einem leisen Kopfnicken, sondern ging die steinige Fahr-
straße hinan, als wäre sie schon ein abgeschiedener Geist, der weder
irdische Beschwerden fühlen, noch Menschenrede achten könne. Dicht
hinter ihr schritt die Rosine mit dem stillen Gesicht, das Alle ge-
wohnt waren. Nur war es heute so bleich, daß mitleidige Weiber
es sich mit Achselzucken und Kopfschütteln zeigten, während das
Gesicht der Alten von einem frischen Roth angehaucht war. Sie
nahm sich auch nicht die Zeit, auf der halben Höhe auszurasten, wo
eine Bank am Felsen stand. Es war, als triebe sie die Ahnung
vorwärts, daß sie keine Minute zu verlieren habe.

(c) Das Bürgertum in den Städten wurde wohlhabender, doch
fehlte ihm noch das freie Selbstvertrauen und die kühne Unterneh-
mungslust unserer heutigen Zeit. Die Regierung selbst mußte alles
betreiben, Anlage von Fabriken, Spinnereien, ꝛc. durch Prämien
und Privilegien anregen, oder selbst einzelne Geschäfte als Staats-
monopole übernehmen. Indessen erwuchs in den größeren Städten
ein reicher Kaufmannsstand, und schon zeichneten sich, z. B. in Berlin,
auch jüdische Familien durch Glanz und Reichthum, bald sogar durch
Bildung aus. Sonst herrschte noch meist der alte, fromme, nüch-
terne, beschränkte, aber ehrenfeste Bürgersinn; nur einige geweckte
Köpfe begannen der neuen Aufklärung nachzustreben und an der
aufblühenden Dichtung teilzunehmen.

(d) Komm du hervor, du Bringer bittrer Schmerzen,
Mein teures Kleinod jetzt, mein höchster Schatz—
Ein Ziel will ich dir geben, das bis jetzt
Der frommen Bitte undurchdringlich war—
Doch d i r soll es nicht widerstehn— Und du
Vertraute Bogensehne, die so oft
Mir treu gedient hat in der Freude Spielen,
Verlaß mich nicht im fürchterlichen Ernst!
Nur jetzt noch halte fest, du treuer Strang,
Der mir so oft den herben Pfeil beflügelt—
Entränn' er jetzo kraftlos meinen Händen,
Ich habe keinen zweiten zu versenden.

ADVANCED FRENCH.

[N.B.—Répondez aux questions dans l'ordre même où elles vous sont posées. Les réponses doivent toutes être en français. La traduction anglaise des passages français doit être en aussi bon anglais que possible.]

1. Traduisez en français :—

(a) English travellers are the best and the worst in the world. Where no motives of pride or interest intervene, none can equal them for profound and philosophical views of society, or faithful and graphical descriptions of external objects; but when either the interest or reputation of their own country comes in collision with that of another, they go to the opposite extreme.

Hence, their travels are more honest and accurate, the more remote the country described. I would place implicit confidence in an Englishman's descriptions of the regions beyond the cataracts of the Nile; of unknown islands in the Yellow Sea; of the interior of India; or of any other tracts which other travellers might be apt to picture out with the illusions of their fancies; but I would cautiously receive his account of his immediate neighbors, and of those nations with which he is in habits of most frequent intercourse.— WASHINGTON IRVING.

(b) Nothing in the early existence of Britain indicated the greatness which she was destined to attain. Her inhabitants, when first they became known to the Tyrian mariners, were little superior to the natives of the Sandwich Islands. She was subjugated by the Roman arms; but she received only a faint tincture of Roman arts and letters. Of the western provinces which obeyed the Cæsars she was the last that was conquered and the first that was flung away. No magnificent remains of Roman porches and aqueducts are to be found in Britain. No writer of British birth is reckoned among the masters of Roman poetry and eloquence. — MACAULAY.

2. Répondez aux questions suivantes : —
Qui était Pierre André ?
Qui était Marianne Chevreuse ?
Qu'est-ce que le père de Philippe Gaucher avait écrit à Pierre André ?
Comment se termine le roman intitulé *Marianne*, et quel est l'auteur de ce roman ?

3. Racontez l'histoire de M. Destournelles telle que vous la trouvez dans la comédie intitulée *Mademoiselle de la Seiglière*.

4. Racontez une des fables suivantes, et écrivez, si vous le pouvez, six ou huit vers d'une autre : *Le Loup et l'Agneau*, *le Renard et la Cigogne*, *le Chêne et le Roseau*, *le Lion et le Moucheron*, *le Lion et le Rat*, *l'Enfant et le Maître d'École*.

5. Racontez, d'après Corneille, l'histoire des Horaces et des Curiaces.

6. Écrivez huit ou dix lignes sur *l'Avare*.

7. Traduisez en anglais : —

(*a*) Je vous écris à côté d'un poêle, la tête pesante et le cœur triste, en jetant les yeux sur la rivière de la Sprée, parce que la Sprée tombe dans l'Elbe, l'Elbe dans la mer, que la mer reçoit la Seine, et que notre maison de Paris est assez près de cette rivière de Seine ; et je dis : Ma chère enfant, pourquoi suis-je dans ce palais, dans ce cabinet qui donne sur cette Sprée, et non pas au coin de notre feu ? Rien n'est plus beau que la décoration du palais du soleil dans *Phaéton*, Mademoiselle Astrua est la plus belle voix de l'Europe ; mais fallait-il vous quitter pour un gosier à roulades et pour un roi ? Que j'ai de remords, ma chère enfant ! que mon bonheur est empoisonné ! que la vie est courte ! qu'il est triste de chercher le bonheur loin de vous ! et que de remords si on le trouve !

Je suis à peine convalescent ; comment partir ? Attendez-moi, aimez-moi, recevez-moi, consolez-moi, et ne me grondez pas. — VOLTAIRE.

(*b*) POIRIER, *seul.* — Ah ! mais il m'ennuie, mon gendre. Je vois bien qu'il n'y a rien à tirer de lui . . . Ce garçon-là mourra dans la gentilhommerie finale. Il ne veut rien faire, il n'est bon à rien . . . Il me coûte les yeux de la tête . . . Il est maître chez moi . . . Il faut que ça finisse. (*Il sonne. — Entre un domestique.*) Faites monter le portier et le cuisinier. (*Le domestique sort.*) Nous allons voir, mon gendre ! . . . J'ai assez fait le gros dos et la patte de velours. Vous ne voulez pas faire de concessions, mon bel ami ? A votre aise ! je n'en ferai pas plus que vous : restez marquis, je redeviens bourgeois. J'aurai du moins le contentment de vivre à ma guise.

(*c*) POIRIER, *à Gaston.* — Dame ! le bilan est facile à établir : vous avez reçu cinq cent mille francs de la dot de ma fille. La corbeille de noces et les frais d'installation en ont absorbé cent mille. Vous venez d'en donner deux cent dix-huit mille à vos créanciers ; il vous en reste donc cent quatre-vingt-deux mille, qui, placés au taux légal, représentent neuf mille livres de rente . . . Est-ce clair ? Est-ce avec ce revenu que vous nourrirez vos amis de carpes à la Lithuanienne et de volailles à la Concordat ? Croyez-moi, mon cher Gaston, restez chez moi, vous y serez encore mieux que chez vous. Pensez à vos enfants . . . qui ne seront pas fâchés de trouver un jour dans la poche du marquis de Presles les économies du bonhomme Poirier. A revoir, mon gendre ; je vais régler le compte de monsieur Vatel. (*Il sort.*)

LOGARITHMS AND TRIGONOMETRY.

[One hour allowed; omit any two questions *except* 6.]

1. Find the logarithm of 0.1 in a system the base of which is 20.

2. The sine of an angle in the third quadrant is $-m$. Find the secant and the tangent of this angle.

3. Reduce $\csc x + \ctn x$ to a single function of $\dfrac{x}{2}$.

4. Obtain an expression for $\cos(x+y)\cos(x-y)$ in terms of the cosine of one angle and the sine of the other.

5. A gunboat lies 10 miles N.E. of a blockaded port. A privateer leaves the port, sailing south at the rate of eight miles an hour. In what direction, and at what rate, must the gunboat sail to overhaul the privateer in three hours?

6. A ship leaves Cape Cod (42° 2′ N., 70° 3′ W.), and sails N.E. 200 knots, E. 300 knots. Find, by Middle Latitude and Parallel Sailing, the latitude and longitude reached.

7. Obtain an expression for $\cos 3x$ in terms of $\cos x$.

SOLID GEOMETRY.

One hour allowed.

1. Prove that the intersections of two parallel planes with a third plane are parallel; and that parallel lines intercepted between two parallel planes are equal.

2. Prove that the section of a pyramid made by a plane parallel to the base is a polygon similar to the base.

What is the corresponding proposition concerning a cone?

3. Prove that two spherical triangles on the same sphere are equal or symmetrical if the three angles of one are respectively equal to the three angles of the other.

When are two spherical triangles called equal? when symmetrical?

4. Define a regular polyedron. Show that no regular polyedron bounded by hexagons is possible.

5. The radius of a sphere is 5 feet. Find the area of the curved surface of the segment and the volume of the segment cut off by a plane 3 feet from the centre of the sphere. (Take $\pi = 3\frac{1}{7}$.)

ANALYTIC GEOMETRY.

One hour allowed.

1. Prove that if two ellipses have the same major axis, and if, at points where they are cut by a perpendicular to this axis, tangents are drawn, these tangents will intersect on the major axis produced.

2. Given the base of a triangle and the length of the line drawn from one end of the base to the middle point of the opposite side: find the locus of the vertex. What is the name and what the position of the curve?

3. Find the equation of a tangent at a given point of the hyperbola $x^2 - y^2 = a^2$; of the hyperbola $2xy = b^2$.

Prove that these hyperbolas cross each other at right angles.

4. Find the equation of a diameter of a parabola in terms of the slope of the chords which it bisects.

N.B. The *slope* of a line is the value of m, when its equation is written in the form $y = mx + b$.

MECHANICS.

One hour allowed.

[ASK FOR LOGARITHMIC TABLES at the beginning of the hour, if they are not furnished to you. You will not need them till you reach the last part of the *second question.*]

1. A triangle is cut off from a square, by a line joining the middle points of two adjacent sides of the square. Find the centre of gravity of the remaining pentagon; proving that its distance from the centre of the square $= \frac{1}{21}$ of the diagonal of the square.

2. A uniform gate, 6 feet wide and 4 feet high, and weighing 80 pounds, hangs by two hinges, which are at the top and bottom of the gate; but so adjusted that the whole weight is borne by the support of the upper hinge. Find the direction and magnitude of the resultant pressure of the gate on the support of each hinge.

3. A body, weighing 100 pounds, placed on a rough plane, inclined 36° 20′ to the horizon, is just prevented from sliding down the plane by a force of 10 pounds, directed up the plane. Find the *coefficient of friction* between the body and the plane; and find the greatest force, directed up the plane, which could act on the body without dragging it up the plane.

Find the greatest angle of inclination of the plane, at which no force would be needed to prevent sliding.

4. A square plate, ABCD, lies on a smooth table. Strings, attached to the corners of the plate, pass over smooth pulleys at the edge of the table, and sustain weights, which hang freely, and are such as to produce equilibrium. The string attached at A has the direction of the diagonal CA produced, and bears a weight of 37.2 ounces; the string attached at B has the direction of the side AB produced, and bears a weight of 48.6 ounces; the strings attached at C and D are parallel to each other. Find the weight which each of these strings bears, and the direction of the string.

June, 1887.

ELEMENTARY.

ENGLISH.

Write a composition — with special attention to clearness of arrangement, accuracy of expression, and quality rather than quanity of matter — on one of the following subjects : —

1. An outline of the Story of Quentin Durward.

2. The escape of Isabelle of Croye from the Castle Hall of Schonwaldt.

3. How Quentin Durward outwitted the Bohemian Hayraddin.

4. The character of King Louis XI. as represented by Scott.

5. The Meeting of Louis XI. and the Duke of Burgundy, at Peronne.

6. A Glimpse of William de la Marck, the Boar of Ardennes.

SPECIMENS OF BAD ENGLISH.
Write your number on this paper.

Correct on this paper all the errors you discover in the following sentences : —

1. Being commissioned to relieve the beleaguered city, she sat out at the head of a force whose numbers were swelled by accessions all along the march.

2. It is not too much to say that he is known most and best by a single story; one which we read in childhood and seem never to quite forget.

3. It is most efficacious when taken fasting and mixed with an equal quantity of hot water.

4. De la Marck, in short, saw he would not be supported, even by his own band, in any farther act of immediate violence.

5. Tom stared at me, and I wished I was home.

6. Mr. Hastings did not reveal this to Mr. Marley, who, by the way, had fallen in love with Miss Hardcastle, whom he thought was the bar-maid.

7. When every worldly maxim arrayed itself against him; when blasted in fortune, and disgrace and danger darkened around his name she loved him the more ardently for his very sufferings.

8. In seeing Miss Anderson's Juliet I think I have seen the part as well acted as I am likely to.

9. There was a grand baloon ascension which landed in West Wareham.

10. Last Saturday evening we celebrated the first annual existance of our paper amid the enthusiasm of hundreds of people.

11. Probably there was never known such a gathering in town since its foundation, and the result of an establishment of a newspaper in town with such a widespread circulation shows fairly what and who pursues its columns.

12. He was one whom nature seemed to have first made generously and then to have added music as a dominant power.

13. A feeling of sympathy for his fellow man, although in bondage, has at last induced the faculty to put into execution the long-dreamt of idea of laying board walks throughout the college yard.

14. Some of this wax Ulysses gave to each sailor to put in his ears and prevent him hearing the Sirens.

15. One finds in the reviews of to-day, articles ranging from a sermon to a story and of course many excellent ones, but the efficacy of these latter are destroyed by the stiff, unfamiliar style in which they are written and which usually does away with whatever interest we may take in the subject.

16. We wish to congratulate '87 on her well-earned success, as by winning this race she placed the victor's wreath on her head which will be remembered long after the members of the present seniors are scattered in the four corners of the world.

17. Soliciting your inquiry either in person or letter before you shall locate your home at this Island in the Ocean.

. I am, Most Respectfully,

X. Y.

GREEK.

[SUBJECT.—Tissaphernes, over-confident because of an accession of troops from the interior, bids Agesilaus leave Asia. His answer, and the subsequent course of events.]

TRANSLATE:—

Ἐπεὶ δὲ μέγα φρονήσας ὁ Τισσαφέρνης ἐπὶ τῷ καταβάντι στρατεύματι παρὰ βασιλέως προεῖπεν Ἀγησιλάῳ πόλεμον, εἰ μὴ ἀπίοι ἐκ τῆς Ἀσίας, οἱ μὲν ἄλλοι σύμμαχοι καὶ Λακεδαιμονίων οἱ παρόντες μάλα ἀχθεσθέντες

5 φανεροὶ ἐγένοντο, νομίζοντες ἐλάττω τὴν παροῦσαν εἶναι δύναμιν Ἀγησιλάῳ τῆς βασιλέως παρασκευῆς, Ἀγησίλαος δὲ μάλα φαιδρῷ[1] τῷ προσώπῳ[2] ἀπαγγεῖλαι Τισσαφέρνει τοὺς πρέσβεις ἐκέλευσεν ὡς πολλὴν χάριν αὐτῷ ἔχοι, ὅτι ἐπιορκήσας αὐτὸς μὲν πολεμίους τοὺς
10 θεοὺς ἐκτήσατο, τοῖς δ' Ἕλλησι συμμάχους ἐποίησεν. ἐκ δὲ τούτου εὐθὺς τοῖς μὲν στρατιώταις παρήγγειλε συσκευάζεσθαι ὡς εἰς στρατείαν, ταῖς δὲ πόλεσιν, εἰς ἃς ἀνάγκη ἦν ἀφικνεῖσθαι στρατευομένῳ[3] ἐπὶ Καρίαν, προεῖπεν ἀγορὰν παρασκευάζειν. ἐπέστειλε δὲ καὶ
15 Ἴωσι καὶ Αἰολεῦσι καὶ Ἑλλησποντίοις πέμπειν πρὸς ἑαυτὸν εἰς Ἔφεσον τοὺς συστρατευσομένους. ὁ δὲ Τισσαφέρνης, καὶ ὅτι ἱππικὸν οὐκ εἶχεν ὁ Ἀγησίλαος, ἡ δὲ Καρία ἄφιππος ἦν, καὶ ὅτι ἡγεῖτο αὐτὸν ὀργίζεσθαι αὐτῷ διὰ τὴν ἀπάτην, τῷ ὄντι νομίσας ἐπὶ τὸν αὐτοῦ
20 οἶκον εἰς Καρίαν αὐτὸν ὁρμήσειν, τὸ μὲν πεζὸν ἅπαν διεβίβασεν ἐκεῖσε, τὸ δ' ἱππικὸν εἰς τὸ Μαιάνδρου πεδίον περιῆγε, νομίζων ἱκανὸς εἶναι καταπατῆσαι τῇ ἵππῳ τοὺς Ἕλληνας, πρὶν εἰς τὰ δύσιππα[4] ἀφικέσθαι.

XEN. *Hell*. III. 4, 11, 12.

ANSWER THE FOLLOWING: —

(*a*) Decline, in the singular number, the noun· to which the form πόλεσιν (12) belongs. Compare the adjective to which the form ἐλάττω (5) belongs.

(*b*) In what tense, mood, and voice is ἀφικέσθαι (23)? Give the present indicative first person singular. Inflect the second aorist optative middle.

(*c*) Give the principal parts of ἀγγέλλω (7); and analyze the form διεβίβασεν (21) by naming the augment, tensestem, etc.

[1] φαιδρός, *radiant, cheerful.*   [2] πρόσωπον, *countenance.*
[3] στρατευομένῳ: sc. αὐτῷ.   [4] δύσ-ιππα: sc. χωρία.

(d) Give the derivation of φανερός (5), by naming the stem from which it is formed and its suffix, and give as many Greek words from the same stem, with their meanings, as you can recall.

(e) State the use of the participles καταβάντι (1) and συστρατευσομένους (16).

(f) Account for the tense of ὁρμήσειν (20), and explain the construction of καταπατῆσαι (22).

(g) Account for the case of παρασκευῆς (6), and of προσώπῳ (7).

(h) Account for the mood of ἔχοι (9).

LATIN.

I. TRANSLATE: —

Qua re animadversa Pompeiani in quodam monte constiterunt. Hunc montem flumen subluebat. Caesar milites cohortatus, etsi totius diei continenti labore erant confecti noxque jam suberat, tamen munitione flumen a monte
5 seclusit, ne noctu aquari Pompeiani possent. Quo perfecto opere illi de deditione missis legatis agere coeperunt. Pauci ordinis senatorii, qui se cum iis conjunxerant, nocte fuga salutem petiverunt. Caesar prima luce omnes eos qui in monte consederant ex superioribus locis in planitiem
10 descendere atque arma proicere jussit. Quod ubi sine recusatione fecerunt passisque palmis projecti ad terram flentes ab eo salutem petiverunt, consolatus consurgere jussit et pauca apud eos de lenitate sua locutus, quo minore essent timore, omnes conservavit, militibusque suis com-
15 mendavit, ne qui eorum violaretur, neu quid sui desiderarent. Hac adhibita diligentia ex castris sibi legiones alias occurrere et eas quas secum duxerat invicem requiescere

atque in castra reverti jussit, eodemque die Larisam pervenit.

1. Mark the quantity of every vowel in *Caesar milites cohortatus, etsi totius diei continenti labore erant confecti noxque jam suberat.*

2. Give the principal parts of *constiterunt* (line 1), *conjunxerant* (line 7), *petiverunt* (line 8), *consederant* (line 9), *passis* (line 11), *requiescere* (line 17), *reverti* (line 18).

3. Decline *ordinis* (line 7), *nocte* (line 7), *locis* (line 9).

4. Give all the participles of *facio* and *loquor*, with the meaning of each.

5. Explain the mood and tense in *ne noctu aquari Pompeiani possent* (line 5).

6. Explain the mood in *quo minore essent timore* (line 13). Why is *quo* used?

7. Explain the case of *missis legatis* (line 6), *fuga* (line 8), *prima luce* (line 8), *Larisam* (line 18).

II. TRANSLATE : —

Cimonem Athenienses non solum in bello, sed etiam in pace diu desideraverunt. Fuit enim tanta liberalitate, cum compluribus locis praedia hortosque haberet, ut numquam in eis custodem imposuerit fructus servandi gratia,
5 ne quis impediretur, quo minus ejus rebus, quibus quisque vellet, frueretur. Semper eum pedissequi[1] cum nummis sunt secuti, ut, si quis opis eius indigeret, haberet quod statim daret, ne differendo videretur negare. Saepe, cum aliquem videret minus bene vestitum, suum amiculum dedit.

1. Explain the construction of *fructus servandi*, and state what other expression might have been used.

[1] *Footmen, attendants.*

2. Explain the case of *tanta liberalitate* (line 2), and *rebus* (line 5).

3. Why is "his" expressed by *ejus* in line 5, but by *suum* in line 9?

GERMAN.

[No. I., if well translated, will be enough. A good rendering of II. will compensate in some measure for deficiencies in I.]

I. TRANSLATE INTO ENGLISH:—

Auf eine Zeit ging das Hühnchen mit dem Hähnchen in den Nußberg, und sie machten mit einander aus, wer einen Nußkern fände, sollte ihn mit dem andern teilen. Nun fand das Hühnchen eine große, große Nuß, sagte aber nichts davon und wollte den Kern allein essen. Der Kern war aber so dick, daß es ihn nicht hinunter schlucken konnte, und er ihm im Hals stecken blieb, daß ihm angst wurde, es müßte ersticken. Da schrie das Hühnchen „Hähnchen, ich bitt' dich, lauf was du kannst, und hol mir Wasser, sonst erstick ich." Das Hähnchen lief, was es konnte, zum Brunnen und sprach „Born, du sollst mir Wasser geben: das Hühnchen liegt auf dem Nußberg, hat einen großen Nußkern geschluckt und will ersticken." Der Brunnen antwortete „lauf erst hin zur Braut und laß dir rote Seide geben." Das Hühnchen lief zur Braut „Braut, du sollst mir rote Seide geben: rote Seide will ich dem Brunnen geben, der Brunnen soll mir Wasser geben, das Wasser will ich dem Hühnchen bringen, das liegt auf dem Nußberg, hat einen großen Kern geschluckt und will daran ersticken." Die Braut antwortete „lauf erst und hol mir mein Kränzlein, das blieb an einer Weide hängen." Da lief das Hähnchen zur Weide und zog das Kränzlein von dem Ast und brachte es der Braut, und die Braut gab ihm rote Seide dafür, die brachte es dem Brunnen, der gab ihm Wasser dafür. Da brachte das Hähnchen das Wasser zum Hühnchen, wie es aber hinkam, war dieweil das Hühnchen erstickt und lag da tot und regte sich nicht. Da war das Hähnchen so traurig, daß es laut schrie, und kamen alle Tiere und beklagten das Hühnchen: und sechs Mäuse bauten einen kleinen Wagen das Hühnchen darin zum Grabe zu fahren; und als der Wagen fertig war, spannten sie sich davor, und das Hähnchen fuhr. Auf dem Wege aber kam der Fuchs, „wo willst du hin, Hähnchen?" „Ich will mein Hühnchen begraben." „Darf ich mitfahren?"

„Ja, aber setz dich hinten auf den Wagen,
vorn könnens meine Pferdchen nicht vertragen."

Da setzte sich der Fuchs hinten auf, dann der Wolf, der Bär, der Hirsch, der Löwe und alle Tiere in dem Wald. So ging die Fahrt fort, da kamen sie an einen Bach. „Wie sollen wir nun hinüber?" sagte das Hähnchen. Da lag ein Strohhalm am Bach, der sagte „ich will mich quer darüber legen, so könnt ihr über mich fahren." Wie aber die sechs Mäuse auf die Brücke kamen, rutschte der Strohhalm und fiel ins Wasser, und die sechs Mäuse fielen alle hinein und ertranken. Da ging die Not von neuem an, und kam eine Kohle und sagte „ich bin groß genug, ich will mich darüber legen, und ihr sollt über mich fahren." Die Kohle legte sich auch an das Wasser, aber sie berührte es unglücklicher Weise ein wenig, da zischte sie, verlöschte und war tot. Wie das ein Stein sah, erbarmte er sich und wollte dem Hähnchen helfen und legte sich über das Wasser. Da zog nun das Hähnchen den Wagen selber, wie es ihn aber bald drüben hatte und war mit dem toten Hühnchen auf dem Land und wollte die andern, die hinten auf saßen, auch heran ziehen, da waren ihrer zu viel geworden, und der Wagen fiel zurück, und alles fiel mit einander in das Wasser und ertrank. Da war das Hähnchen noch allein mit dem toten Hühnchen, und grub ihm ein Grab und legte es hinein, und machte einen Hügel darüber, auf den setzte es sich und grämte sich so lang, bis es auch starb; und da war alles tot.

II. Translate into German:—

Romulus built the city of Rome. The inhabitants were called Romans. They were a very brave people. They loved their country and fought to defend it. They would sooner have died than have lost their liberty. It was dearer to them than life. They waged many wars with the Carthaginians, with varying success. At last they conquered the Carthaginians and destroyed their city.

FRENCH.

I. TRANSLATE :—

"Et après?" *dis-je* au capitaine, après avoir rallumé sa pipe, qu'il avait laissée s'éteindre. — "Après, je n'ai plus voulu retourner sur mer. Vous voyez, *j'avais perdu* tout ce que j'aimais, ma femme, mon fils, mon bateau. Un marin qui a perdu son bateau est un homme déshonoré." — "Mais, capitaine, pourquoi dire que vous avez perdu votre fils? Qui vous dit que vous ne le retrouverez pas un jour?"

La figure du capitaine Belleau *prit* alors une expression que ne lui avaije jamais vue. La colère décomposait ses traits et en faisait je ne sais quel animal hideux, au lieu de l'homme bienveillant, quoique rude, qu'il était naturellement: "Le misérable!" s'écria-t-il d'une voix qui fit trembler le parquet de la chambre; "le misérable! qu'il ne reparaisse jamais devant moi!" — "Qu'a-t-il donc fait?" *demandai-je*, stupéfait d'une telle explosion. — "Monsieur Telmer," me répondit le vieux marin, déjà un peu remis, et avec une dignité qui m'étonna; "voici plus de cent cinquante ans que les Belleau n'épousent que des filles de marins; mon aïeul, mon père, moi-même, nous avons été fidèles aux traditions de la famille. J'espérais que mon fils le serait aussi; déjà ma sœur s'occupait de le marier. Une charmante jeune fille, la nièce de mon vieil ami Pernadec, une des victimes du terrible cyclone d'il y a deux ans, aurait fait l'affaire. Il a mieux aimé aller à la ville et s'amouracher de la fille d'un confectionneur, qui est aujourd'hui sa femme, la malheureuse! Jamais je ne la *reconnaîtrai* comme ma belle-fille! Jamais je ne le reconnaîtrai plus comme mon fils! Il est mort pour moi." Et en prononçant ces paroles le vieux marin ebranla d'un formidable coup de poing la table auprès de laquelle nous étions assis, et fit voler au loin verres, assiettes et bouteilles. La porte alors s'ouvrit, comme si ce coup de poing en eût fait sauter la serrure. Mais elle livra passage à un grand et vigoureux garçon dont l'aspect sembla pour un moment pétrifier le vieillard. — ALFRED MANIÈRE.

[A good translation of the above passage is all that is required to pass the examination; the following questions are added to enable candidates to make up for any slight deficiencies in the translation.]

II. Conjugate *dis-je, j'avais perdu, prit, demandai-je, je reconnaîtrai*, and give the principal tenses of the verbs to which they belong.

III. Translate in French: —

(*a*) I have not yet finished your book; I will send it to you to-morrow.

(*b*) Do not speak to me: speak to him!

(*c*) I do not want these books; I want those that you bought this morning.

(*d*) I could not speak; I was struck with admiration.

IV. Write twelve lines in French on the following subject: *Why I want to go to Harvard.*

HISTORY OF THE UNITED STATES.

[Take 1 and three others.]

1. Fort Orange, Jamestown, Ticonderoga, Valley Forge, Louisburg, Fort Duquesne, — where?

2. The causes of the French and Indian war.

3. [Take one.] (a) The provisions of the Stamp Act.
(b) The Surrender at Saratoga.
(c) Jay's Treaty.

4. What was the Compromise of 1850? Was it carried out?

5. Describe very briefly the condition of the middle class in Virginia before the Revolution.

6. What were the "gag-resolutions"? What was the attitude of John Quincy Adams regarding them?

HISTORY OF ENGLAND.

[Take 1 and three others.]

1. Give the situation of Kent, Norfolk, Oxford, Gloucester, Westminster, and the Medway.

2. [Take one.] St. Dunstan. Archbishop Cranmer.

3. [Take one.] The treaty of Wedmore. The battle of the Standard. The battle of Naseby.

4. Explain: wergeld, relief, scutage, benevolences, and ship-money.

5. [Take one.]

(a) The two great Parties in the Long Parliament.
(b) London Coffee-houses in the 17th century.

6. Difficulties and dangers of travelling in England in the 17th century.

ANCIENT HISTORY.

I.

(*a*) [Take FIVE.] Elis, Locris, Megara, Mytilene, Corcyra, Arginusae, Leuctra, Chaeronea, — where? Mention (with dates) historical events connected with four of these places.

(*b*) [Take FIVE.] Caudium, Thurii, Saguntum, Zama, Praeneste, Pharsalus, Pydna, Heraclea, — where? Mention (with dates) historical events connected with four of these places.

II.

[Take any two.]

1. [Take TWO.] (*a*) The reforms of Kleisthenes.
   (*b*) The peace of Nicias.
   (*c*) The destruction of Corinth.

2. What grievances were complained of by the allies of Athens during the Athenian supremacy? In what respects did Sparta use the supremacy differently from Athens?

3. [Take TWO.] Peisistratos, Cimon son of Miltiades, Pheidias, Kleon.

4. [Take TWO.]
   (*a*) Commercial importance of the Greek festivals.
   (*b*) The Greek ideal of an educated man.
   (*c*) The success of Pericles as a democratic leader.

III.

[Take any two.]

1. Mention in order (with dates, but without description) the successive stages of the Roman conquest of Italy. What means did the Romans use to strengthen their hold on Italy?

2. [Take TWO.] Regulus, Germanicus, Trajan.

ALGEBRA.

3. Explain rogatio, interrex, jus auspiciorum, jus honorum, patrum auctoritas. Describe the Hortensian law, or the Valerian laws.

4. What were the chief grievances of the Italians at the time of the Gracchi? Was Tiberius Gracchus a revolutionist?

ALGEBRA.

[Write legibly and without crowding; give the work clearly and find all possible answers. The shortest methods are preferred.]

1. Solve the following equation: —

$$\sqrt{x-3} + \sqrt{3x+4} + \sqrt{x+2} = 0.$$

Find two answers, and verify the positive answer, by showing that it satisfies the equation.

2. A broker sells certain railway shares for $3240. A few days later, the price having fallen $9 per share, he buys, for the same sum, 5 more shares than he had sold. Find the price and the number of shares transferred on each day.

3. Solve the following equation, finding four values of x: —

$$x^4 + (2a^2 + 3ab - 2b^2)^2 = 5(a^2 + b^2)x^2.$$

4. Reduce the following expression to its simplest form as a single fraction: —

$$\left(\frac{1-x^3}{1+x^3} - \frac{1-x}{1+x}\right) \div \left(\frac{1+x^2}{1-x^2} + \frac{1+x}{1-x}\right).$$

PLANE GEOMETRY.

[In solving problems use for π the approximate value $3\frac{1}{7}$.]

1. Prove that in an isosceles triangle the angles opposite the equal sides are equal.

One of the equal sides of a certain isosceles right triangle is $10\sqrt{2}$ units long; what is the length of the perpendicular dropped upon the hypotenuse from the vertex of the opposite angle?

2. Prove that the product of the two segments of any chord drawn through a fixed point which is within a circle has the same value in whatever direction the chord is drawn. If the radius of a circle be 5 feet and the distance of a point P from the centre be 3 feet; what is the value of the product of the segments of any of the chords which pass through P? How long are the longest and shortest of these chords?

3. Prove that if two circumferences touch each other externally, and if two straight lines be drawn through the point of contact, two of the lines which join the middle points of the chords thus formed are parallel. Under what circumstances will the middle points of the chords lie at the corners of a parallelogram?

4. Prove that two regular polygons of the same number of sides are similar polygons.

State (without proving) the method of inscribing a regular hexagon in a circle; of inscribing a regular dodecagon; of inscribing an equilateral triangle. How would you then circumscribe a figure of either of these kinds about the circle?

5. The altitude of an equilateral triangle is 9 feet: find the radii and areas of the inscribed and circumscribed circles.

PHYSICAL SCIENCE.

FIRST ALTERNATIVE.

PHYSICS.

Candidates who offer (1) of the New Method will take the Astronomy questions instead of Physics questions 3 and 4.

[In this paper take g as 32 ft. per second.]

1. Which could you throw farther, a solid iron sphere 1 in. in diameter, or a solid wooden sphere of the same size? Tell as exactly as you can why this is so.

2. (a) The horizontal reach of a certain inclined plane is 8 ft., its height is 6 ft., its length, therefore, is 10 ft. A force applied parallel to the incline draws a mass of 100 lbs. from the bottom to the top. How great a force is required and how much work does it do? Disregard friction.

or

(b) A ball is sent vertically upward with a velocity of 80 ft. per second. What will be its height above the starting-point after 4 seconds?

3. What reasons have you for believing sound to be a *wave-motion* of *air*?

4. What point on the Fahrenheit scale of temperature corresponds to 20° on the centigrade scale?
How would you test the accuracy of the freezing-point and boiling-point of a thermometer?

5. (a) Explain by means of a diagram the action of a convex lens used as a "simple microscope," *i.e.* to give a magnified and erect image of an object. Where must the object be placed with respect to the principal focus of the lens?

or

(b) Describe the construction and action of a Nicol prism.

6. (*a*) Describe very carefully and fully the construction and action of the electrophorus.

or

(*b*) Describe very carefully and fully the process of electrotyping with copper.

ASTRONOMY.

1. Define " plane of the ecliptic."
What is a solar day? mean solar day? sidereal day?

2. Define nebula, constellation, Milky Way. What reason have we for thinking the "fixed stars" to be much farther from us than the sun is?

SECOND ALTERNATIVE.

[Candidates may omit any one question except the first.]

1. Describe fully, but concisely, some experiment upon which you have spent not less than one and a half hours of laboratory work.

2. If a carriage wheel be resting upright upon the ground, and be prevented from slipping at the bottom, how great a force applied horizontally at the top will just neutralize a force equal to the weight of 50 lbs. applied horizontally in the opposite direction at the centre of the wheel?

3. Define carefully the *dyne* and *erg*, or the *poundal* and *foot-poundal*.

4. If a body be acted on by a constant force which imparts to it in 1 second a velocity of 1 m. per second, how far will it have moved in 5 seconds, starting from rest?

5. Define *density* and *specific gravity*, distinguishing between the two. A certain solid floats in water with only $\frac{2}{3}$ of its volume submerged; what is the specific gravity of this solid?

PHYSICAL SCIENCE. 49

6. Into 110 grams of water at 15° C. contained in a vessel the thermal capacity of which is equal to that of 10 grams of water, are put 200 grams of a certain solid at 100° C., and the resulting temperature of the whole is 25° C. Calculate the specific heat of the solid.

7. What is photometry? What difficulties, if any, have you encountered in making experiments in photometry?

8. Describe carefully and fully some galvanic cell that you have used.

ADVANCED.

GREEK.

[SUBJECT.—Telemachus protects Odysseus at the banquet and defies the suitors.]

Τηλέμαχος δ' 'Οδυσῆα καθίδρυε, κέρδεα[1] νωμῶν,[2]
ἐντὸς ἐυσταθέος μεγάρου, παρὰ λάινον οὐδὸν,
δίφρον[3] ἀεικέλιον καταθεὶς ὀλίγην τε τράπεζαν·
πὰρ δ' ἐτίθει σπλάγχνων μοίρας, ἐν δ' οἶνον ἔχευεν   260
ἐν δέπαϊ χρυσέῳ, καί μιν πρὸς μῦθον ἔειπεν·
" ἐνταυθοῖ νῦν ἧσο μετ' ἀνδράσιν οἰνοποτάζων·
κερτομίας δέ τοι αὐτὸς ἐγὼ καὶ χεῖρας ἀφέξω
πάντων μνηστήρων, ἐπεὶ οὔ τοι δήμιός ἐστιν
οἶκος ὅδ', ἀλλ' 'Οδυσῆος, ἐμοὶ δ' ἐκτήσατο κεῖνος.   265
ὑμεῖς δὲ, μνηστῆρες, ἐπίσχετε θυμὸν ἐνιπῆς[4]
καὶ χειρῶν, ἵνα μή τις ἔρις καὶ νεῖκος ὄρηται."
Ὣς ἔφαθ', οἱ δ' ἄρα πάντες ὀδὰξ ἐν χείλεσι φύντες
Τηλέμαχον θαύμαζον, ὃ θαρσαλέως ἀγόρευε.
τοῖσιν δ' Ἀντίνοος μετέφη, Εὐπείθεος υἱός·   270
" καὶ χαλεπόν περ ἐόντα δεχώμεθα μῦθον, Ἀχαιοὶ,
Τηλεμάχου· μάλα δ' ἡμῖν ἀπειλήσας ἀγορεύει.
οὐ γὰρ Ζεὺς εἴασε Κρονίων· τῷ κέ μιν ἤδη
παύσαμεν ἐν μεγάροισι, λιγύν[5] περ ἐόντ' ἀγορητήν."
Ὣς ἔφατ' Ἀντίνοος· ὁ δ' ἄρ' οὐκ ἐμπάζετο[6] μύθων.   275
κήρυκες δ' ἀνὰ ἄστυ θεῶν ἱερὴν ἑκατόμβην
ἦγον· τοὶ δ' ἀγέροντο κάρη κομόωντες Ἀχαιοὶ
ἄλσος[7] ὕπο σκιερὸν ἑκατηβόλου Ἀπόλλωνος.
Οἱ δ' ἐπεὶ ὤπτησαν κρέ ὑπέρτερα[8] καὶ ἐρύσαντο,

μοίρας δασσάμενοι δαίνυντ' ἐρικυδέα δαῖτα· 280
πὰρ δ' ἄρ' Ὀδυσσῆι μοῖραν θέσαν οἳ πονέοντο
ἴσην, ὡς αὐτοί περ ἐλάγχανον· ὣς γὰρ ἀνώγει
Τηλέμαχος, φίλος υἱὸς Ὀδυσσῆος θείοιο.
Hom. Odys. XX. 257-283.

[1] wiles. [2] νωμάω (νέμω), animo versare. [3] seat. [4] angry threats. [5] shrill. [6] care for. [7] grove. [8] outer (ὑπέρ).

II. ANSWER THE FOLLOWING:—

(a) Give the Attic equivalents of the following forms: κέρδεα (257); χρυσέῳ (261); ὅ (269); τοί (277). Give the Homeric form of the genitive singular of μέγαρον (274).

(b) Give the Attic equivalents of the following forms: ἐόντα (271); κέ (273); παύσαμεν (274); κομόωντες (277). Explain the assimilation in the last form.

(c) Name the parts (with their meanings) of which the following words are compounded: οἰνοποτάζων (262); κερτομίας (263); ἐρικυδέα (280).

(d) Point out the cases of tmesis in 260.

(e) Account for the case of χειρῶν (267), and for the mood and tense of παύσαμεν (274).

(f) State the difference in use of ὡς and ὣς (282).

(g) Write out verses 275, 276, dividing them into feet, and marking the caesural pause in each verse.

(h) In what particular do these two caesural pauses differ from one another? Account for the quantity of the first syllable of the third foot in verse 275.

[SUBJECT.—Odysseus comes to the land of the Cyclopes.]

Ἔνθεν δὲ προτέρω πλέομεν ἀκαχήμενοι[1] ἦτορ. 105
Κυκλώπων δ' ἐς γαῖαν ὑπερφιάλων,[2] ἀθεμίστων[3]
ἱκόμεθ', οἵ ῥα θεοῖσι πεποιθότες ἀθανάτοισιν
οὔτε φυτεύουσιν χερσὶν φυτὸν οὔτ' ἀρόωσιν,

ἀλλὰ τά γ' ἄσπαρτα καὶ ἀνήροτα πάντα φύονται,
πυροὶ⁴ καὶ κριθαὶ⁵ ἠδ' ἄμπελοι, αἴτε φέρουσιν   110
οἶνον ἐριστάφυλον,⁶ καί σφιν Διὸς ὄμβρος ἀέξει.
τοῖσιν δ' οὔτ' ἀγοραὶ βουληφόροι οὔτε θέμιστες,
ἀλλ' οἵ γ' ὑψηλῶν ὀρέων ναίουσι κάρηνα
ἐν σπέσσι γλαφυροῖσι, θεμιστεύει δὲ ἕκαστος
παίδων ἠδ' ἀλόχων, οὐδ' ἀλλήλων ἀλέγουσιν.   115

¹ ἀκαχίζω, *grieve*. ² Literally '*overgrown*' (φύω, *make grow*), but used here metaphorically. ³ Cf. θέμις, *law, usage* (τίθημι). ⁴ *wheat*. ⁵ *barley*. ⁶ Cf. σταφυλή, *bunch of grapes*.

II. ANSWER THE FOLLOWING:—

(a) Give the Attic equivalents of the following forms: θεοῖσι (107); σφιν (111); ὀρέων (113). Give the Homeric form of the genitive singular of οἶνος (111).

(b) Give the Attic equivalents of the following forms: πλέομεν (105); ἀρόωσιν (108); ἀέξει (111). Explain the assimilation in ἀρόωσιν (108).

(c) Write out verse 105, dividing it into feet, and marking the caesural pause.

(d) In what particular does this caesural pause differ from the one in the next verse? Account for the quantity of the first syllable of the first foot in verse 107.

[SUBJECT.—Syloson, in the market-place at Memphis in Egypt, gives his red mantle to Darius, afterwards the king of Persia.]

τοῦτον τὸν Συλοσῶντα κατέλαβε εὐτυχίη τις τοιήδε·
λαβὼν χλανίδα καὶ περιβαλόμενος πυρρὴν ἠγόραζε ἐν
τῇ Μέμφι. ἰδὼν δὲ αὐτὸν Δαρεῖος, δορυφόρος τε ἐὼν
Καμβύσεω¹ καὶ λόγου οὐδενός κω μεγάλου ἐπεθύμησε
5 τῆς χλανίδος καὶ αὐτὴν προσελθὼν ὠνέετο.² ὁ δὲ
Συλοσῶν ὀρέων τὸν Δαρεῖον μεγάλως ἐπιθυμέοντα τῆς
χλανίδος θείῃ τύχῃ χρεόμενος λέγει· Ἐγὼ ταύτην

LATIN.

πωλέω³ μὲν οὐδενὸς χρήματος, δίδωμι δὲ ἄλλως,⁴ εἴπερ
οὕτω δεῖ γενέσθαι πάντως. αἰνέσας ταῦτα ὁ Δαρεῖος
10 παραλαμβάνει τὸ εἷμα. ὁ μὲν δὴ Συλοσῶν ἠπίστατό
οἱ τοῦτο ἀπολωλέναι δι' εὐήθειαν,⁵ ὡς δὲ τοῦ χρόνου
προβαίνοντος Καμβύσης τε ἀπέθανε καὶ τῷ μάγῳ ἐπα-
νέστησαν οἱ ἑπτά⁶ καὶ ἐκ τῶν ἑπτὰ Δαρεῖος τὴν βασι-
ληίην ἔσχε, πυνθάνεται ὁ Συλοσῶν, ὡς ἡ βασιληίη
15 περιεληλύθοι ἐς τοῦτον τὸν ἄνδρα, τῷ κοτὲ αὐτὸς ἔδωκε
ἐν Αἰγύπτῳ δεηθέντι τὸ εἷμα.

HEROD. III. 139, 140.

[1] Cambyses, son of Cyrus the Great. [2] Conative imperfect. [3] sell.
[4] gratis. [5] good-nature. [6] The seven Persian nobles who overthrew the Magus.

(e) Name the parts (with their meanings) of which the following words are compounded: εὐτυχίη (1); δορυφόρος (3); εὐήθεια (11).

(f) Give the Attic equivalents of the following forms: ἐπιθυμέοντα (6); χρεόμενος (7); βασιληίη (14).

(g) Account for the case of χρήματος (8) and of χρόνου (11).

(h) Explain the use of the participle ἐπιθυμέοντα (6), and of the infinitive ἀπολωλέναι (11).

LATIN.

CICERO AND VIRGIL AT SIGHT.

TRANSLATE : —

I.

Nam relatio[1] illa salutaris et diligens fuerat consulis, animadversio quidem et iudicium senatus: quae cum reprehendis, ostendis qualis tu, si ita forte accidisset, fueris illo tempore

[1] for the punishment of the Catilinarian Conspirators.

consul futurus: stipendio, mehercule, et frumento Catilinam esse putasses iuvandum. quid enim interfuit inter Catilinam et cum, cui tu senatus auctoritatem, salutem civitatis, totam rem publicam provinciae praemio vendidisti? quae enim L. Catilinam conantem consul prohibui, ea P. Clodium facientem consules adiuverunt. voluit ille senatum interficere; vos sustulistis; leges incendere: vos abrogastis; vim inferre patriae: quid est vobis consulibus gestum sine armis? incendere illa coniuratorum manus voluit urbem: vos eius domum, quem propter urbs incensa non est. ac ne illi quidem, si habuissent vestri similem consulem, de urbis incendio cogitassent; non enim se tectis privare voluerunt, sed his stantibus nullum domicilium sceleri suo fore putaverunt. caedem illi civium, vos servitutem expetistis; hic vos etiam crudeliores: huic enim populo ita fuerat ante vos consules libertas insita, ut ei mori potius quam servire praestaret.

Give the derivation of *animadversio, relatio, salutaris, vendidisti.*

Give the principal parts of *adiuverunt, sustulistis, inferre.*

Give the construction of *consulis, praemio, patriae, fueris. cum reprehendis.* Should you expect subjunctive? Why? *provinciae.* What was a Roman province? and why should any one want it?

II.

At cantu commotae Erebi de sedibus imis
Umbrae ibant tenues simulacraque luce carentum,
Quam multa in foliis avium se milia condunt,
Vesper ubi aut hibernus agit de montibus imber,
Matres atque viri defunctaque corpora vita
Magnanimum heroum, pueri innuptaeque puellae,
Impositique rogis iuvenes ante ora parentum;
Quos circum limus niger et deformis arundo
Cocyti tardaque palus inamabilis unda

Alligat et noviens Styx interfusa coercet.
Quin ipsae stupuere domus atque intima Leti
Tartara caeruleosque implexae crinibus anguis
Eumenides, tenuitque inhians tria Cerberus ora
Atque Ixionii vento rota constitit orbis.
Iamque pedem referens casus evaserat omnis
Redditaque Eurydice superas veniebat ad auras
Pone sequens, — namque hanc dederat Proserpina legem —
Cum subita incautum dementia cepit amantem,
Ignoscenda quidem, scirent si ignoscere Manes :
Restitit Eurydicenque suam iam luce sub ipsa
Immemor heu! victusque animi respexit.

Give the derivation of *simulacra, magnanimum, dementia*.
Compare *niger, superas*.
Construction of *angues, ignoscere, scirent*.
suam. Why not *eius*?
How do you know what *tarda* agrees with?
Mark the principal caesura in fourth line. Is this the most common place for it? What other places of the caesura are common?

GREEK COMPOSITION.

TRANSLATE : —

Until [1] he was twelve years old Cyrus was educated among the Persians, and followed [2] the more simple mode of life [3] which was prescribed [4] by the Persian customs. But afterwards he went to his grandfather Astyages, king of the Medes. And he was amazed when he first saw his grandfather decked [5] with purple tunics and necklaces [6] and bracelets,[7] which were customary with the Medes; still, when his grandfather decked him with a beautiful robe,[8] child as he was [9] and ambitious, he was greatly delighted. When his mother asked him whether his father or his grandfather seemed to him more beautiful, he replied that his father was by far the most beautiful man of all the Persians, but of all the Medes whom he had seen in the streets and in the palace his grandfather seemed to be the most beautiful.

[1] μέχρι with genitive.   [2] χράομαι.   [3] δίαιτα.   [4] προστάττω.   [5] κοσμέω.   [6] στρεπτός.   [7] ψέλιον.   [8] στολή.   [9] ἅτε with participle.

LATIN COMPOSITION.

TRANSLATE INTO LATIN: —

When we read in Cornelius Nepos about the life of Epaminondas we cannot help admiring the self-control and sense of justice which that Greek leader showed. We learn from the answer he made to the ambassador of King Artaxerxes how little he valued money in comparison with honor and love for his country. The ambassador had corrupted a young friend of Epaminondas, and was trying through him to win over the leader himself. But when he understood why the ambassador had come, he said: "There is no need of money, for if what the king desires is for the interest of Thebes, I will gladly do it for nothing; if otherwise, there is not gold enough in the whole world to persuade me to injure my country." Then he bade the ambassador leave the city as soon as possible that he might not teach others to do wrong, and he made the youth through whose means the ambassador had come to him return immediately all the money he had received.

GERMAN.

I. Translate into German:—

„Peter Schlemihl" is the story of a man who had lost his shadow. It was written by Chamisso. The author of this pretty story was born in France, but he lived a long time in Germany and soon learned to love his new home. He also wrote many poems, which are read in the schools of Germany and of this country. One of the best of his poems is called „Das Riesenspielzeug." It tells about a "giant-maiden," who carried some peasants and oxen to her father, and asked, "Are they not beautiful playthings?" But her father was angry, because she had taken the peasants from their work. He said to his daughter, "You must not take those little people away from their fields and houses, although they are so very small and would make such a pretty plaything for you. If you do not let them work, we shall have no bread to eat." Then the girl carried them back again to their little huts under the green trees.

II. Translate:—

(a) Melchthal. Ertragen sollt' ich die leichtfert'ge Rede
Des Unverschämten: „Wenn der Bauer Brod
Wollt' essen, mög' er selbst am Pfluge ziehn!"
In die Seele schnitt mir's, als der Bub' die Ochsen,
Die schönen Thiere, von dem Pfluge spannte;
Dumpf brüllten sie, als hätten sie Gefühl
Der Ungebühr, und stießen mit den Hörnern;
Da übernahm mich der gerechte Zorn,
Und meiner selbst nicht Herr, schlug ich den Boten.
Walther Fürst. O, kaum bezwingen wir das eigne Herz;
Wie soll die rasche Jugend sich bezähmen!
Melchthal. Mich jammert nur der Vater — er bedarf
So sehr der Pflege, und sein Sohn ist fern.

Der Vogt ist ihm gehässig, weil er stets
Für Recht und Freiheit redlich hat gestritten.
Drum werden sie den alten Mann bedrängen,
Und Niemand ist, der ihn vor Unglimpf schütze.
— Werde mit mir, was will, ich muß hinüber.

(*b*) v. Tellheim. Wohl denn, so hören Sie, mein Fräulein.
— Sie nennen mich Tellheim; der Name trifft ein. — Aber Sie
meinen, ich sey der Tellheim, den Sie in Ihrem Vaterlande gekannt
haben, der blühende Mann, voller Ansprüche, voller Ruhmbegierde;
der seines ganzen Körpers, seiner ganzen Seele mächtig war; vor
dem die Schranken der Ehre und des Glücks eröffnet standen; der
Ihres Herzens und Ihrer Hand, wenn er schon Ihrer noch nicht
würdig war, täglich würdiger zu werden hoffen durfte. — Dieser
Tellheim bin ich eben so wenig, als ich mein Vater bin. Beide sind
gewesen. — Ich bin Tellheim, der verabschiedete, der an seiner Ehre
gekränkte, der Krüppel, der Bettler. — Jenem, mein Fräulein, ver-
sprachen Sie sich: wollen Sie diesem Wort halten?

(*c*) Wer in den ersten Jahren nach dem Tode Friedrich's des
Großen die Straßen einer mäßigen Stadt betrat, die er im Jahr
1750 durchschritten hatte, der mußte die größere Kraft ihrer Be-
wohner überall erkennen. Noch stehn die alten Mauern und Thore,
aber es wird darüber verhandelt, die Eingänge, welche für Menschen
und Lastwagen zu enge sind, von dem alten Ziegeljoch zu befreien,
mit leichtem Gitterwerk zu schließen, an anderen Stellen der Mauer
neue Pforten zu öffnen. Der Wall um den Stadtgraben ist mit
breitgegipfelten Bäumen bepflanzt, und in dem dichten Schatten der
Linden und Kastanien halten jetzt die Städter ihren diätetischen
Spaziergang, athmet das Kindervolk frische Sommerluft. Auch die
kleinen Gärten an der Stadtmauer sind verschönert, neue fremde
Blüthen glänzen zwischen den alten und umgeben das künstliche
Fragment einer Säule, oder einen kleinen Genius von Holz, der mit
weißer Oelfarbe überzogen ist; hier und da erhebt sich ein Sommer-
haus entweder als antiker Tempel, oder auch als Hütte von be-

moofter Rinde zur Erinnerung an die unschuldsvollen Urzustände des Menschengeschlechts, in denen die Gefühle so unendlich reiner und der Zwang der Kleider und der Convenienz so viel geringer war.

III. Give a brief description of life in the royal castle at Berlin at the time of the boyhood of Frederick the Great.

IV. TRANSLATE (*at sight*) : —

Noch fehlte es an Bekleidung, Verpflegung, Bewaffnung. Aber es begann jetzt ein rührender Wetteifer in freiwilligen Gaben. Auch der Aermste brachte sein Scherflein. Wo in dem ausgesogenen Lande Geld fehlte, griff man zu anderen Mitteln. Eheleute und Verlobte brachten die goldenen Trauringe und erhielten eiserne dafür zurück: „Gold gab ich für Eisen" lautete die schöne Inschrift. Jenes arme Fräulein (Ferdinanda von Schmettau) brachte den einzigen Schmuck, den sie besaß: ihr schönes Haupthaar. Das Weib ließ den Gatten, die Verlobte den Bräutigam, die Mutter den Sohn willig ziehen: Schmach hätte den Zurückbleibenden getroffen. An der Spitze der Frauenvereine, die sich zur Unterstützung der Kämpfenden, zur Pflege der Verwundeten, zur Sammlung von Liebesgaben bildeten, stand die edle Prinzeß Wilhelm, Marianne von Hessen-Homburg, nebst acht anderen Prinzessinnen des königlichen Hauses. — Der christliche Sinn, die einst verspottete und vergessene Religion, war mit heiliger Macht in allen Seelen wieder aufgelebt. Unter Glockenklang, mit feierlich-kirchlicher Segnung, zogen die Scharen aus in den „heiligen Krieg."

FRENCH.

N.B.—Take up the questions exactly in the order in which they are on the paper. The answers must all be in French.

1. Traduisez en français : —

(*a*) Mr. Rushworth was from the first struck with the beauty of Miss Bertram, and, being inclined to marry, soon

fancied himself in love. He was a heavy young man, with
not more than common sense; but as there was nothing dis-
agreeable in his figure or address, the young lady was well
pleased with her conquest. Being now in her twenty-first
year, Maria Bertram was beginning to think matrimony a
duty; and as a marriage with Mr. Rushworth would give her
the enjoyment of an income larger than her father's, as well
as insure her the house in town, which was now a prime
object, it became, by the same rule of moral obligation, her
evident duty to marry Mr. Rushworth, if she could. — JANE
AUSTEN.

(*b*) It was ten o'clock. The coach of the lieutenant of
the Tower was ready. Monmouth requested his spiritual
advisers to accompany him to the scaffold, and they consented; but they told him that, in their judgment, he was
about to die in a perilous state of mind, and that, if they
attended him, it would be their duty to exhort him to the
last. As he passed along the ranks of the guards he saluted
them with a smile, and mounted the scaffold with a firm
tread. Tower Hill was covered up to the chimney tops with
an innumerable multitude of gazers, who, in awful silence,
broken only by sighs and the noise of weeping, listened for
the last accents of the darling of the people. — MACAULAY.

2. Racontez une de ces deux comédies : *Le Gendre de M.
Poirier; Mademoiselle de la Seiglière.*

3. Racontez une des fables suivantes de La Fontaine : *Le
Corbeau et le Renard, le Loup et l'Agneau, le Renard et la
Cigogne, le Lion et le Moucheron, le Lion et le Rat.*

4. Écrivez une demi-douzaine de vers extraits d'une fable
de La Fontaine.

5. Racontez en une quinzaine de lignes la comédie de
Molière intitulée *l'Avare.*

6. Écrivez une douzaine de lignes sur Pierre Corneille.

7. Traduisez en anglais : —

En me parlant de tragédie, monsieur, vous réveillez en moi une idée que j'ai depuis longtemps de vous présenter la Mort de César, pièce de ma façon, toute propre pour un collège où l'on n'admet point de femmes sur le théâtre. La pièce n'a que trois actes, mais c'est celui de tous mes ouvrages dont j'ai le plus travaillé la versification. Je m'y suis proposé pour modèle votre illustre compatriote, et j'ai fait ce que j'ai pu pour imiter de loin
        la main qui crayonna
L'âme du grand Pompée et celle de Cinna.

Il est vrai que c'est un peu *la grenouille qui s'enfle pour être aussi grosse que le bœuf;* mais enfin je vous offre ce que j'ai. Il y a une dernière scène à refondre, et sans cela il y a longtemps que je vous aurais fait la proposition. En un mot, César, Brutus, Cassius et Antoine sont à votre service quand vous voudrez.

Je suis bien sensible à la bonne volonté que vous voulez bien témoigner pour le petit Champbonin, que je vous ai recommandé. C'est un jeune enfant qui ne demande qu'à travailler, et qui peut, je crois, entrer tout d'un coup en rhétorique ou en philosophie. Nous sommes bon gentilhomme et bon enfant, mais nous sommes pauvre. Si l'on pouvait se contenter d'une pension modique, cela nous accommoderait fort : et elle serait au moins payée régulièrement, car les pauvres sont les seuls qui payent bien.

Adieu, monsieur ; comptez sur l'amitié, sur l'estime, sur la reconnaissance de V. Point de cérémonie ; je suis quaker avec mes amis. Signez-moi un A. — VOLTAIRE.

8. Expliquez l'allusion que contiennent les mots imprimés en italiques dans le passage précédent.

LOGARITHMS AND TRIGONOMETRY.

[One hour allowed; omit any two questions, *except* 6.]

1. In a certain system of logarithms, the logarithm of $\frac{1}{4}$ is 2. What is the logarithm of 16 in the same system? What is the base?

2. Given $\sin x + \cos x = n$. Find $\sin x$. What are the limiting values of n?

3. Reduce $\frac{1}{2}(\tan x + \operatorname{ctn} x)$ to a single function of $2x$.

4. Obtain, from fundamental formulas, a formula for the sum of the cosines of two angles, in terms of the half-sum and the half-difference of the angles.

5. Two roads in a level plane cut each other at right angles at a point A. A surveyor, standing at B on one of the roads, sees two houses, C and D, on the other road, C lying between A and D. He knows that $AB = 225$ yards, and $AC = 150$ yards, and measures the angle $CBD = 41° 17'$. What is the distance CD?

6. Find, by Middle Latitude Sailing, the bearing and distance from Savannah (32° 05' N., 81° 05' W.) to Trinidad (10° 39' N., 61° 31' W.).

7. Reduce $\dfrac{4 \tan x (1 - \tan^2 x)}{(1 + \tan^2 x)^2}$ to a single function of $4x$.

SOLID GEOMETRY.

1. Prove that if a line and a plane are parallel, the intersection with the plane of any plane containing the line is parallel to the line.

2. Prove that a triangular prism is one-half of a parallelopiped of double the base and the same altitude.

3. Prove that the volume of a triangular prism is equal to the product of the area of a lateral face by one-half its distance from the opposite edge.

4. Prove that the sum of two face angles of a triedral angle is greater than the third. What proposition concerning a spherical triangle follows immediately from this theorem?

5. Show that the sum of the angles of a spherical triangle is greater than two and less than six right angles.

6. State without proof the rule for finding the area of the surface of a sphere in terms of the radius; and that for the volume of a sphere in terms of the radius.

7. The altitude of the torrid zone is about 3200 miles. Find its area in square miles (radius $= 4000$ miles).

ANALYTIC GEOMETRY.

1. Define the parabola, and obtain its equation in the form $y^2 = 2mx$. What are the co-ordinates of the focus? What is the equation of the directrix? Define the *latus rectum*, and find its length.

2. Obtain the equation of the circle which passes through the vertex of the parabola and the extremities of the double ordinate through the focus. Find the centre and radius of this circle.

3. Obtain the equations of the tangent and normal at the point (x_1, y_1) of the parabola. Prove that the normal makes equal angles with the principal axis and with the line joining (x_1, y_1) with the focus.

4. Prove that, if two tangents to a parabola are perpendicular to each other, they meet on the directrix.

5. Find the equation of the locus of the middle points of a set of chords of the hyperbola all of which pass through the vertex.

MECHANICS.

1. Two forces, one of 3 pounds and one of 5 pounds, act at a point of a body in directions which make with each other an angle of 60°. Find the magnitude of the resultant of these forces and show that its line of action makes with the greater of them an angle whose sine is $\dfrac{3\sqrt{3}}{14}$, that is, 0.371+.

2. A grocer uses correct weights with a false balance whose arms are 10 and 11 inches long respectively. In selling two pounds of sugar, he first puts enough sugar in one of the two scale pans (A) to balance a pound weight placed in the other (B). He then puts enough sugar in pan (B) to balance a pound weight placed in (A), and gives the customer the quantities of sugar thus weighed out, under the impression that he has given him just 2 pounds. How much has the customer really received?

3. A weightless string bears at one end a weight P, $= 4\sqrt{3}$ pounds, and is tied at the other end to a peg, A, fixed in the wall. Between A and P the string passes through a smooth ring, which slides freely on it and carries a weight of 12 pounds, and then over a smooth peg, B, in the same horizontal line with A. Find the tension of the string and the strain which B has to bear. Would these quantities be larger or smaller if B were below the horizontal plane in which A lies?

4. A horizontal force of 10 pounds must be exerted on a certain body, P, which lies on the rough horizontal top of a table, in order to set P in motion, but when the table is tipped up so that the top makes an angle of 45° with the vertical, P justs slides down of itself: how heavy is P? What force exerted downwards in a direction making an

PHYSICAL SCIENCE. 65

angle of 60° with the vertical would make P move if the table top were level? What force in a direction making an angle of 30° with the vertical?

5. A uniform ladder which weighs 100 pounds rests with its top against the smooth wall of a house and makes an angle of 60° with the horizon. The coefficient of friction between the bottom of the ladder and the pavement is $\frac{1}{2}$. Will the foot of the ladder slip out if a man rest his whole weight of 150 pounds on the top of the ladder?

DATA.

$\sin 30° = \frac{1}{2}$ $\sin 120° = \sqrt{3}$
$\cos 30° = \frac{1}{2}\sqrt{3}$ $\cos 120° = -\frac{1}{2}$
$\sin 45° = \sqrt{\frac{1}{2}}$ $\sin 150° = \frac{1}{2}$
$\cos 45° = \sqrt{\frac{1}{2}}$ $\cos 150° = -\frac{1}{2}\sqrt{3}$
$\sin 60° = \frac{1}{2}\sqrt{3}$ $\sqrt{3} = 1.732 +$
$\cos 60° = \frac{1}{2}$ $\sqrt{\frac{1}{3}} = 0.577 +$

PHYSICAL SCIENCE.

[This paper must not be taken as indicating the character of future examination papers in Advanced Physics, which will more closely resemble the papers of Physics C and in Physics 2 of previous years. Such papers will be found in the collections of Final Examination Papers issued annually by the University.]

1. The errors which affect a result are divided into two classes: 1st, constant errors, or those which always increase or diminish the result by a given amount; and 2d, accidental errors, or those which tend sometimes to increase and sometimes to diminish the result. Show that the mean (or average) of several observations is less affected by accidental errors than on the average the separate observations are.

2. How would you go to work to construct a gram weight if all standards of mass were lost?

3. The *apparent* weight of a certain solid is 140 grams in air of mean density (0.0012) and 49 grams in water of density 0.999, the weights used being brass of density 8.4. Find the *absolute* density of the solid, correcting approximately for the buoyancy of air and for the deviation of the water from standard density.

4. Describe as minutely as possible any experiment in sound, heat, or light from which you have obtained a numerical result which agrees within one per cent with that which you suppose to be the true result.

5. (*a*) Explain the construction of a vernier-gauge or of a micrometer-gauge; or (*b*) state the general principles by which verniers are constructed.

6. What precautions are necessary in order to obtain accurate results with a Nicholson's hydrometer or with a densimeter of any description?

7. Explain the reduction of the answer to absolute units (dynes or poundals) in any experiment which you have performed involving a measure of force.

8. Describe or explain any experiment in which you have measured work or energy, naming the unit of work or energy employed.

9. State the law which connects electromotive force, resistance, and electric current, and show that if the external resistance of the circuit be small, it is possible to increase greatly the number of cells in the circuit without greatly increasing the current.

FOR ADVANCED STANDING.

ENGLISH A.

[Make your answers thorough, and pay attention to form as well as to substance.]

I.

Write a short composition on one of the following subjects: —

1. The Honyhuhnms.
2. A Character from Fielding.
3. Pope's Homer.
4. A Sketch of Dryden's Life.
5. An Outline of one of Pope's Works.

II.

Discuss the use of *should* and *would* in the following passage: —

"If I were as rich as Mr. Darcy," cried a young Lucas, who came with his sisters, "I should not care how proud I was. I would keep a pack of foxhounds, and drink a bottle of wine every day."

"Then you would drink a great deal more than you ought," said Mrs. Bennett; "and if I were to see you at it, I should take away your bottle directly."

The boy protested that she should not; she continued to declare that she would; and the argument ended only with the visit.

III.

Describe briefly some person or place that you know.

IV.

1. Reduce to a syllogism the following argument, pointing out the major term, the minor term, the middle term, the major premise, the minor premise, and the conclusion: —

"Dirt defies the king." If the old proverb be true, Sapolio is greater than royalty itself.

2. Discuss the relation between the Argument from Example and the Argument from Sign.

V.

Give your opinion of the literary worth of the following passage, arranging your criticism under the heads of (*a*) Clearness, (*b*) Force, (*c*) Elegance, and (*d*) General Remarks: —

Power, of some kind or other, will survive the shock in which manners and opinions perish; and it will find other and worse means for its support. The usurpation which, in order to subvert ancient institutions, has destroyed ancient principles, will hold power by arts similar to those by which it has acquired it. When the old feudal and chivalrous spirit of fealty, which, by freeing kings from fear, freed both kings and subjects from the precautions of tyranny, shall be extinct in the minds of men, plots and assassinations will be anticipated by preventive murder and preventive confiscation, and that long roll of grim and bloody maxims, which form the political code of all power not standing on its own honor, and the honor of those who are to obey it. Kings will be tyrants from policy when subjects are rebels from principle.

PHYSICS A.

1. Describe the thermo-electric pile, and galvanometer.
2. What experiments show that heat is produced by friction?
3. What is the mechanical equivalent of heat?
4. How is it measured?
5. What is heat supposed to be?
6. What is the condition of a gaseous body?
7. What is essential to the production of light, as well as heat?
8. What experiments show the energy of molecular motions?
9. How is the melting-point altered by pressure?
10. On what does the boiling-point of a liquid depend?
11. Illustrate the difference between potential and actual energy.
12. What experiments illustrate the spheroidal condition of matter?
13. Explain the trade winds.
14. How do they affect the climate of Europe and America?
15. What are Faraday's experiments on relegation?

CHEMISTRY A.

1. The symbol $C_4H_{10}O$ gives what information in regard to the substance called ether?
2. The expression $Zn + (2\ HCl + Aq) = (ZnCl_2 + Aq) + H_2$ gives what information in regard to the process it represents?

CHEMISTRY.

3. The composition of alcohol is as follows: —

    Carbon   52.18
    Hydrogen 13.04
    Oxygen   34.78
                 100.00

The density of the vapor of alcohol is 23 times that of hydrogen. Calculate the symbol of alcohol.

4. Describe the three laws which govern chemical changes, and illustrate by examples.

5. How many liters of hydrogen gas can be made from 100 grams of zinc by the reaction given above?

6. A volume of gas (free to expand under constant pressure) measures 600 centimeters at the freezing-point. What would it measure at 182° C. provided all other conditions remained unchanged?

$H = 1$. $O = 16$. $C = 12$. $Zn = 65$.

The weight of one liter (1000 c. m.) of hydrogen gas is $\frac{9}{100}$ of a gram. Absolute temperature equals centigrade temperature plus 273°.

CLASSIFIED PAPERS.

LATIN.

TRANSLATION AT SIGHT AND SENTENCES.

July, 1887.

I. TRANSLATE Bell. Gall. VIII. 38.

II. TRANSLATE : —

1. You wish to go away at the beginning of summer.

2. He answered that the Suevi would return to their homes across the Rhine.

3. "Let me come to Rome," he said, "to persuade the Senate not to favor our enemies."

4. By learning the causes of all things we are freed from the fear of death.

September, 1887.

I. TRANSLATE Bell. Gall. VIII. 43.

suspensi, compare *in suspense*.

II. TRANSLATE : —

1. Caesar, seeing that his soldiers were hard pressed, sent Labienus to encourage them.

2. In our times, if the flames cannot be extinguished by water, they tear down the houses, a method (*ratio*) which they used also in ancient times at Rome.

3. Our soldiers ran much faster than the enemy.

4. It was for Cicero's interest to unite with Brutus and Cassius.

September, 1886.

I. TRANSLATE Caes. Bell. Gall. VIII. 28.

II. TRANSLATE:—

1. Caesar, wishing to find out how much courage his men had, commanded them to storm the town in a night attack.

2. The numbers of the enemy were, however, too great for our men to withstand.

3. A Gallic chief was captured and sent to the senate at Rome and by them was pardoned.

July, 1886.

I. TRANSLATE:—

1. The consul sent two messengers to warn the king not to make an attack upon his allies.

2. Let us forget the wrongs which our enemies have done us, and take care that we do no wrong to others ourselves.

3. You, who have so much money, may lead such a life, but it is not possible for those who are in want to do so.

4. Since this is so, you ought to choose the work which you like best to do, and then do it with all your might.

II. TRANSLATE:—

Cum in Pontum venisset copiasque omnes in unum locum coëgisset, quae numero atque exercitatione bellorum mediocres erant (excepta enim legione sexta, quam secum adduxerat Alexandria veteranam multis laboribus periculisque functam reliquae erant tres legiones, una Deiotari, duae, quae in eo proelio, quod Cn. Domitum fecisse cum Pharnace scripsimus, fuerant), legati a Pharnace missi Caesarem adeunt atque imprimis deprecantur, ne eius adventus hostilis esset: facturum enim omnia Pharnacen, quae imperata essent. maximeque commemorabant nulla Pharnacem auxilia contra Caesarem Pompei dare voluisse, cum Deiotarus, qui dedisset, tamen ei satisfecisset. Caesar respondit se fore aequissimum Pharnaci, si quae polliceretur repraesentaturus esset. monuit autem, ut solebat, mitibus verbis legatos, ne aut Deiotarum sibi obicerent, aut nimis eo gloriarentur beneficio, quod auxilia Pompeio non misissent. nam se neque libentius facere quicquam quam supplicibus ignoscere, neque provinciarum publicas iniurias condonare iis posse, qui fuissent in se officiosi.

September, 1885.

I. TRANSLATE: —

1. I came from Rome to Athens in four days.

2. It is a great question whether Caesar favored the conspiracy of Catiline or not.

3. I am much pleased that you have used the gifts of fortune wisely, and have been content with what the gods have thought you worthy to receive.

4. What would you give to live a hundred years?

II. TRANSLATE Bell. Gall. VII. 39.

June, 1885.

I. TRANSLATE: —

1. The soldier said that he should have stayed at Rome unless his brother had come from Capua.

2. The consul was persuaded to pardon those who had threatened him with death.

3. This very war, which has lasted nine years, could be finished in a year if we might enroll all the Italian soldiers.

4. The consul received orders through his lieutenant to allow the town to be fortified by the Greeks with strong fortifications.

II. TRANSLATE Bell. Civ. I. 22.

September, 1884.

I. Translate Bell. Civ. I. 14.

Explain the case of *Romam*, and the mood and tense of *profugeret*. Give the principal parts of *invasit, profectus, colligunt, attribuit*. What were *gladiatores*?

II. Translate: —

1. Pythagoras was born at Samos, but afterwards betook himself to Italy and taught philosophy for many years at Croton and Metapontum.

2. After the battle of Pharsalus, Caesar used the utmost clemency toward the conquered.

3. If you say this, no one will believe you.

4. Caesar, having crossed the river, encamped at the top of a hill which was 500 paces distant from the stream, and sent out scouts (*exploratores*) to find out the plans of the enemy.

June, 1884.

I. Translate: —

1. I do not doubt that Hector was the bravest of the men who fought at Troy.

2. The old Roman soldier would have been ashamed if he had surrendered in order to save his life.

3. The Arcadians were older than the moon itself if we may believe what they say of themselves.

4. Caesar ordered the town to be taken by the cavalry by a night attack.

II. Translate Bell. Civ. I. 44.

September, 1883.

I. Translate Caes. Bell. Gall. VII. 70.

II. Translate: —

1. They declared that they would tell all they knew, unless money were given them.

2. The Greeks came with an army to besiege the town.

3. I am afraid that the man will die before the physician arrives.

4. Are you not ashamed of your avarice?

5. When Corinth was taken, Mummius returned to Rome with great booty.

6. No commander was ever more beloved by his soldiers than Germanicus.

June, 1883.

I. TRANSLATE: —

1. The kings of the most distant lands sent ambassadors to congratulate Augustus on his victory.

2. Remember the kindnesses which you have received and forget the injuries.

3. Do you advise me to attempt so important a thing without consulting the gods?

4. He ordered those houses at Naples to be destroyed by the soldiers by fire.

TRANSLATE Bell. Civ. III. 30 (to "per Graecos deferuntur").

September, 1882.

I. TRANSLATE: —

1. We must go away from Athens to-morrow, and shall arrive at Rome within two days.

2. Is there any town in Italy greater than Rome?

3. Pardon him, and you will not repent of the deed.

4. They sent ambassadors to Carthage to demand satisfaction.

II. TRANSLATE Caes. Bell. Gall. VII. 78, 79 (from "Sententiis dictis constituunt" to "munitionibus considunt").

June, 1882.

I. TRANSLATE Nepos, Pelop. XVI. 5 (from "Conflictatus autem est" to "agro donarunt").

II. TRANSLATE:—

1. Have you forgotten who commanded the Carthaginians at Zama?

2. Having got possession of the town, he ordered the prefect to close all the gates.

3. He advised the consul to go to Ephesus, the chief town of that region.

4. The soldier confessed that he was sorry for his cowardice, and begged Caesar to pardon him.

XENOPHON AT SIGHT AND SENTENCES.

September, 1887.

TRANSLATE:—

1. The enemy put the army to flight.[1]

2. When it became evening[2] the horsemen came from the city.

3. The woman admired the discipline[3] of the army.

4. But he himself marched to the garrisons[4] and there remained.

5. If the barbarians have broken the truce, the gods will fight on our side.

6. Cyrus is said to have said that he wished to learn this.

7. Let the hoplites be at hand with their arms.

8. The king's brother made an alliance with him.

[1] τρέπομαι.   [2] ἑσπέρα.   [3] τάξις.   [4] φρούριον.

September, 1886.

[SUBJECT.—Pharnabazus resolves to make vigorous war upon the Lacedaemonians.]

I. TRANSLATE Xen. Hell. IV. 8. 6 and 7, to εἰς τὴν Λακεδαίμονα.

ἐπέραινε = *he made no progress towards.* εὐτρεπίζεσθαι = *to conciliate.*
περὶ παντὸς ἐποιεῖτο = *set above everything.*

II. TRANSLATE:—

1. The messengers took him by the girdle and led him away.
2. If the citizens should be willing, the generals would send away their soldiers.
3. He assembled the barbarians and told them to fight.
4. I am afraid that Cyrus will die.
5. I said this that they might be wiser.
6. According to the agreements he denied that there was another road.
7. While he was saying this he heard the trumpet.
8. If Cyrus dies, we shall be afraid.

July, 1886.

[SUBJECT.—Naval operations of Athens and Sparta in the East.]

I. TRANSLATE Xen. Hell. IV. 8. 23 and 24.

ἐλάττω ... ἢ ὥστε = *too small ... to.* ἐπὶ συμμαχίᾳ τῇ = *according to the alliance with.* συμμαχίαν = *a force of allies.*

II. TRANSLATE:—

1. He asked them who said this.
2. They were willing to wait, and Cyrus sent a messenger to the king.

3. If he should kill Orontes, the generals would be more faithful.

4. I ordered him to remain for two days that I might converse with him.

5. They took care to become friends of the soldiers.

6. If they do not obey their commanders, these soldiers will be worsted.

7. Let him give the peltasts pay for three months.

8. Tissaphernes said that Darius was ill.

September, 1885.

[SUBJECT. — Agesilaus' campaign in Asia Minor. The Persians disconcerted. The satrap Tissaphernes executed.]

I. TRANSLATE Xen. Agesil. I. 32 and 35.

αἰτιᾶσθαι = to blame. ποιεῖσθαι = to consider. ἐλευθεροῦν = to set (it) free. διακρίνεσθαι = to decide. ἄθυμος = discouraged. ἐρρωμένος = vigorous.

II. TRANSLATE : —

1. Order the cavalry to proceed slowly.

2. The general says that he has persuaded the allies to fight.

3. He was greatly troubled[1] because he had been reviled by his own brother.

4. When our dead are buried, we will cross the river.

5. Who will be elected general, if this brave leader dies?

6. There were many orators at Athens worthy of admiration.

7. If you dare to do this, we will absolutely oppose you.

8. He will delay his march that he may make a review of the army.

[1] ἀνιάω.

June, 1885.

[SUBJECT.—An oath of alliance proposed by Athens after Leuctra to be sworn to by her Peloponnesian allies.]

I. TRANSLATE Xen. Hell. VI. 5. 1.

ἀκολουθεῖν = to follow.   διατιθέναι = to treat.   μετέχειν = to share.
κοινωνεῖν = to be partners.   ἐμμένειν = to abide by.   αὐτόνομος = independent.

II. TRANSLATE:—

1. These brave men were beheaded by order of the satrap.

2. If the general sends for ships, you will be at a loss what to do.

3. Who believes that Socrates was put to death justly?

4. Let us send two messengers to announce[1] what we must do.

5. He must exercise both himself and his horses.

6. If we should give up our arms, the king would inflict punishment on our leaders.

7. He announced that the exiles were fleeing at full speed.

8. He had feared that he might be encircled in the mountains.

September, 1884.

[SUBJECT.—Cyrus, inquiring for Abradates, is told how he died.]

I. TRANSLATE Cyrop. VII. 3. 2–6.

θαμίζων = to be often with one.   στῖφος = column.   ὠχεῖτο = to ride.
προσκεκομικίναι = to carry.   ὀρύττειν = to dig.   κεκοσμηκυῖα = adorn (for burial).

II. TRANSLATE:—

1. The citizens ransomed their children with money.

2. But he promised to give each man five minae of silver.

3. The army will slaughter the cattle, that it may procure itself food.

4. The Greeks encamped near a great park.

5. Let us all strive to conquer the king's army.

6. They asked who the man was.

7. And she was said to have given much money to Cyrus.

8. They hear the soldiers shouting, "The Sea! The Sea!"

June, 1884.

[SUBJECT.—The capture of Sardis by Cyrus the Great.]

I. TRANSLATE Cyrop. VII. 2. 1–4.

κλίμακας = *ladders.* ἀποτομώτατα: cf. ἀποτέμνω. ἐρύματος = *fortification.* φρουρῶν = *garrison.*

II. TRANSLATE :—

1. Those who command, therefore, must be much more vigilant.

2. Without the knowledge of the soldiers he sent a messenger to him and bade him be of good courage.

3. Let us send for the hoplites as quickly as possible.

4. But this became evident on the following day.

5. I am not willing to go, fearing that he may take me and inflict punishment on me.

6. They went off and burned the wagons and the tents.

7. Cyrus kept finding many pretexts, as *you* also well know.

8. But I hope that the enemy will not stay, when they see us on the heights.

September, 1883.

I. TRANSLATE Xen. Hell. V. 3. 4–6.

II. TRANSLATE : —

1. He commanded the guide not to lead them where there was not food for the beasts of burden.

2. We must hope till our messenger comes back.

3. Having said many wonderful things, the soldier went away.

4. The soothsayer declared that there would be a storm.

5. But the day happens to be very fine.

6. Do not believe the soothsayers, if they predict evils.

7. When the infantry heard the trumpet, they straightway grounded arms.

June, 1883.

[SUBJECT. — Military operations near Olynthia.]

I. TRANSLATE Xen. Hell. V. 3. 1–3.

λεηλατέω, *to plunder.* τειχήρεις, *beleaguered.*

II. TRANSLATE : —

1. We should have taken the city, if the hostile horsemen had not followed (us).

2. We sent a messenger to learn who they were.

3. They said they would gladly become our allies.

4. If we give them pay, they will be our friends.

5. We ought to send them pay for three months.

6. This army guards the king himself.

7. The next day they did not appear.

8. The enemy no longer attacked us, fearing lest they should be conquered.

PHYSICS.
July, 1886.
Avery or Gage.

1. Describe such experiments as you have made to test the physical properties of air. If you have never made any such experiments, describe those you have seen or read of.

2. Define inertia. Define force. Define work. Would it, according to your definition, require work to set a mass in motion on a smooth level plane in a vacuum?

3. A cord, whose weight may be neglected, passing over a frictionless pulley bears a mass of 25 grm. at one end and a mass of 15 grm. at the other end. If this system of cord and weights starts from rest, under the influence of gravity, how much kinetic energy will the weights have after two seconds? What unit of energy do you employ?

4. Name and describe the use of the main parts of a non-condensing steam-engine.

5. Describe very carefully some two-fluid galvanic [or voltaic] cell. Could you obtain a strong shock directly from such a cell? Describe the apparatus you would employ with such a cell, if you wished to get the most powerful shock possible.

6. Show, by drawing a figure, how to find the position and size of the image of a body placed between a concave mirror and its principal focus. How does a real image differ from a virtual one?

[Arrange the answers in their proper order.]

Rolfe and Gillet.

1. Describe such experiments as you have made to test the physical properties of air. If you have never made any such experiments, describe those you have seen or read of.

PHYSICS. 83

2. A vertical screw, with threads ½ in. apart vertically, is turned by a lever 2 ft. long. What is the ratio of the power to the weight lifted?

3. A piece of wood which weighs 20 grm. in air is attached to a sinker that weighs 25 grm. under water. The two together weigh 15 grm. under water. What is the specific gravity of the wood?

4. Show fully the difference between ordinary evaporation and boiling. Describe the action of the wet-and-dry-bulb hygrometer.

5. Describe very carefully some two-fluid galvanic [or voltaic] cell. Could you obtain a strong shock directly from such a cell? Describe the apparatus you would employ with such a cell, if you wished to get the most powerful shock possible.

6. Let two lines, drawn at right angles to each other, represent the edges of two mirrors, and let a luminous point be placed within the right angle. Show very carefully, by means of a diagram, how to find all the images of this point in the two mirrors.

June, 1885.

[Candidates may take either of these papers, but not selections from different papers.]

ROLFE AND GILLET.

1. If a body be shot upward with a velocity of 100 ft. a second, how far will it rise in 3 seconds?

2. A piece of wood weighing 6 lbs. in air is fastened to a piece of lead which alone in water weighs 7 lbs. The two together weigh 5 lbs. in water. Find the specific gravity of the wood.

3. Describe carefully the construction and action of a thermo-electric pile or battery.

4. How does polarized light differ from ordinary light? Describe some method of polarizing light.

5. Explain the construction and action of the "compensation balance-wheel" of a watch or clock.

6. Describe some experiment showing the interference of sound-waves.

7. Describe the construction and action of the voltameter.

Avery.

1. Define a "gravity unit of force" and an "absolute unit of force" in a manner calculated to make the matter plain to a person unacquainted with physics.

2. A body weighing 50 lbs. is moving at the rate of 8 miles an hour. What is its kinetic energy? What is the unit of energy in this case?

3. A piece of wood weighing 6 lbs. in air is fastened to a piece of lead which alone in water weighs 7 lbs. The two together weigh 5 lbs. in water. Find the specific gravity of the wood.

4. Describe carefully the construction and action of a thermo-electric pile.

5. Describe some experiment showing the interference of sound-waves.

6. Describe what is seen to take place in water as it is raised, by means of heat applied at the bottom of the vessel, from the ordinary temperature to the boiling-point.

7. Can a convex mirror be used to throw upon a screen the image of an object before it? If so, tell how the object and the screen must be placed for this purpose. If not, tell why not.

June, 1884.
ROLFE AND GILLET.

1. If a body in falling from a state of rest through 4.9 meters, acquires a velocity of 9.8 meters per second, through what distance must it fall from rest in order to acquire a velocity of 4.9 meters per second?

2. Describe the construction and action of the *governor* of a steam-engine.

3. State briefly Helmholtz's theory of dissonance in musical sounds.

4. Explain "Fraunhofer's lines," and tell what use is made of them.

5. What is the exact meaning of the expression *humidity in the air?* Describe some form of hygrometer.

6. Describe carefully some form of galvanic cell.

AVERY.

1. If a body in falling from a state of rest through 4.9 meters acquires a velocity of 9.8 meters per second, through what distance must it fall from rest in order to acquire a velocity of 4.9 meters per second?

2. A piece of metal weighs 14 grm. in air, 12 grm. in water, and 11 grm. in another liquid. Find the specific gravity of the metal and that of the unknown liquid.

3. Describe carefully some form of galvanic cell.

4. Explain the beats of musical sounds. Upon what conditions does the velocity of sound depend?

5. What weight of water at $90°$ C. will just melt 5 lbs. of ice which is at $-5°$ C.?

6. Give carefully a rule for constructing real images formed by a concave spherical mirror.

June, 1883.

Rolfe and Gillet or Avery.

1. Describe briefly the construction of the hydrostatic press, and state the principle of it.

2. Describe the construction and action of the safety valve of a steam boiler.

3. What is meant by the term *harmonics*, or *overtones*, in music? What is the condition of the air in an open pipe giving its fundamental note?

4. What is the principal focus of a concave mirror? What are conjugate foci?

5. What is an induced current of electricity? Describe the construction and action of any induction coil.

6. State and explain the effect of increase of pressure upon the boiling-point of a liquid.

7. How is an astatic magnetic needle constructed? How must such a needle be placed in order to be of service in a galvanometer?

Arnott.

1. If a certain body weigh 100 lbs. at the earth's surface, what would it weigh at a point 8000 miles distant from that surface, the effect of centrifugal force being disregarded and the radius of the earth being called 4000 miles?

2. What is meant by the statement that gases and liquids are perfectly elastic?

3. What momentum will a 10-lb. weight have after falling 2 seconds from a position of rest?

4. Define energy, and illustrate the difference between kinetic and potential energy.

5. If in a pair of nut-crackers the nut be placed 1 inch from the hinge, how much pressure must be applied at a distance of 6 inches from the hinge in order to crack the nut, supposing the latter capable of sustaining a direct pressure of 10 lbs.?

6. If a simple pendulum 40 inches long would vibrate in one second, what would be the length of a pendulum vibrating in one-half a second?

7. State the three so-called *laws of friction* between solids. What is meant by the *angle of repose* for any two given substances?

September, 1882.

ROLFE AND GILLET.

[The acceleration of gravity may be taken as 32 feet.]

1. Describe the action of the common air-pump.

2. A body is thrown upward with such a velocity that it will continue to rise four seconds. What height will it have reached at the end of the second second?

3. Is the condenser more commonly used with high-pressure or low-pressure engines? Why?

4. What is the condition of the air at the node of an organ pipe?

5. Does a double-concave lens diverge or converge rays of light? What is the principal focus of a lens?

6. What is meant by the specific heat of a substance?

7. Describe the construction of the ordinary frictional electrical machine.

ARNOTT.

1. A body is thrown upward with such a velocity that it will continue to rise four seconds. What height will it have reached at the end of the second second?

2. Describe the construction and use of Atwood's machine.

3. What is meant by the mechanical equivalent of heat?

4. Give the conditions necessary for stable, unstable, and neutral equilibrium respectively.

5. What is the relation of the power to the weight in case of a single movable pulley?

6. How does the time of vibration of a pendulum depend on its length?

7. Give the laws of friction between solids.

June, 1882.
Rolfe and Gillet.

1. Describe the experiment of the Magdeburg hemispheres and tell what the experiment shows.

2. How far would a body fall in three seconds in a vacuum?

3. Explain "beats" produced by musical sounds.

4. Upon what does the color of bodies depend?

5. What is the apparent position of a point seen by reflection in a plane mirror? Show how to determine the apparent position of an arrow under the same circumstances.

6. Are liquids and gases good or bad conductors of heat? What is convection of heat?

7. Describe the construction and use of the gold-leaf electroscope.

Arnott.

1. Illustrate the difference between cohesion, or adhesion, and chemical attraction.

2. How far would a body fall in three seconds in a vacuum?

3. Illustrate the difference between kinetic and potential energy.

4. Explain the advantage obtained by use of the lifting-screw.

5. What are the laws of friction between solids?

6. How would you find the centre of gravity of a plane figure? Give examples of stable, unstable, and neutral equilibrium.

7. How much work would be done in lifting a 10-lb. weight a distance of 50 feet from the surface of the earth?

September, 1880.
MINIMUM PHYSICS.
[Omit any four.]

1. What are some of the properties of bodies resulting from cohesion?

2. What is the result of two coexistent motions? Illustrate by the motion of a projectile.

3. Show that the energy of a moving body is proportional to the square of its velocity.

4. What is the position of centre of gravity of an equilateral triangle of a conical surface?

5. What are the simple machines? What is the gain with the inclined plane?

6. What is the centre of oscillation? of percussion? Can either coincide with the centre of gravity? If so, when?

7. Describe and account for sounding flames.

8. Explain the *mirage*.

9. What is the cause which makes a liquid assume the spheroidal state?

10. Describe formation of voltaic arc. What is the cause of the *heat* developed?

PLANE GEOMETRY.
September, 1886.

[In solving problems use for π the approximate value $3\frac{1}{7}$.]

1. Prove that the straight line drawn parallel to the bases of a trapezoid so as to bisect one of the non-parallel sides bisects the opposite side also, and is equal to half the sum of the parallel sides.

2. Prove that an angle formed by two secants intersecting without a circumference is measured by one-half the difference of the intercepted arcs.

3. Show that the common interior tangent of two circles of radii 4 inches and 8 inches respectively, whose centres are 18 inches apart, cuts the line joining these centres at a distance of 6 inches from the centre of the smaller circle.

4. Prove that two triangles which have an angle of the one equal to an angle of the other are to each other as the products of the sides including the equal angles.

If two mutually equiangular polygons have the sides enclosing a certain angle of the one respectively equal to the sides enclosing the corresponding angle of the other, are the two polygons necessarily equal? Give an example to illustrate your answer.

5. Prove that the locus of the middle points of all the chords of a given circle, which pass through a given point P without the circumference, is a certain arc of the circle which has for a diameter the line which joins P with the centre of the given circle.

July, 1886.

[In solving problems use for π the approximate value $3\tfrac{1}{7}$.]

1. Prove that the lines which join the middle points of the sides of any triangle divide the triangle into four equal triangles, and show that the area of each of the parts into which an isosceles right triangle whose hypotenuse is 8 might be thus subdivided would be 4.

2. Prove that through any three points, not in the same straight line, one circumference can be made to pass, and but one. What is the locus of the centres of all the circumferences that can be made to pass through *two* given points?

3. Show that, if two circles touch each other externally, that portion of a common exterior tangent which is included between the points of contact with the two circumferences is a mean proportional between the diameters of the circles.

4. The areas of two mutually equiangular parallelograms are to each other as the products of the two sides which include corresponding angles. Assuming that this proposition is true when the corresponding sides of the two parallelograms are commensurable, prove strictly by the "Method of Limits" that it is still true when the sides of the one parallelogram are respectively incommensurable with the corresponding sides of the other.

5. Prove that if all the sides of a regular hexagon be produced until each side meets the next but one, the star-shaped figure thus produced will have twice the area of the original hexagon; and find the area of the hexagon obtained by joining by straight lines the consecutive points of the star.

June, 1885.

[In solving problems use for π the approximate value $3\tfrac{1}{7}$.]

1. Prove that every point in the bisector of an angle is equally distant from the sides of the angle. If the converse of this proposition is true, state and prove that also.

2. Prove that in the same circle, or in equal circles, equal chords are equally distant from the centre.

A line, MN, 10 inches long, is inscribed in a circle whose radius is 13 inches. From C, the centre of the circle, a perpendicular is let fall upon MN and extended until it cuts the circumference in Q. Prove that the path traced out by the middle point of the chord MQ, as MN is moved from one of its inscribed positions to another, is the arc of a circle, and find the radius of this circle.

3. Prove that if two straight lines be drawn through the point of contact of two circles which have a common tangent, the chords of the intercepted arcs will be parallel.

4. Assuming that a line drawn parallel to the base of a triangle divides the other two sides proportionally when these sides have a common measure, prove strictly, by the doctrine of limits, that the same proposition is true when the sides of the triangle are incommensurable.

5. Prove that the triangle formed by joining the middle point of one of the non-parallel sides of a trapezoid to the extremities of the opposite side, is equivalent to one-half the trapezoid.

6. The length of a side of a certain regular hexagon is 6. Find the area of the hexagon and the circumference and area of the circle inscribed in a regular hexagon whose area is 4 times as great.

September, 1884.

1. Prove that the lines drawn from opposite vertices of any parallelogram to middle points of opposite sides are parallel, and divide one of the diagonals into 3 equal parts.

2. (a) Prove that through 3 points not in the same straight line one circle can be drawn, and only one.

(b) A certain equilateral triangle has sides 12 inches long. What is the radius of the circle circumscribed about it?

3. (a) What do you mean by the limit of a variable quantity?

(b) Prove that in same circle 2 angles at centre are to each other as the arcs they intercept (by doctrine of limits when incommensurable).

4. (a) Prove that sum of squares of sides of any parallelogram equal sum of the squares of the diagonals.

(b) The sides of a certain parallelogram are 4 inches and 6 inches respectively. Find the hypotenuse of a right triangle whose sides are equal to the diagonals of this parallelogram.

5. The radii of 2 circles are 8 inches and 3 inches, and the distance between their centres is 15 inches. Find the length of their common exterior tangent.

6. The perimeter of a certain hexagon is 48 feet. Find the area of the circle inscribed in an equivalent square.

June, 1884.

[In solving problems use for π the approximate value $3\frac{1}{7}$.]

1. Show how to draw a parallelogram which shall be equivalent to a given trapezoid, and prove that the straight line which connects the middle points of the non-parallel sides of any trapezoid is parallel to the parallel sides and is equal to half their sum.

2. Prove that an angle formed within a circumference by the intersection of two chords is measured by half the sum of the two arcs which the sides of the angle subtend.

A, B, C, and D are 4 points lying in order upon a certain circumference. The arcs AB, BC, and CD have the values 86°, 43°, and 108° respectively. Find the angle formed by the intersection of the chords AC and BD, and also the angles formed without the circumference by the intersection of the chords AB and CD produced.

3. Assuming that two rectangles which have equal altitudes are to each other as their bases, when these bases are commensurable, prove by the doctrine of limits that the same proportionality exists when the bases are incommensurable.

4. Prove that, if AB is the side of an equilateral triangle inscribed in a circle of which O is the centre and AOC a diameter, the triangle BOC will be equilateral.

If AO is 10 inches long, what will be the area of the triangle ABC?

5. Prove that the figure formed by joining consecutively the four middle points of the sides of any quadrilateral is equivalent to one-half the quadrilateral.

6. The area of a certain square is 49 sq. ft.: write down the length of the circumference and the area of the circle inscribed in the square.

September, 1883.

1. Prove that every point in the bisector of an angle is equally distant from the sides of the angle, and hence show that the 3 bisectors of 3 angles of a triangle meet in a point.

2. Prove that if 2 circles are concentric, all tangents to the inner which are terminated by the circumference of the outer circle are equal to each other.

3. Show how to draw a line which shall bisect the angle made by two intersecting straight lines.

4. The area of a regular hexagon inscribed in a circle equals $24\sqrt{3}$. Find area of circle, and of its circumscribed square.

5. The least chord which can be drawn through point P within a circle is 8 inches long, but the distance between P and the nearest point of circumference is only 2 inches. Find radius of circle.

Prove that if through a fixed point without a circle a secant be drawn, the product of the whole secant and its external segment will have the same value in whatever direction the secant be drawn.

June, 1883.

1. What must you know about the sides, angles, or diagonals of a quadrilateral in order to be able to infer that it is a parallelogram?

Prove that the diagonals of a parallelogram bisect each other.

2. Prove that in the same circle or in equal circles, equal chords are equally distant from the centre, and that of two unequal chords the less is at the greater distance from the centre.

In a certain circle a chord whose length is 16 inches is at a distance of 6 inches from the centre: find the radius of the circle and the length of a chord whose distance from the centre is only 4 inches.

3. Prove that if a perpendicular be drawn from the vertex of the right angle to the hypotenuse of a right triangle, each side about the right angle will be a mean proportional between the hypotenuse and the adjacent segment.

If a chord, AB, 5 inches long be drawn in a circle whose diameter is 13 inches, find the perpendicular distance of B from the diameter drawn through A.

4. Prove that regular polygons of the same number of sides are similar.

The area of a regular decagon circumscribed about a certain circle is 10 square inches; find the area of a similar figure circumscribed about a circle whose radius is 16 times as great as that of the first.

5. Prove that the area of a regular hexagon inscribed in any circle is a mean proportional between the areas of the inscribed and circumscribed equilateral triangles.

September, 1882.

1. State, without proving that your construction is correct, how you could describe on a given line 4 inches long a segment of a circle which should contain an angle of 45°. How long would the radius of your circle be?

2. Prove that if a straight line drawn parallel to the base of a triangle bisects one of the sides it bisects the other side also; and the portion of the line intercepted between the two sides is equal to one-half the base.

3. Prove that if through a fixed point without a circle a secant be drawn, the product of the whole secant and its external segment will have the same value in whatever direction the secant be drawn.

4. Prove that the perimeters of regular polygons of the same number of sides are to each other as the radii of the circumscribed circles, or as the radii of the inscribed circles, and hence show that the ratio of the circumference to the diameter is the same in all circles.

5. Two triangles are on the same base and between the same parallels; through the point of intersection of their sides is drawn a straight line parallel to the base, and terminated by the sides which do not intersect: prove that the segments of this straight line are equal.

June, 1882.

1. What must you know about the sides or angles of two triangles in order to be able to infer that the triangles are equal?

Prove that two triangles are equal when the three sides of the one are respectively equal to the three sides of the other.

2. Two chords of a circle which intersect within the circumference divide the latter into four parts whose lengths taken in order are 89°, 43°, 117°, and 111°. Find, without proof, the angles which the chords make with each other.

Prove that an angle formed by two secants intersecting without the circumference is measured by one-half the difference of the intercepted arcs.

3. Define similar polygons, and prove that two triangles are similar when they are mutually equiangular.

4. State, without proof, how you would inscribe a regular decagon in a given circle.

5. Prove that in a right-angled triangle the straight line joining the right angle to the centre of the square on the hypotenuse will bisect the right angle.

[Suggestion.—Draw a circumference on the hypotenuse as a diameter.]

September, 1881.

1. Define similar triangles. Prove that two triangles which are mutually equiangular are similar.

2. Prove that the angle made by a tangent to a circle and

a chord drawn through the point of tangency is measured by one-half the intercepted arc.

3. Prove that a tangent to a circle is perpendicular to the radius drawn to the point of tangency.

4. Prove that the two pairs of opposite sides of any quadrilateral circumscribed about a circle have the same sum.

June, 1881.

1. State and prove how to inscribe a circle in a given triangle.

2. Prove that an angle formed by two chords of a circle, and which has its vertex between the centre and the circumference, is measured by one-half the intercepted arc plus one-half the arc intercepted by its sides produced.

3. What is the sum of the interior angles of a polygon of n sides? Give the proof.

4. State, without proof, how to draw a straight line through the middle point of the base of a triangle so that the triangle shall be bisected.

5. Any point D in the base BC of a triangle ABC is joined with the vertex A by a straight line, and from E, the middle point of the base, a line is drawn parallel to DA to meet one of the sides of the triangle in F. Prove that the straight line which joins D with F bisects the triangle.

September, 1880.

1. Prove that the tangent to a circle is perpendicular to the radius drawn to point of tangency. State the converse.

2. Show how to draw a circumference through a given point and tangent to a given line at a given point of it.

3. Show how to draw tangent to circle from point without.

4. Let tangent be drawn from point P to circle, with radius equal to 4 feet, at a point T of circumference, and let O be centre of circle. If the circumference bisects OP and angle $TPO = 30°$, what are the areas of the circle, the triangle TPO, and the part of the circle within the triangle?

5. Define similar polygons. Prove that two similar polygons may be decomposed into same number of triangles similar each to each.

6. Prove that areas of similar triangles are proportional to the squares of homologous sides.

What is the ratio of areas of similar polygons.

July, 1880.

1. Prove that the perpendiculars erected at the middle points of the sides of a triangle meet in a common point.

2. Prove that the three perpendiculars from the vertices of a triangle to the opposite sides meet in a common point. [SUGGESTION.—Draw a parallel to each side through the opposite vertex.]

3. Prove that the area of any polygon circumscribed about a circle is measured by one-half the product of the perimeter of the polygon and the radius of the circle.

4. In a circle with a radius of 6 feet, a regular hexagon is inscribed, and about the circle a polygon is circumscribed with a perimeter of 40 feet. Find the areas of the hexagon, the polygon, and of the part of the circle without the hexagon.

5. Prove that in a right triangle the perpendicular from the vertex of the right angle upon the hypotenuse divides

the hypotenuse into segments, such that each side is a mean proportional between the whole hypotenuse and the adjacent segment.

6. Prove that the square described on the hypotenuse of a right triangle is equivalent to the sum of the squares described on the other sides.

ALGEBRA.

September, 1886.

1. Solve the equation

$$\frac{\frac{1}{5}[2b(x+1)]^2}{4bx^3 + 5ax} - a\left(\frac{1}{x} - \frac{5ax - 4b}{4bx^2 + 5a}\right) = 0;$$

and reduce the answers to their simplest forms.

2. Solve the equation $x^{-3} - x^3 = 7(x^3 + 1)$.

3. A and B have 4800 circulars to stamp for the mail, and mean to do them in two days, 2400 each day. The first day A, working alone, stamps 800 circulars, and then A and B together stamp the remaining 1600, the whole job occupying 3 hours. The second day A works 3 hours and B 1 hour, but they accomplish only $\frac{9}{10}$ of their task for that day. Find the number of circulars which each stamps per minute, and the length of time that B works on the first day.

4. Find the value of x from the proportion

$$\frac{5ac}{b^2}\sqrt[3]{ab^2} : \sqrt[4]{\frac{9c^3}{a^2}} = x : \frac{3a^2}{2}\sqrt{\frac{3c}{ab}};$$

and express the answer with the use of only one radical sign.

5. Given the three expressions

$$2x^4 + x^3 - 8x^2 - x + 6,$$
$$4x^4 + 12x^3 - x^2 - 27x - 18,$$
$$4x^4 + 4x^3 - 17x^2 - 9x + 18;$$

find the greatest common divisor and the least common multiple of the *first two* of these expressions; also those of *the whole group of three.*

July, 1886.

1. A boat's crew, rowing at half their usual speed, row three miles down a certain river and back again, in the middle of the stream, accomplishing the whole distance in 2 hours and 40 minutes. When rowing at full speed, they go over the same course in 1 hour and 4 minutes. Find (in miles per hour) the rate of the crew, when rowing at full speed, and the rate of the current.

(Notice *both* solutions of this problem.)

2. Solve the equation

$$3\sqrt{x^3 + 17} + \sqrt{x^3 + 1} + 2\sqrt{5x^3 + 41} = 0.$$

Substitute the answers, when found, in the equation, and show in what manner the equation is satisfied.

3. Solve the equations

$$x + \frac{4y+1}{x+2y} = 2(y+1), \quad x + 3y + 1 = 0.$$

4. Solve the equation

$$\frac{(a+2b)x}{a-2b} = \frac{a^2}{a-2b} - \frac{4b^2}{x};$$

and reduce the answers to their simplest form.

5. Find the greatest common divisor and the least common multiple of $4x^3 - 4x^2 - 5x + 3$ and $10x^2 - 19x + 6$.

6. Find the 6th and 25th terms of the 29th power of $(x - y)$; reducing the numerical coefficients to their prime factors, and not performing the multiplications.

Find the 6th term of the 29th power of $\left(\dfrac{\sqrt[2]{a}}{b} - \dfrac{b^2}{2a}\right)$, reducing exponents to their simplest form, and combining similar factors.

June, 1885.

1. Three students, A, B, and C, agree to work out a series of difficult problems, in preparation for an examination; and each student determines to solve a fixed number of problems every day. A solves 9 problems per day, and finishes the series 4 days before B; B solves 2 more problems per day than C, and finishes the series 6 days before C. Find the number of problems, and the number of days given to them by each student.

2. Solve the following equation, reducing the answers to their simplest form: —

$$\dfrac{2}{1 + 3x} - \left(\dfrac{a(1 + 2x)}{b(1 + 3x)} - \dfrac{b(3x - 1)}{a(2x + 1)}\right) = 0.$$

3. Solve the equation

$$\dfrac{\sqrt{3}}{\sqrt{2x - 1} - \sqrt{x - 2}} = \dfrac{1}{\sqrt{x - 1}}.$$

4. A certain whole number, composed of three digits, has the following properties: 10 times the middle digit exceeds the square of half the sum of the digits by 21; if 99 be added to the number, the order of the digits is inverted; and if the number be divided by 11, the quotient is a whole number, of two digits, which are the same as the first and last digits of the original number. Find the number.

ALGEBRA. 103

5. Given $\dfrac{x+6y}{7x-2y} = 8$; find the value of $\dfrac{10x-3y}{2x-y}$.

6. Find the greatest common divisor of
$$3x^4 - x^3 - 2x^2 + 2x - 8$$
and $\qquad 6x^3 + 13x^2 + 3x + 20.$

7. Find the square root of
$$4 - 12x + 5x^2 + 26x^3 - 29x^4 - 10x^5 + 25x^6.$$

June, 1884.

1. A landowner laid out a rectangular lot containing 1200 square yards. He afterwards added three yards to one dimension of his lot, and subtracted $1\frac{1}{2}$ yards from the other, thereby increasing the area of his lot by 60 square yards. Find the dimensions of the lot before and after the change. How do you explain the *negative* solution?

2. Solve the equation
$$\frac{x+1}{c} - \frac{2}{cx} = \frac{x+2}{ax-bx};$$
reducing the answers to their simplest forms.

3. Solve the equations
$$x^2 + y^2 = 52, \quad xy + 24 = 0.$$
Find all the sets of answers, and state which answers belong together.

4. Multiply $a^{\frac{2}{3}} - a^{\frac{1}{3}} + 1 - a^{-\frac{1}{3}} + a^{-\frac{2}{3}}$ by $a^{\frac{1}{3}} + 1 + a^{-\frac{1}{3}}$.

Simplify the following expression:
$$\sqrt[26]{\left[\sqrt[3]{x^2} \cdot \sqrt{\left(\frac{\sqrt{x}}{\sqrt[3]{x}}\right)^5}\right]^3}.$$

104 ALGEBRA.

5. Prove that, if the corresponding terms of two proportions be multiplied together, the result is a proportion.

6. Find the greatest common divisor of
$9x^5 - 7x^3 + 8x^2 + 2x - 4$ and $6x^4 - 7x^3 - 10x^2 + 5x + 2$.

September, 1883.

1. A man setting out on a journey drives at the rate of a miles per hour to the nearest railway station distant b miles from his house. On arriving at the station he finds that the express for his destination has left c hours before. At what rate should he have driven in order to reach the station just in time for the express? Having obtained the general solution, find what the answer becomes in the following cases:—

(1) $c = 0$, (2) $c = \dfrac{b}{a}$, (3) $c = -\dfrac{b}{a}$.

In case (2) how much time does the man have to drive from his house? In case (3) what is the meaning of the negative value of c?

2. Solve the equation
$$(2x-1)^{\frac{1}{2}} - (3x+1)^{\frac{1}{2}} = (x-4)^{\frac{1}{2}}.$$

3. Solve the equation
$$\frac{ax}{a^2x-2} - \frac{1}{a}\left(\frac{x-3}{a^2x-2} - \frac{1}{x}\right) = \frac{2}{2x-a^2x^2},$$
reducing answers to lowest terms. What do answers become if $a = -1$?

4. Reduce to lowest terms
$$\frac{6x^5 - 2x^4 - 11x^3 + 5x^2 - 10x}{9x^5 + 3x^4 - 11x^3 + 9x^2 - 10x}.$$

ALGEBRA.

5. Value of a^0? } Give *reasons*.
   Value of a^{-n}

6. Solve $\begin{cases} x\dot{y} + 4 = 0. \\ 9x^2 - y^2 = 7. \end{cases}$

Find all the answers, and state what values of x and y belong together.

June, 1883.

1. Solve the equation
$$\frac{1}{x} = 2 - \frac{4ax^2 - 3b(x-2)}{2a(x^2+1) + 3b}.$$

2. A man walks at a regular rate of speed on a road which passes over a certain bridge, distant 21 miles from the point which the man has reached at noon. If his rate of speed were half a mile per hour greater than it is, the time at which he crosses the bridge would be an hour earlier than it is. Find his actual rate of speed, and the time at which he crosses the bridge. Explain the *negative* answer.

3. Find the prime factors of the coefficient of the 6th term of the 19th power of $(a-b)$. What are the exponents in the same term, and what is the sign?

4. Reduce the following fraction to its lowest terms:—
$$\frac{x^4 + 2x^2 + 9}{x^4 - 4x^3 + 10x^2 - 12x + 9}.$$

5. Prove that, if $a:b=c:d$,
$$\frac{a+b}{c+d} = \frac{a-b}{c-d} = \frac{a}{c} = \frac{b}{d}.$$

6. Solve the equations $xy = 4 - y^2$, $2x^2 - y^2 = 17$.

Find all the answers, and show what values of x and y belong together.

September, 1882.

1. Simplify
$$\frac{x - 3a + \dfrac{4a^2}{a+x}}{x - \dfrac{2a^2}{a+x}}.$$

2. Solve the equations
$$\frac{x}{a} + \frac{y}{b} = 1, \quad \frac{a}{x} + \frac{b}{y} = 4.$$

3. Find the factors of the least common multiple of
$$3x^5 + 2x^4 + x^2 \text{ and } 3x^4 + 2x^3 - 3x^2 + 2x - 1.$$

4. Solve the equation
$$(3 + b^2)(x^2 - x + 1) = (3b^2 + 1)(x^2 + x + 1).$$

5. Find the terms which do not contain radicals in the development of
$$\left(\sqrt{2a} - \sqrt{\frac{b}{a}} \right)^4.$$

6. A hires a certain number of acres for $420. He lets all but four of them to B, receiving for each acre $2.50 more than he pays for it. The whole amount received from B is $420. Find the number of acres.

7. Which is the larger, $\sqrt[3]{10}$ or $\sqrt[5]{46}$? Give the reason for your answer.

June, 1882.

1. Simplify
$$\frac{a^2 - bc}{(a-b)(a-c)} + \frac{b^2 + ca}{(b+c)(b-a)} + \frac{c^2 + ab}{(c-a)(c+b)}.$$

ALGEBRA.

2. A man bought a certain number of sheep for $300; he kept 15 sheep, and sold the remainder for $270, gaining half a dollar a head. How many sheep did he buy, and at what price?

3. Find the greatest common divisor of

$$2x^5 - 11x^2 - 9 \text{ and } 4x^5 + 11x^4 + 81.$$

4. Solve the equation

$$\frac{(4a^2 - b^2)(x^2 + 1)}{4a^2 + b^2} = 2x.$$

Reduce the answers to their lowest terms.

5. Find the square root of

$$x^3 + 2x^{\frac{5}{2}} - 3x^2 - 4x^{\frac{3}{2}} + 4x.$$

6. A and B can do a piece of work in 18 days; A and C can do it in 45 days; B and C in 20 days. Find the time in which A, B, and C can do it, working together.

September, 1881.

1. Solve the equation

$$\frac{4a^2}{x+2} + \frac{4a^2 - b^2}{x(x^2 - 4)} = \frac{b^2}{x-2}.$$

2. Multiply $\dfrac{x+y}{x-y} - \dfrac{x-y}{x+y} - \dfrac{4y^2}{x^2 - y^2}$ by $\dfrac{x+y}{2y}$.

3. Solve the equations

$$\frac{m}{x} + \frac{n}{y} = a, \quad \frac{n}{x} + \frac{m}{y} = b.$$

4. Find the greatest common measure of

$$x^4 - 115x + 24 \text{ and } 24x^4 - 115x^3 + 1.$$

5. A man bought a number of railway shares when they were at a certain rate per cent discount for $8500; and afterwards, when they were at the same rate per cent premium, he sold all but 20 of them for $9200. How many did he buy, and what did he give for each of them?

6. Find the last four terms of
$$(a^{\frac{1}{2}} - 2b^{\frac{1}{3}})^{20},$$
reducing the numerical part of each term to its prime factors.

September, 1880.

1. Simplest form of
$$\left(\frac{x+y}{x-y} + \frac{x^2+y^2}{x^2-y^2}\right) \div \left(\frac{x-y}{x+y} - \frac{x^3-y^3}{x^3+y^3}\right).$$

2. G.C.D. and L.C.M. of
$$x^6 + 3x^5 + 3x^4 + 9x^3 - 4x^2 - 12x$$
and
$$x^6 + 3x^5 - x^3 - 3x^2.$$

3. Find 6th term of $\left(\dfrac{a\sqrt{a}}{\sqrt[9]{b^2}} - 6\sqrt{b^3}\right)^{17}$, reducing the literal part of the term to its simplest form, and leaving the numerical part as a product of its prime factors.

4. A reservoir, supplied by several pipes, can be filled in 15 hours, every pipe discharging into it the same fixed number of hhds. per hour. If there were 5 more pipes, and every pipe discharged per hour 7 hhds. less, the reservoir would be filled in 12 hours. If the number of pipes were 1 less, and every pipe discharged per hour 8 hhds. more, the reservoir would be filled in 14 hours. Find number of pipes and capacity of reservoir.

ALGEBRA.

5. Solve $\dfrac{2x+1}{b} - \dfrac{3x+1}{a} = \dfrac{1}{x}\left(\dfrac{1}{b} - \dfrac{2}{a}\right).$

Work out completely and carefully, and reduce answers to simplest forms.

July, 1880.

1. Reduce to its simplest form
$$\dfrac{1}{x + \dfrac{2}{1 - \dfrac{x-2}{2x+1}}}.$$

2. Divide $6x^{m+3n} - 19x^{m+2n} + 20x^{m+n} - 7x^m - 4x^{m-n}$ by $3x^{2n} - 5x^n + 4$.

3. Find the fourth term of $\left(\dfrac{2\sqrt{a}}{3} - \dfrac{6\sqrt[3]{b^2}}{a}\right)^{21}$, reducing it to its simplest form.

4. Find the greatest common measure and the least common multiple of $2x^5 - 11x^2 - 9$ and $4x^5 + 11x^4 + 81$.

5. A man walks 2 hours at the rate of $4\frac{1}{2}$ miles per hour. He then adopts a different rate. At the end of a certain time, he finds that if he had kept on at the rate at which he set out, he would have gone three miles further from his starting-point; and that if he had walked three hours at his first rate and half an hour at his second rate, he would have reached the point he has actually attained. Find the whole time occupied by the walk and his final distance from the starting-point.

6. Solve the equation
$$\dfrac{a}{b(2x-1)} - \dfrac{b(2x+1)}{a(x^2-1)} = \dfrac{1}{(2x-1)(x+1)} + \dfrac{1}{(2x-1)(x-1)}.$$

Reduce the answers to their simplest forms. (Work out completely and carefully.)

ALGEBRA.

September, 1879.

1. Several friends, on an excursion, spent a certain sum of money. If there had been 5 more persons in the party, and each person had spent 25 cents more, the bill would have amounted to $33. If there had been 2 less in the party, and each person had spent 30 cents less, the bill would have amounted to only $11. Of how many did the party consist, and what did each spend?
Find all possible answers.

2. Solve the equations
$$2x + 4y + 27z = 28,$$
$$7x - 3y - 15z = 3,$$
$$9x - 10y - 33z = 4.$$

3. Solve the equation
$$\frac{x+3b}{8a^2-12ab} + \frac{3b}{4a^2-9b^2} = \frac{a+3b}{(2a+3b)(x-3b)}.$$
Reduce the answers to their simplest forms. (Work out completely and carefully.)

4. Calculate the 6th term of
$$\left(\frac{\sqrt[3]{a}}{\sqrt[4]{2}\sqrt[11]{b^3}} - \frac{\sqrt{2}}{3a^4\sqrt[10]{b}}\right)^{27}.$$
Reduce the answer to its simplest form, cancelling all common factors of numerator and denominator, performing the numerical multiplications, and giving a result which has only one radical sign and no negative or fractional exponents.

5. Simplify the fraction
$$\frac{\dfrac{2x+y^3}{2x-y^3} + \dfrac{4x^2+y^6}{4x^2-y^6}}{\dfrac{2x-y^3}{2x+y^3} - \dfrac{8x^3-y^9}{8x^3+y^9}}.$$

ALGEBRA. 111

6. Find the greatest common measure and the least common multiple of

$$4x^5 + 14ax^4 - 18a^3x^2 \text{ and } 24ax^3 + 30a^3x + 126a^4.$$

June, 1878.

1. Two workmen, A and B, are employed on a certain job at different wages. When the job is finished, A receives \$27.00, and B, who has worked 3 days less, receives \$18.75. If B had worked for the whole time, and A 3 days less than the whole time, they would have been entitled to equal amounts. Find the number of days each has worked, and the pay each receives per diem.

2. Find the value of x from the proportion

$$\left(\frac{10\sqrt[3]{a^2}}{3\sqrt[4]{b^5}}\right)^2 : x = \sqrt{\frac{5a\sqrt[3]{a^2}}{4\sqrt[5]{a^2}\cdot b^9} : \frac{9b^{-3}}{\sqrt{5}}}.$$

Express the answer in its simplest form, free from negative and fractional exponents.

3. Simplify the expression

$$\frac{\dfrac{x^2+y^2}{x^2-y^2} - \dfrac{x^2-y^2}{x^2+y^2}}{\dfrac{x-y}{x+y} + \dfrac{x+y}{x-y}}.$$

4. Write out the first five terms and the last five terms of $(x-y)^{13}$.

5. Find the value of x from the equations

$$ax + by = l,$$
$$cy + dz = m,$$
$$ex + fz = n.$$

6. Find the greatest common divisor and the least common multiple of $6x^2 + 7x - 5$ and $2x^3 - x^2 + 8x - 4$.

7. Solve the equation
$$\frac{x+13a+3b}{5a-3b-x} - \frac{a-2b}{x+2b} = 1.$$

ANCIENT HISTORY AND GEOGRAPHY.

September, 1886.

I.

1. Give an account of the races which inhabited Italy before the founding of Rome.

2. What were the principal Greek colonies on the shores of the Mediterranean? For what were three of them celebrated?

II.

3. Describe the three forms of the Roman *comitia* and trace the development of the *comitia tributa*.

4. What were some causes of the victory of Rome in the Punic wars? The effect of this victory upon Italy?

5. Explain *patria potestas, princeps senatus, municipium, ager Romanus, equites.*

III.

6. Describe the battle of Salamis, and show its importance in Greek history.

7. Describe as fully as possible the early training of Alexander of Macedon and his conquest of Asia.

8. [Take any three.] Solon, Plato, Herodotus, Lysander, Aeschylus. When and where did they live, and for what were they noted?

July, 1886.

I.

1. Indicate or describe the geographical position of the mountains Parnassus and Olympus; of the rivers Achelous, Liris, and Ticinus; of the cities Megalopolis and Panormus.

2. Give the names of the political divisions and the chief cities of Italy which were situated upon the Mare Superum. Where were Tyre, Lamia, and Saguntum?

II.

3. What were the institutions and natural ties which tended to keep alive a national spirit among the Greeks?

What part did the Amphictyonic council play in the history of Greece?

4. The Peace of Nicias; of Callias. Give a brief account, with dates.

How do you account for the Supremacy of Thebes?

5. Critias, Demetrius, Aeschylus, Thucydides. Give a brief account of three.

III.

6. The Valerian and Horatian laws. The agrarian law of Tiberius Gracchus.

7. Mention the curule magistrates, and describe the powers and duties of any two of them.

8. Aemilius Paulus, Sulla. Where did they live, and for what were they noted? Explain *plebiscitum, senatus consultum, lustrum, novus homo.*

June, 1885.

I.

1. Name the principal divisions of Greece. Give the situation of six of the most celebrated cities.

2. Name the countries included in the Roman dominions at the end of the Mithridatic war.

II.

1. The form of government among the Greeks in the Heroic Ages. What other forms of government were afterward adopted?

2. Give an account of the Sicilian expedition.

3. Give the dates and state briefly the causes of Athenian, Spartan, Theban and Macedonian supremacy in Greece.

III.

1. The importance in Roman history of the dates B.C. 48; 44; 42; 31.

2. Comment briefly upon: "The real lesson to be learned from the overthrow of the Roman Commonwealth is that states which boast themselves of their own freedom should not hold other states in bondage."

3. Give the names and dates of the Claudian Emperors, with some account of one of them.

June, 1885.

I.

1. (*a*) The Aryan settlement of Europe.

(*b*) What peoples were settled in Spain before the Roman conquest?

2. Indicate the extent of the geographical knowledge of the ancients and name the principal countries known to them.

II.

1. "This war might be looked on as a war between Ionians and Dorians, between democracy and oligarchy." What war? Explain the remark quoted. Give dates of the chief events of the war.

2. State the extent of the empire of Alexander the Great. What were some of the effects of Alexander's conquests?

3. B.C. 490, 480, 405, 387, 371, 338, 331, 323: to what events in the history of Greece do these dates point?

III.

1. The curule magistrates. Name them and state their functions.

2. What was the condition of the Italian states under Rome?

3. Marius and Sulla.

June, 1884.

I.

1. Enumerate (or indicate upon a map if you prefer) the countries conquered by Rome and included in the Empire of Augustus. Give a summary account of the conquest of two of them.

2. Describe accurately the situation of *six* of the following places, and name an important historical event connected with each, with the date: Corinthus, Cynoscephalae, Arbela, Carthago, Cunaxa, Hierosolyma, Agrigentum, Sphacteria, Aquae Sextiae, Numantia.

II.

1. Give a brief account of the public services of three leading men at Athens, at the period of the Persian wars.

2. The Thirty Tyrants.

3. Name in proper order, with dates, the chief events of the Peloponnesian War. Also the chief events in the life of Philip of Macedon.

III.

1. Events at Rome in the years B.C. 451–449.

2. The Roman Senate — its number, its mode of election, and its powers and duties.

3. The Battle of Philippi and the Battle of Actium, with the period between (with dates).

September, 1883.

I.

1. Name and place the chief seaports of the Mediterranean.

2. Draw an outline map of ancient Italy, showing the chief rivers, towns, and political divisions.

II.

1. The Thebans in Greek history.
2. Changes in form of government at Athens.
3. Pisistratus; Pericles; Conon; Timoleon.

III.

1. What was the Ager Romanus? What political questions arose in relation to it?

2. Government of Italy, and treatment of Italians by Rome.

3. Story of the Decemvirs.

SPECIMENS OF BAD ENGLISH.

September, 1886.

Correct on this paper all the errors you discover in the following sentences, the work of candidates for admission to Harvard College: —

1. Then hear Lady Macbeth call her husband a coward and saying that she herself wished to be a man.

2. He was the author of Paradise Lost and Regained also of many "Arguments."

3. But to make the other part clear, Tony Lumkin's mother wished him to marry her niece; but the dislike for each other was mutual on their part, but pretended they were deeply in love in Mrs. Hardcastle's sight.

4. Mr. Hardcastle has drilled his servants, and given the part which he will perform, to each one.

5. At the inn he meets the half-brother of the young lady, who is enjoying himself in his way. He directs him to his father's house as an inn, in order to witness the consternation of his step-father, at the thought of his house being taken for an inn.

6. Tony was a wild and awkward fellow, while, on the other contrary, Miss Hardcastle was very obedient and graceful.

7. Oliver Goldsmith presents in this story a striking aray of intricate and laughable positions which a man, without bordering upon the improbable, can imagine circumstances to place him.

8. The play, "She Stoops to Conquer," represents the mistakes of a young man, who has been sent by his father

to visit a friend of his, thinking it possible to arrange a match between that friend's daughter and his son.

9. Neither she nor Tony entertain any thoughts of marriage.

10. Mrs. Hardcastle wishes Tony Lumpkin to marry Miss Neville, while he, in reality, objects, although he is afraid to appear so.

11. Macbeth would have preferred to have compassed his design without resorting to the end he did.

12. It has always been a question in my mind whether Shakespere intended the ghost of Banquo to really appear on the stage as an ideal ghost, or whether it was his intention to convey the impression that the ghost was a creation of Macbeth's diseased mind.

13. At last, goaded on by his wife he does the deed, and murders the old king, as he slept.

14. The climax of Macbeth's life was now approaching. Still he trusted to the prophesy that he would not die, "Until Birnam Wood comes unto Dunsinane."

15. She wouldn't have liked it if she knew that Miss Neville were engaged to Hastings.

16. Mr. Hardcastle was watching eagerly for a young man to make him a visit, whom he hoped some day would be his son-in-law.

June, 1886.

1. These chapters prove that the boy Grant and the man Grant were as nearly alike as bud and flower — that the latter cannot be accounted for without the former is studied.

2. It is a pity these things are not more studied by the electorate, and that in addition to reading Mr. Gladstone's

SPECIMENS OF BAD ENGLISH.

and Mr. Chamberlain's speeches, they would sometimes read also Lord Granville's despatches.

3. This is one of the reasons why the author did, and every one else ought, to love nature.

4. A convent, a lunatic asylum, or a husband — either will do.

5. Colonel Enderby stepped out on to the gravel.

6. If I was you, I wouldn't let my husband talk in that way.

7. One alumnae recently pledged $5000 for improvements in the opportunities for physical culture at Vassar, on condition that $15,000 more should be raised by alumnae.

8. A celebrated anatomist, a profound chemist, and one of the first physiologists in Europe, it was a relief to him to turn from these subjects.

9. In proportion as either of these two qualities are wanting, the language is imperfect.

10. Madame Voss had a clearer insight to the state of her niece's mind than had her husband.

11. A British and Yankee skipper were sailing side by side.

12. She had not spoken hardly above a word during that interview.

13. We may fairly regard the book as a collection of youthful reflections as to the advisability of publishing which the poet had not yet made up his mind, and perhaps had he lived would have suppressed.

14. He considered it his duty to remonstrate with a woman whom he plainly saw was very much out of place there.

15. On reaching the office he heard a door creak in the basement, and upon going down stairs some one ran up.

16. The roof covers quite a considerable area of ground.

17. Lord D——, whose good nature was unbounded and which, in regard to myself, had been measured by his compassion perhaps for my condition, faltered at this request.

18. I never heard him say he had, and I would be likely to know.

19. These figures are certainly conclusive as to the ability of veterans to more than hold their own under existing circumstances.

20. The Yale News complains of smoking in their gymnasium.

September, 1885.

1. No pupil ever graduated from this school who was more earnest, thorough, and painstaking in their work.

2. We should like to name the sum, but it would be making public out of private affairs, and therefore must be omitted.

3. The game opened decidedly in favor of Brinley, although the friends of Knapp, flushed with his victory over J. S. Clark yesterday, and who is considered the best except Sears, expected great things from him.

4. She was so intent on the sport, that she allowed the sun to severely blister her hands.

5. Figuratively speaking, the Bostons literally swept the ground with the Providences at the South end yesterday afternoon.

6. Her complement of officers from the Captain down have filled their posts with credit to themselves and to the appreciation of all who have patronized the line.

7. Mrs. John Jones, while laying a covering cloth upon her parlor carpet got it entangled in her feet by which she was thrown down breaking the hip bone.

8. Exhibitors are requested not to lose their tags, nor to put them on the dogs, when practicable, until just before presenting them at the door.

9. No ready-thinking, progressive New England girl will for a moment be satisfied with any half-way measures, but will prefer to be put on a basis with her brother, and be willing to stand the same tests of ability and scholarship; and this is as it should be.

10. I was unable to give that close application to the work which I would have wished.

11. My dogs ate the New Process Dog Biscuit from the beginning ravishly, which surprised me, for the other kinds of biscuit the dogs had to be starved and coaxed to eat them.

12. Finding at your office, and having consulted you, you advised me to visit the other school before deciding, which I did, but came to the conclusion that your facilities were far superior to all others.

13. One word with regard to the corps of teachers: as instructors their equals cannot be surpassed.

14. He had to give up the stage on account of his health being utterly broken down.

15. He gives this lecture by invitation of several lovers of the horse, who meet the expenses of the same.

June, 1885.

1. Pitt and Fox both died a month after each other.

2. His mother was a tight-rope dancer, who lost her life while performing that feat.

3. Charles died a promising young clergyman, to the intense grief of his family and a large circle of friends.

4. The patent "Austria" skate fastens itself by stepping into it.

5. Here we were obliged to wait for daybreak in order to make a landing, which, being made in a small boat, was rendered very difficult on account of the swiftness of the current.

6. After a hearty breakfast we left the camp, at which we had arrived the night before, about half-past seven on a cool September morning, in an old-fashioned farm wagon, for we had some distance to go, and the walking through the tall broom-grass of the prairie is fatiguing in the extreme.

7. Mr. Smith presents his Compliments to Mr. Jones, and finds he has a Cap which isn't mine. So, if you have a Cap which isn't his, no doubt they are the Ones.

8. My Christian and surname begin and end with the same letters.

9. Charlemagne patronized not only learned men, but also established several educational institutions.

10. Because there are a few savage tribes who have no beliefs whatsoever, is no more, on the contrary not as great, a cause than to say, there is or are divine beings.

11. The crows whirled over his head, at which he now and then shied a stone.

12. They found grandmamma and luncheon there, with open arms and inviting dishes to welcome them.

13. I had heard of him [Keats] as an original, but peculiar, genius, the rich budding of whose thoughts was destined never to be perfected by an untimely death.

14. Quite a number of Harvard's most noted professors were present at Prof. Thompson's lecture, President Eliot being among the number.

15. Mrs. Jones, who is now 84, gave her first ball more than 60 years ago, at her house in Bowling Green, which shows the rapid growth of the city.

16. Nonquitt does not possess a store of any kind; not even a barber-shop. The ladies miss the former; the latter is an inconvenience to the gentlemen.

17. Mme. Adelina Patti having consented to appear as Martha, and Mme. Scalchi as Nancy, that favorite opera will be performed on Tuesday evening next.

18. The Amherst college senate has overhauled the '86 Olio, it being claimed that articles were published in that production which had been especially forbidden by the faculty.

19. When moulting we should take great care of canary birds.

20. These tickets will be good from Saturday A.M. until Sunday night, and by paying a small sum in addition, will be good from Friday afternoon to Monday night, so that those who wish to accompany the nine on the whole trip, can use the same tickets.

September, 1884.

1. Mr. Miller will give $100 to any person who will do the above feat with their eyes wide open.

2. He performs feats right among the audience, without apparatus, and repeating them any number of times, which he openly offers a reward of fifty dollars to any person who tells how they are done and will do them as he does.

3. The appearance of the yacht was man-of-war like,

coupled with a luxuriousness which reminded one of the Queen's private yacht.

4. Please state here your exact age, name and address, and mail it.

5. One of the most touching parts of "Henry Esmond," is surely, the description, which Thackeray gives of his boyhood.

6. The aspect of that boy, with his large sad eyes must have struck all who saw him as one who was naturally accustomed to look upon the dark side of affairs.

7. In the character of Shylock we can see the best as well as the worst faults of Irving's acting.

8. She tells him to be sure he takes neither more or less than a pound or he will forfeit his life.

9. The icy hand of Death stalked in, and breathed upon her.

10. But behold here Friendship, which Carlyle says exists no more, which last I do not believe at all.

11. To realize how great his misfortune was in this respect, let us ask ourselves how we would like to be ignorant of whom our parents were, and to find out at middle age that one was a wretch and the other a foreigner.

12. Irving, I think tries to elevate and to make "Shylock" appear more in the light of an injured and wronged man, than as the sly and grasping rogue that he is.

13. But then, what difference did it make whether one more lived or died, when men killed each other, and themselves, just as soon as they would an animal?

14. He seems to have accepted bribes and bribed others to a great extent, to have been ambitious, also mean, and to

SPECIMENS OF BAD ENGLISH. 125

have been very jealous of anyone under him making military fame, as is shown by his treatment of General Webb, which Mr. Thackeray in the impersonation of Henry Esmond resents exceedingly.

15. That affair turned out very differently than I expected it to.

16. Well Portia and Bassanio were married, the time of payment came and went but the ships came not, the Jew called upon Antonio for the money and on his refusal to pay he (Shylock) brings Antonio before the Court of Venice for the purpose of enforcing the fulfillment of the bond.

17. Blind chance, or a fortuitous concourse of atoms have been supposed to offer a sufficient account of the world's origin.

18. Then we have a poet intent on "the best and master thing," and who prosecutes his journey home.

19. Fraternal love, sometimes almost everything, is at others worse than nothing.

20. This cider is made from selected fruit, warranted pure, and free from artificial gases.

June, 1884.

1. The wealth of the many make a very little show in statistics; the wealth of the few make a great show in statistics.

2. By "Good Use" is meant the correct use of correct words in their correct, places, no more than necessary, and to always use the simplest words.

3. I think the style bad and that he has a good deal of the old woman in his way of thinking.

4. If you were able to go to church tomorrow, you will hear an excellent sermon.

5. One sailor said: "I never saw anything to equal it, and as long as I live I will never be able to forget those terrible and pitiful cries for help."

6. The Commission in their report also speaks of S.'s Copyright.

7. In their compartment of the train going back to Paris who should they see but Mr. Stuyvesant, who had been to Versailles, not as a pleasure trip, but on a matter of business.

8. Then we honor most of all, perhaps, he whose anniversary comes this month, the great Luther.

9. If the person who took a black silk umbrella out of Sever 32 by mistake, he would much oblige the owner by returning the same to ———.

10. It keeps in good repair, does the writing well, and is a real pleasure to operate it.

11. There are points where, in my mind Wordsworth reaches as high if not higher, than any poet of his time.

12. It happens, therefore, that there are active and influential members of such conventions whom their fellow-delegates, who know them at all, know perfectly well ought to be in "durance vile."

13. Charles was the first to die, although out of his slender gains he had put by as much as would have provided comfortably for Mary after his death.

14. He is endorsed by the citizens of Springfield, Mass., and also by Major General Howard, which document he will be happy to show at any time.

SPECIMENS OF BAD ENGLISH. 127

15. President McCosh and Eliot each of whom was a member of the University crew of their respective colleges excelled in athletics.

16. In fact, there is no case of disease among Horses and Cattle where these valuable Powders are not called for, and by their timely administration will save the lives of many valuable animals.

17. Everything Scott described he has made famous and none can go to the Highlands but what they must visit the places he describes.

18. In these days it does not seem hardly possible that any man with such an education and poetic genius as Coleridge himself possessed would have expressed such an opinion.

19. An arrangement which sandwiches a sermon or a biblical lecture between each chapter of the story — a great convenience for skippers.

20. Accordingly as a man combines these characteristics, will he be an admirer of Scott or Dickens.

September, 1883.

1. I don't see anything so very particular in having a few almanacks; other people have them I believe, as well as we.

2. Neither Emily nor Valencourt were conscious how they reached the chateau.

3. We should not punish a breach of the Sabbath nor any offence against the Mosaic law.

4. In intellectual and moral strength Maggie Tulliver is what George Eliot was; in physical beauty she is what George Eliot would have chosen to have been.

5. Mr. Freeman may not know but little more history than he would if Macaulay had never written.

[From papers written by candidates for admission to Harvard College.]

6. But when he learned that Orlando was son of the deposed Duke's friend, his brow clouded, and he bade Orlando to immidiately leave the city, or his life would be in danger.

7. This forbearance toward every one even his enemies strikes us at once as we read of his forbearance toward the Pope although he might easily have found weapons far better than those of the Pope and which he certainly could have used with as much skill.

8. The son of the old noble, being treated illy by his oldest brother, goes to the court of the userping Duke. There he wrestles with the pugilist and overcomes him, which feat in connection with his good looks has a very bad effect upon Rosalind the daughter of the true duke, in other words she falls in love with him.

9. But when the king asked him: " who was his father" and learning him to be the sun of Sir Rowland de Bois his countenance changed and he said: I would you were any other man's son, than Sir Rowland, for he was an enemy to me and so you must be.

10. Celia weds Oliver, the brother of Orlando, who has again kindly received the latter to his home. The deep and true affection of Orlando and Rosalind, the ridiculous sayings of Touchstone, and the artless Audrey, are all pleasing factors which go to make up the tale.

11. Orlando tells Rosilind, whom he thinks is a shepherd boy, how he is in love with a lady who had once rewarded him at a wrestling match, and that if he could only find her, he would offer himself to her.

12. After several days had transpired Rosalind told Orlando that she would, on a certain day cause Rosalind to be present when he could have her as his wife.

13. At last the appointed day arrived, and from far and near people flocked to see the sport, among whom being Celia, Frederic's daughter, and Rosalind, her cousin, daughter of the banished duke.

14. The day for the match came, and when, shortly before the eventful time, Orlando walked onto the field, his face and youthful look attracted the attention of Duke Frederic, and Rosalind and Celia.

15. Everybody except his brother, tried to persuade him from his made intention, but he would not hear them.

16. Orlando was urged on, by his brother, to the match, who wished to destroy him, and who, failing in this, at last caused him to flee to the forest.

17. Hospitality was one of Addison's characteristics, and he rarely met a friend, but what he asked him to his lodgings to have a talk over a bottle of wine.

18. In Parliament Addison never spoke but once.

June, 1883.

CORRECT:—

1. This is what Mr. Ingram has done for an American poet whose verse is more justly weighed now than when he was living, and which is not found wanting.

2. Nature had endowed him with considerable abilities, and peculiarly adapted to the scene of their display.

3. Dryden was born in 1631, and Boileau in 1636, and were thus contemporaries.

4. In Handwriting and Orthography, a great number of intelligent and studious candidates are generally nearly equal in merit, so that it is in arithmetic that the tug of war transpires.

5. But that the editor of such a magazine as that in which this effusion appeared should think it worth while to print, and presumably to pay for it, is a phenomenon which suggests two interesting reflections.

6. Nothing tickles a reader's vanity nor tends to establish sympathy with the author so much as for him to discover in print some truth which he has himself learned by observation.

7. There was no charity so fashionable, and consequently no ball so well attended; everybody was more or less interested, everybody of importance appeared at it, showing themselves for a few moments at least.

8. She was the wife only of an earl, but the earl was a knight of the garter.

9. Neither Johnson nor Bacon were men whom he could have been expected to see through with a wide and tolerant eye.

10. I am creditably informed of your incapacity that way.

11. In short, the allegory, proverbially the most headstrong of figures, has served its purpose as a stepping stone to the higher attainments of the intellect.

12. I think it not likely, if I live, that I will be long of returning to Scotland.

13. *Resolved* also that we will and do denounce any man as sycophant, who has, or shall, ask permission of James F. Cooper to visit the Point in question.

14. We notice that Mr. A., whomsoever he may be, suggested that the term used in addressing the boys should be "young gentlemen," and not "young men."

15. Different as are their opinions, they have derived a mutual benefit from each other's society.

16. Upon the whole, therefore, the Squire had very fair reason to be satisfied that he had rode his hobby throughout the day without any other molestation.

17. In this manner he led me through the length of the whole Mall, fretting at his absurdities, and fancying myself laughed at as well as he by every spectator.

18. What's the use of laying in bed when one has had enough of sleep?

19. I was at first fearful of contracting any engagement with him, because being younger than me, he might be more apt to change.

20. He never went to church, and had not eaten or drank in any house but his own since he had come to Belton.

June, 1882.

1. The vote of the trustees on the resolution sustaining President Bartlett, was 6 in the affirmative, 4 in the negative, with one member of the board absent, who it is claimed by the opposition would have voted in the negative.

2. "I only said I wouldn't go, without one of the servants come up to Sir Leicester Dedlock," returns Mr. Smallweed.

3. Neither Senators Dawes nor Hoar were in their seats to-day.

4. She was smaller in stature than either of her three sisters, to all of whom had been acceded the praise of being fine women.

5. Happily neither she nor her mother had completely parted with their senses.

6. "If I review Virgil for instance in April, I will forget much of it before July, having so much other work on my hands."

7. "Lying off the Battery, we would be as easily accessible as are vessels at the city piers."

"When will you be ready for business?" asked the reporter.

"By the spring of 1883; but not before. . . . We shall have a stock company, but there will be comparatively little stock issued. We shall place a large amount of bonds. This will enable us to avoid onerous taxation from the city."

8. He folded it and put it in his breast pocket and laid down once more, and it was not referred to again.

9. Although Mr. Jonas conducted Charity to the hotel and sat himself beside her at the board, it was pretty clear that he had an eye to "the other one" also, for he often glanced across at Mercy, and seemed to draw comparisons between the personal appearance of the two, which were not unfavorable to the superior plumpness of the younger sister."

10. "This is a phenomena common to an immense number of diseases."

11. "Mr. Stanley was the only one of his predecessors who slaughtered the natives of the region he passed through.

12. "She was a good deal hurt, and her hand so severely

injured that unless she has the forefinger amputated, she will entirely lose the use of it.

13. "The farmstead was always the wooden, white-painted house of which all the small country towns are composed.

14. If I were old enough to be married, I am old enough to manage my husband's house.

15. The seventeenth century evidently had a different notion of books and women than that which flourishes in the nineteenth.

16. "It would not suit the rules of art nor of my own feelings to write in that style."

GREEK PROSE COMPOSITION.

September, 1887.

TRANSLATE INTO GREEK:—

If you think this is so,[1] you are free[2] to make this transaction[3] instantly of-no-effect[4] by ordering Seuthes to give you the money. For it is plain that Seuthes, if I have money from him, will require[5] it of me, and will require it fairly if I do not assure[6] the transaction[3] for him with-a-view-to[7] which I took-the-bribe.[8] But I consider that I fall far short[9] of having what is yours; indeed,[10] I swear to you by all the gods that I have not even what Seuthes promised me individually.[11]

[1] i.e. that I have been bribed by Seuthes. [2] ἔξεστι. [3] πρᾶξις. [4] μάταιος.
[5] ἀπαιτέω. [6] βεβαιόω. [7] ἐπί with dat. [8] δωροδοκέω. [9] lack much. [10] γάρ.
[11] ἰδίῃ.

June, 1887.

TRANSLATE INTO GREEK:—

Xenophon, however, wished to make the march along with them, because he thought it safer. But he was persuaded to advance alone by Neon, who had heard that Cleandrus, the harmost[1] in Byzantium, was to arrive with ships. Now he gave this advice in order that no others might share[2] [the[3] opportunity[3]], but that they themselves and their soldiers might sail off on the triremes. And Cheirisophus, at once[4] discouraged[5] by what had happened and[4] incensed[6] against[6] the army, allowed him to do just what he wished. Indeed, if Cheirisophus had not been discouraged, he would have done many great things which no one else was able to accomplish.

[1] ἁρμοστής. [2] μετέχω. [3] omit. [4] ἅμα μὲν . . . ἅμα δέ. [5] ἀθυμέω. [6] μισέω.

July, 1886.

TRANSLATE INTO GREEK:—

When this had happened many times, Darius was at a loss,[1] and the barbarians on learning this sent a herald with presents for Darius, a bird and a mouse[2] and a frog.[3] When the Persians asked the meaning[4] of these gifts,[5] he answered that he had been commanded to give them and to go away. He bade the Persians, if they were wise, to find out the meaning themselves. On hearing this the Persians began to deliberate. And the opinion of Darius was that the Scythians offered[6] themselves and earth and water to him.

[1] ἀπορέω. [2] μῦς. [3] βάτραχος. [4] νοῦς. [5] a part. of δίδωμι. [6] δίδωμι.

September, 1885.

The Syracusan[1] general suspected[2] that the Athenians were intending to go away, and thought it to be a dreadful[3] thing that[4] so large an army should withdraw[5] safely by land. He therefore urged⁶ that all the Syracusans should go out and block-up⁷ the roads. But the authorities⁸ said this was impracticable,⁹ for this reason: On that day there happened to be a sacrifice in the city, and the greater part of the citizens had fallen to drinking.¹⁰ So they had no hope that they would take up their arms and go out again.

¹ Συρακόσιος. ² ὑπονοέω. ³ δεινός. ⁴ εἰ. ⁵ ὑποχωρέω. ⁶ κελεύω.
⁷ ἀποικοδομέω. ⁸ ἄρχων. ⁹ ἄπορος. ¹⁰ τρέπομαι πρὸς πόσιν.

June, 1885.

The Athenians once sailed into the Nile,¹ and, getting possession of² the river, became masters of³ the largest part of Egypt.⁴ At this time Artaxerxes was king of the Persians; and to these Egypt was subject.⁵ The king, hearing what had happened, was vexed at⁶ the affair, and sent Megabazus, a Persian, to Lacedaemon, supplied with money, that by means of⁷ this he might persuade the Lacedaemonians to invade Attica. His hope was⁸ that the Athenians would go off home again, if they learned that their country was being ravaged.⁹

¹ Νεῖλος. ² κρατέω. ³ κατέχω. ⁴ Αἴγυπτος. ⁵ ὑπήκοος.
⁶ βαρέως φέρω. ⁷ use δίδωμι. ⁸ ἐλπίζω. ⁹ φθείρω.

September, 1884.

When Clearchus heard about the heralds, he ordered them to wait until he should be at leisure.¹ Then after marshalling² his troops he sent word to admit³ them. They said: "We come from the king to ask if the Greeks will make a truce⁴"; and he answered: "Tell the king that we must fight; for no one shall talk⁵ to Greeks about a truce if he does not first provide⁶ them with food." The heralds departed, but returned quickly and said⁷: "The king praised the words of Clearchus."

¹ σχολὴν ἄγειν. ² compound of τάσσω. ³ εἰσάγειν. ⁴ σπένδομαι.
⁵ διαλέγομαι. ⁶ παρέχειν. ⁷ announcing.

June, 1884.

The soldiers, on hearing this, suspected[1] that Cyrus was deceiving[2] them, but said they were ready to follow[3] him, if he would give them more pay. For they believed that it would be dangerous for them to leave Cyrus and march homeward, and thought it best to do what Cyrus required,[4] because they hoped he would conquer. What happened[5] at Tarsus makes it plain[6] that it was hard to use Greek mercenaries when they thought they had good reason to complain[7] of injustice.

[1] ὑποπτεύω. [2] ἐξαπατάω. [3] συστρατεύομαι. [4] κελεύω. [5] γίγνομαι.
[6] δηλόω. [7] tr. *they might justly say they had suffered unjust things.*

GREEK.

HERODOTUS AT SIGHT.
September, 1887.

[SUBJECT.—Capture of Croesus by Cyrus the Great, and invocation of Solon by Croesus.]

TRANSLATE Herod. I. 86.

ζωγρέω, *take captive (alive)*. συννήσας (νέω, *heap*). ἀκροθίνια καταγιεῖν (κατά, ἁγίζω), *consecrate first-fruits.* ὅτεῳ δή, indefinite. εὐχήν, *vow.* τοῦ κατακανθῆναι (κατακαίω), genitive after ῥύσεται. ἐσελθεῖν, *came into (his mind).* προστῆναι, like ἐσελθεῖν above. ἀνενεικάμενον (ἀναφέρω): sc. πνεῦμα, *with a deep sigh.*

June, 1887.

[SUBJECT.—Two accounts of the foundation of oracles in Greece and Libya.]

TRANSLATE Herod. II. 54, 55.

ἐκ Θηβέων, *from (Egyptian) Thebes.* πρηθεῖσαν: from πιπράσκω, *sell.* ἀτρεκέως, *exactly.* προμάντιες, *prophets.* πελειάς, *dove.* αὐτούς and σφέας both refer to the Dodoneans.

September, 1886.

[SUBJECT. — The expulsion of the family of Pisistratus from Athens in 510 B.C. by the help of a Spartan army.]

TRANSLATE Herod. V. 64, 65.

¹ ἐπέδρη (Attic ἐφέδρα), *siege*. ² ὑπεκτίθημι, *to put in a safe place*. ³ παρέστησαν (sc. οἱ Πεισιστρατίδαι), *surrendered themselves*. ⁴ ἐπήλυδες (cf. ἐπῆλθον).

July, 1886.

[SUBJECT. — The contest between Isagoras and Clisthenes at Athens after the expulsion of Hippias in 510 B.C. — Cylon's attempt at revolution about 612 B.C.]

TRANSLATE Herod. V. 70, 71.

ἀπό ... πολιορκίης, i.e., when Cleomenes besieged the Pisistratidae in the Acropolis a short time before this. ἐναγέας, *accursed*. φόνου refers to the murders which led to the curse above mentioned (ἐναγέας). αὐτός (*ipse*) refers to Isagoras, who did not belong to the family of Alcmaeonidae as Clisthenes did. Ὀλυμπιονίκης: Cylon gained a victory at Olympia in 640 B.C. (Olym. 35). ἐκόμησε (*plumed himself*), with ἐπί, *aspired to*. ἄγαλμα, the statue of Athena on the Acropolis. οἱ πρυτάνιες τῶν ναυκράρων, *the presidents of naucraries*, ancient officers, of whom little is known. ὑπεγγύους, *liable to punishment*.

September, 1885.

[SUBJECT. — The story which Herodotus heard at Dodona about the foundation of the oracle there and of that in Egyptian Thebes.]

TRANSLATE Herod. II. 55.

πρόμαντις, *priestess*. πελειάς, *dove*.

June, 1885.

[SUBJECT. — The story of Paris and Helen arriving in Egypt.]

TRANSLATE Herod. II. 113.

ἐξῶσται, as adjective; cf. ἐξωθέω, *drive ashore*. ἔστο, *belongs only to* καταφυγών. ἐπιβάληται, *makes upon himself*. ἀπ-ιστέαται, *escape*. ἐξηγευμενοι, *narrating*.

September, 1884.

TRANSLATE Herod. II. 55.

προμάντις, priestesses who gave out the oracles.   πελείας, rock pigeons.

June, 1884.

TRANSLATE Herod. I. 170.

September, 1883.

TRANSLATE Herod. IV. 97.

¹ ἀρηρμένον from ἀρόω.   ² ἀλώμενοι: cf. ἄλη, *a wandering*.

June, 1883.

[SUBJECT.—The overthrow of Oroites by the king's emissary Bagaios.]

TRANSLATE Herod. III. 128.

σφρηγίς, *a seal.*   περιαιρεώμενος, *unsealing.*   ἐπιλέγεσθαι, *to read aloud.*   ὕπ-αρχοι, *governors.*

September, 1887.

HOMER'S ILIAD.

A.

I. TRANSLATE Il. XI. 122–135.

[SUBJECT.—Agamemnon attacks the two sons of Antimachus, who are in a chariot.]

μενεχάρμην, μένω and χάρμη, *battle.*   οὐκ εἴασχ', *forbade.*   ὁμοῖ, *to the same place,* sc. *where he was.*   σιγαλόεντα, λαμπρά.   κυκηθήτην, κυκάω, *confuse.*   Ζώγρει, *quarter.*   κειμήλια, *treasures.*

II. TRANSLATE Il. XXIII. 555–565.

[SUBJECT.—Achilles, finding that Antiochus objects to letting Eumelos have the second prize, sends for a special prize.]

χεῦμα, *rim.*   κασσιτέροιο, *of tin.*   ἀμφιδεδίνηται, *has been circled.*

GREEK. 139

B.

I. TRANSLATE Il. I. 173–181.

Write out vv. 173 and 174, dividing them into feet, and marking the caesural pause in each line. Explain the reference of τόγ' in line 178, the form of μητίετα in line 175, and of σέθεν in line 180. Who were the Myrmidons, and where did they dwell?

II. TRANSLATE Il. II. 379–393.

Explain the mood of ξυνάγωμεν in line 381, of κρινώμεθα in line 385. Where made and from what are θηξάσθω in line 382, καμεῖται in line 389, διακρινέει in line 387? Give the composition of πανημέριοι in line 385, of ἀμφιβρότης in line 389, of ἐΰξοον in line 390.

III. TRANSLATE Il. III. 298–309.

Explain the mood of δαμεῖεν in line 301. What ὅρκια are alluded to in line 299?

September, 1884.

A.

I. TRANSLATE Il. XXI. 128–143.

κεραΐζων, *ravaging.*   δίνῃσι: cf. δίνη, *eddy.*   δηδὰ, δὴν μώνυχας. fr. μόνος and ὄνυχες, *hoofs.*

II. TRANSLATE Il. XXIV. 480–492.

πυκινὴ, πυκνός, lit. *thick.*   περιναιέται: cf. ναίω, *dwell.*

B.

I. TRANSLATE Iliad I. 149–157.

Derivation of κερδαλεόφρον, βωτιανείρῃ, σκιόεντα. Who is the speaker? whom does he address? Mood of πείθηται. Where are ἐλθέμεναι, ἤλυθον, and ἤλασαν made, and from what present indicative?

II. TRANSLATE Il. II. 90–98.

Where are πεποτήαται, δεδήει, and τετρήχει made, and from what present indicative? Attic equivalent for κλισιάων, βαθείης βοόωντες, σχοίατ', and βασιλήων.

III. TRANSLATE Il. III. 284–292.

Who is the speaker? Copy vv. 284 and 290, and divide into feet, marking quantities and caesura. Mood of κτείνῃ, ἀποδοῦναι, and ἐθέλωσιν.

September, 1883.

A.

I. TRANSLATE Il. XII. 230–243.

[SUBJECT. — Hector rebukes Polydamas for dissuading the battle on account of omens.]

In 237, τύνη, σύ. 238, μεταπρεπομαι, *care for.* 240, ζόφος, *west.*

II. TRANSLATE Il. X. 180–189.

[SUBJECT. — Nestor and others come to the captains of guard.]

183, δυσωρήσωσιν, *keep painful watch.* 189, ἀίω, *hear.*

B.

I. TRANSLATE Il. I. 193–205.

Point out four Homeric forms, and give Attic equivalents. Case of κόμης 197, and ἧς 205. Use of article in 204. State briefly results of wrath of Achilles.

II. TRANSLATE Il. II. 20–28.

Homeric forms in 25 and 26, and give Attic equivalents. Case of ἐμέθεν 26, σέυ 27. Why did Zeus send this message by Agamemnon?

III. TRANSLATE Il. III. 234–244.

Derivation of ἑλίκωπας 234, κοσμήτορ 236, ἱππόδαμον 237,

ποντοπόροισιν 240, φυσίζοος 243. Who is speaker in this passage?

IV. TRANSLATE Il. IV. 446–456.

Four Homeric forms and Attic equivalents. Explain form ὄρεσφι 452. Case of αἵματι 451, and τῶν 455.

V. TRANSLATE Il. VI. 175–186.

Homeric forms in 177 and 178 and all equivalents. Case of γαμβροῦ 178, ἀνθρώπων 180, τεράεσσι 183. Whose story is this? how does it come to be related in the Iliad?

LATIN COMPOSITION.

September, 1887.

TRANSLATE INTO LATIN: —

This same year Caesar made all the preparations which were desirable for such an undertaking and sailed from Gaul to Britain. The tide and wind were favorable, so that the passage was accomplished in a very short time; but Caesar found it difficult to land his troops, because there were so many shallow places along the shore where his large ships could not move, while the enemy, rushing a little way into the water, hurled their weapons so fiercely that they killed and wounded many of the Romans and inspired them all with fear. When his men had been fighting thus for some time in vain, Caesar ordered the long ships, which did not require such deep water, to draw off from the others and attack the enemy on the side. As the ship on which the tenth legion sailed approached the barbarians, the standard bearer cried: "Leap into the water, soldiers, unless you wish to betray the eagle to the enemy; I, at least, mean to do my duty to the country and our general." Then he leaped into the sea with the standard, followed by the soldiers, who shouted encouragement to each other as they swam against the enemy.

June, 1887.

TRANSLATE INTO LATIN: —

After Cicero had set forth to the senate and to the citizens of Rome what abominable crimes one of their own number was meditating against the state, and some of the accomplices of the plot had been thrown into prison, the senate took counsel as to what ought to be done. There were two opinions which were each favored by a large number of senators. Then Cicero begged the senate to remember the best interests of the state and to decree the punishment which would most thoroughly crush the conspiracy. Let no thought of him prevent them from condemning the conspirators to death if that seemed the best thing to do. "But if," said he, "you are persuaded that the plan of Julius Caesar is wiser, follow his opinion. Let us not forget that the honor of our country and the safety of our wives and children depend upon the decision we adopt to-day." The country was saved; but Cicero was himself afterwards driven into exile by his enemies for the part he had taken in the punishment of the conspirators.

September, 1886.

TRANSLATE INTO LATIN: —

Cicero was telling the Romans what the senate had decreed the day before in regard to the people who were accused of conspiracy. He said that he had been thanked in the most complimentary terms for having freed the state of such dangerous enemies. Other men had been thanked too, each in proportion to his deserts. Then Lentulus was compelled to resign his praetorship that he might be thrown into prison as a private citizen, because it was unlawful to imprison a magistrate. Speaking of this same matter later, Cicero reminds the people how much more careful the senate had been than the great Marius had once shown himself on a similar occasion. Would not the gods spare and even protect a nation of such justice?

July, 1886.

TRANSLATE INTO LATIN : —

Since this is so, is not my friend worthy to be called a Roman citizen? Ought we to hinder him from enjoying, at home and abroad, those blessings which fall to the lot only of the Romans? Or ought we not rather to bestow the highest honors upon one who had contributed so much to the glory of the state, especially at a time when so many illiterate people can be found who maintain that it is not worth while to spend one's efforts upon literature? We all remember what Sulla did. Once, when a very bad poet handed him a poem written in his honor, he ordered a reward to be given to the poet from the proceeds of the booty which he was then selling at auction. The verse, however, was so bad that Sulla could not help making a condition that the poet should write no more. In the case of the poet whose cause I plead, I have no fear that you will have to repent if you grant him what he asks.

September, 1885.

TRANSLATE INTO LATIN : —

They fought long and sharply, for the Sontiates, relying upon their earlier victories, thought that the safety of all Aquitania depended upon their bravery, and our men were eager to show what they could do under a young leader in the absence of the commander-in-chief and of the other legions. At length, overwhelmed by wounds, the enemy turned to flight. Then Crassus, having resolved to besiege the town, ordered the guards to take their posts as silently as possible and to refrain from all slaughter; for he wished to get possession of as many prisoners as he could, and then by pardoning them to win over the neighboring states. He sent messengers, also, to report his victory at Rome.

June, 1885.

TRANSLATE INTO LATIN: —

Now Cicero had been informed, through a certain woman named Fulvia, of what these conspirators were doing. Therefore he summoned several faithful men, whose assistance he had often used before in times of danger to the state, and, having explained the matter to them in a few words, ordered them to go to the Mulvian Bridge, so-called, and lie hidden there until the accomplices of the plot arrived and then seize them immediately. Thus some of the chiefs of the conspiracy were taken into custody, and Cicero was persuaded by his friends by cogent arguments to bring these prisoners before the senate. In the senate the conspirators were shown their letters and asked whether they recognized their hands and seals. One of them also was questioned about some swords and daggers which had been found at his house, and at first he answered, with a laugh, that he had always been fond of good cutlery; but, when all the evidence was given, turned very pale and confessed his crime.

September, 1884.

TRANSLATE INTO LATIN: —

They fought long and sharply, for the Sontiates, relying upon their earlier victories, thought that the safety of all Aquitania depended upon their bravery, and our men were eager to show what they could do under a young leader in the absence of the commander-in-chief and of the other legions. At length, overwhelmed by wounds, the enemy turned to flight. Then Crassus, having resolved to besiege the town, ordered the guards to take their posts as silently as possible and to refrain from all slaughter; for he wished to get possession of as many prisoners as he could, and then by pardoning them to win over the neighboring states. He sent messages, also, to report his victory at Rome.

June, 1884.

TRANSLATE INTO LATIN: —

At about the same time Publius Crassus arrived in Aquitania, which deserves, in territory and population, to be reckoned a third part of Gaul, and remembering that he had to carry on war in the places where a few years before the lieutenant Lucius Valerius had lost an army and been killed himself, he felt that no ordinary energy was required of him. He therefore provided himself with as much grain and ammunition as possible and ordered the army to march into the country of the Sontiates. He found the enemy encamped at the foot of a high hill, and their chief, relying upon his numbers, thought he could frighten the Romans from attacking him, and sent them word to consult for their safety. Crassus, however, scorned the advice, and, attacking the Gauls by night gained a brilliant victory.

LATIN.
CICERO.
September, 1887.

I. TRANSLATE Cic. Cat. IV. 6.
Give derivation of *concitari, exitiosam, coniurationem.*
Give principal parts of *censeatis, praedicam, misceri, transcendit.*

Explain construction of *consulis, huic, opinione*.

Compare the meanings of *referre ad vos*, and *ad vos delatum sit*.

Compare the moods of (*quidquid*) *est* and (*quantum facinus delatum*) *sit*.

II. TRANSLATE : —

P. Lentulus consul, simul ac de sollemni religione rettulit, nihil humanarum rerum sibi prius quam de me agendum indicavit. Atque eo die confecta res esset, nisi is tribunus plebis, quem ego maximis beneficiis quaestorem consul ornaveram, cum et cunctus ordo et multi eum summi viri orarent et Cn. Oppius socer, optimus vir, ad pedes eius flens iaceret, noctem sibi ad deliberandum postulasset: quae deliberatio non in reddenda, quem ad modum non nulli arbitrabantur, sed, ut patefactum est, in augenda mercede consumpta est. Postea res acta est in senatu alia nulla, et cum variis rationibus impediretur, voluntate tamen perspecta senatus causa ad vos mense Ianuario deferebatur.

June, 1887.

A.

TRANSLATE Cic. Cat. IV. 22 from " Qua re.

bonorumque: what does *que* connect? *memoria:* construction? *gentium:* derivation? *facile:* compare. *possit:* explain mood and tense. *reperietur:* principal parts? *id:* construction? *confringere:* parts and composition? *ulla:* why not *aliqua*? *profecto:* derivation?

B.

Nam relatio[1] illa salutaris et diligens fuerat consulis, animadversio quidem et iudicium senatus : quae cum reprehendis,

[1] for the punishment of the Catilinarian Conspirators.

ostendis qualis tu, si ita forte accidisset, fueris illo tempore consul futurus : stipendio, mehercule, et frumento Catilinam esse putasses iuvandum. quid enim interfuit inter Catilinam et eum, cui tu senatus auctoritatem, salutem civitatis, totam rem publicam provinciae praemio vendidisti? quae enim L. Catilinam conantem consul prohibui, ea P. Clodium facientem consules adiuverunt. voluit ille senatum interficere; vos sustulistis; leges incendere: vos abrogastis; vim inferre patriae: quid est vobis consulibus gestum sine armis? incendere illa coniuratorum manus voluit urbem: vos eius domum, quem propter urbs incensa non est. ac ne illi quidem, si habuissent vestri similem consulem, de urbis incendio cogitassent; non enim se tectis privare voluerunt, sed his stantibus nullum domicilium sceleri suo fore putaverunt. caedem illi civium, vos servitutem expetistis; hic vos etiam crudeliores: huic enim populo ita fuerat ante vos consules libertas insita, ut ei mori potius quam servire praestaret.

July, 1886.

TRANSLATE Cic. Arch. 7 and 8, to "causa dicta est."

Construction of *lege, civitatibus,* and *annos.*
Explain mood of *ascripti fuissent.*
Explain tense of *ascripti fuissent.*
Explain mood of *ferebatur.*
Explain tense of *ferebatur.*
Causa dicta est: show how this is true. What is the rest of the oration about?

TRANSLATE: —

Quid tandem de illa nocte dicit,[1] cum inter falcarios ad M. Laecam nocte ea, quae consecuta est posterum diem nonarum Novembrium me consule, Catilinae denuntiatione convenit? quae nox omnium temporum coniurationis acerrima fuit atque

---

[1] Cornelius, the prosecutor of P. Sulla.

acerbissima: tum Catilinae dies exeundi, tum ceteris manendi
condicio, tum discriptio totam per urbem caedis atque incen-
diorum constituta est; tum tuus pater, Corneli, id quod
tandem aliquando confitetur, illam sibi officiosam provinciam
depoposcit, ut cum prima luce consulem salutatum veniret,
intromissus et meo more et iure amicitiae me in meo lectulo
trucidaret. hoc tempore, cum arderet acerrime coniuratio,
cum Catilina egrederetur ad exercitum, Lentulus in urbe
relinquiretur, Cassius incendiis, Cethegus caedi praeponere-
tur, Autronio ut occuparet Etruriam praescriberetur, cum
omnia ordinarentur, instruerentur, pararentur, ubi fuit Sulla,
Corneli? num Romae? immo longe afuit: num in eis regionibus, quo se Catilina inferebat? multo etiam longius: num in
agro Camerti, Piceno, Gallico, quas in oras maxime quasi
morbus quidam illius furoris pervaserat? nihil vero minus.
fuit enim, ut iam ante dixi, Neapoli; fuit in ea parte Italiae,
quae maxime ista suspitione caruit. — Cic. pro Sulla, 52, 53.

September, 1885.

I. TRANSLATE Cic. Cat. IV. 21 and 22, to "nec beneficio
placare possis."

Explain briefly the historical references in this passage.
Explain the case of *laude, obsidione, omnibus, gloriae;* the
mood of *habeatur, possimus, habeant, possis;* the derivation
of *nobilissimus, regionibus, obsidione, alienigenae.*

II. TRANSLATE: —

Si medius fidius, iudices, non me ipsa res publica, meis
laboribus et periculis conservata, ad gravitatem animi et
constantiam sua dignitate revocaret, tamen hoc natura est
insitum, ut, quem timueris, quicum de vita fortunisque con-
tenderis, cuius ex insidiis evaseris, hunc semper oderis. Sed
cum agatur honos meus amplissimus, gloria rerum gestarum
singularis, cum quotiens quisquam est in hoc scelere convic-

tus, toties renovetur memoria per me inventae salutis, ego
sim tam demens, ego committam, ut ea, quae pro salute
omnium gessi, casu magis et felicitate a me quam virtute et
consilio gesta esse videantur? Quid ergo? hoc tibi sumis,
dicet fortasse quispiam, ut, quia tu defendis, innocens iudi-
cetur? Ego vero, iudices, non modo mihi nihil adsumo in
quo quispiam repugnet, sed etiam, si quid ab omnibus con-
ceditur, id reddo ac remitto. Non in ea re publica versor,
non iis temporibus meum caput obtuli pro patria periculis
omnibus, non aut ita sunt exstincti quos vici aut ita grati
quos servavi, ut ego mihi plus appetere coner quam quantum
omnes inimici invidique patiantur. — Cic. pro Sulla, XXX.

June, 1885.

I. TRANSLATE : —·

Itaque, credo, si civis Romanus Archias legibus non esset,
ut ab aliquo imperatore civitate donaretur, perficere non
potuit. Sulla cum Hispanos donaret et Gallos, credo hunc
petentem repudiasset: quem nos in contione vidimus, cum ei
libellum malus poëta de populo subiecisset, quod epigramma
in eum fecisset, tantummodo alternis versibus longiusculis,
stotim ex eis rebus, quas tunc vendebat, iubere ei praemium
tribui sed ea condicione, ne quid postea scriberet. Qui
sedulitatem mali poëtae duxerit aliquo tamen praemio dignam, huius ingenium et virtutem in scribendo et copiam non
expetisset? quid? a Q. Metello Pio, familiarissimo suo, qui
civitate multos donavit, neque per se neque per Lucullus im-
petravisset? qui praesertim usque eo de suis rebus scribi
cuperet, ut etiam Cordubae natis poëtis, pingue quiddam
souantibus atque peregrinum, tamen auris suas dederet. —
Cic. pro Archia X.

Construction of *civitate?* Formation of *longiusculis?* Construction of *scriberet, duxerit, expetisset, quiddam?* What

metre is meant by *alternis versibus longiusculis?* What is meant by *ex eis rebus quas tunc vendebat?* Who is meant by *huius?* Construction of *cuperet?* Mark the quantity of all the vowels in *sedulitatem.* Derivation of *familiarissimo, peregrinum ingenium?* Force of *sub* in *subiecisset?* Trace the derivation of *donaret* from its elements.

II. TRANSLATE: —

Nunc quoniam, T. Labiene, diligentiae meae temporis angustiis obstitisti meque ex comparato et constituto spatio defensionis in semihorae curriculum coëgisti, parebitur, et quod iniquissimum est accusatoris condicioni et quod miserrimum inimici potestati; quamquam in hac praescriptione semihorae patroni mihi partis reliquisti, consulis ademisti, propterea quod ad defendendum prope modum satis erit mihi temporis, ad conquerendum parum. Nisi forte de locis religiosis ac de lucis, quos ab hoc violatos esse dixisti, pluribus verbis tibi respondendum putas; quo in crimine nihil est umquam abs te dictum, nisi a C. Macro obiectum esse crimen id C. Rabirio; in quo ego demiror meminisse te quid obiecerit C. Rabirio Macer inimicus, oblitum esse quid aequi et iurati iudices iudicarint. An de peculatu facto aut de tabulario incenso longa oratio est expromenda? quo in crimine propinquus C. Rabiri iudicio clarissimo, C. Curtius, pro virtute sua est honestissime liberatus, ipse vero Rabirius non mode in iudicium horum criminum, sed ne in tenuissimam quidem suspitionem verbo est umquam vocatus. — CIC. pro Rabir. II. 6.

June, 1884.

I. TRANSLATE Cat. II. 4. 12, 13 to "apud M. Laecam fuisset necne."

dicant: explain mood. *in exsilium,* etc.: why is that a

reproach? *eicerem:* explain mood and tense. *permodestus:* force of *per?* *iussus est:* explain mood and tense. *paruit:* principal parts. *domi:* construction. *in aedem Iovis,* etc. : where did the Senate usually meet? *rem detuli:* technical meaning. *hostem:* could he say *inimicum?* give your reason. *partem nudam:* explain meaning. *fuisset:* explain mood and tense.

II. TRANSLATE: —

Tu mihi etiam M. Atilium Regulum commemoras, qui redire ipse Karthaginem sua voluntate ad supplicium quam sine eis captivis, a quibus ad senatum missus erat, Romae manere maluerit, et mihi negas optandum reditum fuisse per familias comparatas et homines armatos? vim scilicet ego desideravi, qui, dum vis fuit, nihil egi, et quem, si vis non fuisset, nulla res labefactare potuisset. Hunc ego reditum repudiarem, qui ita florens fuit, ut verear ne qui me studio gloriae putet idcirco exisse, ut ita redirem? quem enim umquam senatus civem nisi me nationibus exteris commendavit? cuius umquam propter salutem nisi meam senatus publice sociis populi Romani gratias egit? de me uno patres conscripti decreverunt ut, qui provincias cum imperio obtinerent, qui quaestores legatique essent, salutem et vitam custodirent.

September, 1883.

I. TRANSLATE Arch. IX. 21.

Explain construction of *terra, opibus, duce, manu, consilio.* Allusions in *L. Lucullum, Pontum, regiis, apud Tenedum pugna.* What bearing has this passage on the general argument of the oration?

II. TRANSLATE: —

[Cicero advocates legalizing the command held by Octavius against Antony by making him propraetor.]

Hoc autem tempore ita censeo decernendum: Quod C.

Caesar, Gaii filius, pontifex, pro praetore, summo rei publicae tempore milites veteranos ad libertatem populi Romani cohortatus sit eosque conscripserit, quodque legio Martia atque quarta summo studio optimoque in rem publicam consensu C. Caesare duce et auctore rem publicam, libertatem populi Romani defendant defenderint, et quod C. Caesar pro praetore Galliae provinciae cum exercitu subsidio profectus sit, equites, sagittarios, elephantos in suam populique Romani potestatem redegerit difficillimoque rei publicae tempore saluti dignitatique populi Romani subvenerit, ob eas causas senatui placere, C. Caesarem, Gaii filium, pontificem, pro praetore, senatorem esse sententiamque loco praetorio dicere: ejusque rationem, quemcumque magistratum petet, ita haberi, ut haberi per leges liceret, si anno superiore quaestor fuisset. Quid est enim, patres conscripti, cur eum non quam primum amplissimos honores capere cupiamus? Legibus enim annalibus quum grandiorem aetatem ad consulatum constituebant, adolescentiae temeritatem verebantur: C. Caesar ineunte aetate docuit ab excellenti eximiaque virtute progressum aetatis exspectari non oportere. —PHIL. V. 46–47.

Provinciae: why not *in provenciam?* Mood of *defendant, liceret, cupiamus, constituebant.* What is meant by *legibus annalibus? si ... ouaestor:* what difference would that have made?

June, 1883.

I. TRANSLATE Cic. Cat. III. 21.

Explain the mood of *neget, esset, videatur, statueretur;* the tense of *esset, duceretur.* Give the derivation of *aversus, praeceps, interitum, nefariis.* What was the "*signum*"?

II. TRANSLATE: —

Sed tamen venenum unde fuerit, quem ad modum paratum sit non dicitur. Datum esse aiunt huic P. Licinio, pudenti adolescenti et bono, Caelii familiari: constitutum factum esse cum servis, ut venirent ad balneas Senias: eodem Licinium esse venturum atque iis veneni pyxidem traditurum. Hic primum illud requiro, quid attinuerit fieri in eum locum constitutum, cur illi servi non ad Caelium domum venerint. Si manebat tanta illa consuetudo Caelii, tanta familiaritas cum Clodia, quid suspitionis esset, si apud Caelium mulieris servus visus esset? Sin autem iam iam suberat simultas, extincta erat consuetudo, discidium exstiterat, hinc illae lacrimae nimirum et haec causa est omnium horum scelerum atque criminum. Immo, inquit, cum servi ad dominam rem istam et maleficium Caelii detulissent, mulier ingeniosa praecepit suis, omnia Caelio pollicerentur: sed ut venenum, cum a Licinio traderetur manifesto comprehendi posset, constitui locum iussit balneas Senias, ut eo mitteret amicos qui delitiscerent, dein repente, cum venisset Licinius venenumque traderet, prosilirent hominemque comprehenderent.—Cic. Cael. XXV. 62.

What is the construction of *suspitionis? suis?* Explain the mood and tense of *attinuerit, pollicerentur, delitiscerent.*

VIRGIL AND OVID.

September, 1887.

I. TRANSLATE Aen. XI. 22-33.

SUBJECT.—[Aeneas orders the burial of the dead, and the return of Pallas' body to his father Evander.]

Scan lines 1, 2, and 3, marking the principal caesuras.

II. TRANSLATE:—

SUBJECT. — [Medea prepares for her moonlight incantations.]

Tres aberant noctes, ut cornua tota coirent
Efficerentque orbem. Postquam plenissima fulsit,
Ac solida terras spectavit imagine luna,

Egreditur tectis vestes induta recinctas,
Nuda pedem, nudos humeris infusa capillos,
Fertque vagos mediae per muta silentia noctis
Incomitata gradus. Homines volucresque ferasque
Solverat alta quies ; nullo cum murmure sepes ;
Immotaeque silent frondes ; silet humidus aër ;
Sidera sola micant. Ad quae sua bracchia tendens
Ter se convertit, ter sumptis flumine crinem
Inroravit aquis, ternisque ululatibus ora
Solvit.

June, 1887.

I. TRANSLATE Aen. X. 821–832.

[SUBJECT.—Lament of Aeneas over the body of Lausus.]

Scan lines 1, 2, and 3, marking the principal caesuras.

II. TRANSLATE :—

Daedalus interea Creten longumque perosus
Exilium, tactusque loci natalis amore,
Clausus erat pelago. ' Terras licet ' inquit ' et undas
Obstruat, at caelum certe patet. ibimus illac.
Omnia possideat, non possidet aëra Minos.'
Dixit. et ignotas animum dimittit in artes,
Naturamque novat. Nam ponit in ordine pennas,
A minima coeptas, longam breviore sequenti,
Ut clivo crevisse putes. Sic rustica quondam
Fistula disparibus paulatim surgit avenis.
Tum lino medias et ceris alligat imas,
Atque ita compositas parvo curvamine flectit,
Ut veras imitetur aves.

September, 1886.

I. TRANSLATE :—

Planus erat lateque patens prope moenia campus,
Assiduis pulsatus equis, ubi turba rotarum

Duraque mollierat subiectas ungula glaebas.
Pars ibi de septem genitis Amphione fortes
Conscendunt in equos, Tyrioque rubentia suco
Terga premunt, auroque graves moderantur habenas.
E quibus Ismenus, qui matri[1] sarcina[2] quondam
Prima suae fuerat, dum certum flectit in orbem
Quadrupedis cursus, spumantiaque ora coërcet,
'Ei mihi!' conclamat, medioque in pectore fixa
Tela gerit, frenisque manu moriente remissis
In latus a dextro paulatim defluit armo.
      OVID, Met. VI. 218-229.
 [1] Niobe.   [2] burden.

II. TRANSLATE Aen. IX. 93-103.

 filius = Jupiter. *Doto* (-*us*), a sea-nymph.

July, 1886.

I. TRANSLATE : —

Est prope Cimmerios longo spelunca recessu,
Mons cavus, ignavi domus et penetralia Somni:
Quo numquam radiis oriens mediusve cadensve
Phoebus adire potest. Nebulae caligine mixtae
Exhalantur humo dubiaeque crepuscula lucis.
Non vigil ales ibi cristati cantibus oris
Evocat Auroram, nec voce silentia rumpunt
Sollicitive canes canibusve sagacior anser.
Non fera, non pecudes, non moti flamine rami,
Humanaeve sonum reddunt convicia linguae.
Muta quies habitat. Saxo tamen exit ab imo
Rivus aquae Lethes, per quem cum murmure labens
Invitat somnos crepitantibus unda lapillas.
Ante fores antri fecunda papavera florent
Innumeraeque herbae, quarum de lacte soporem
Nox legit et spargit per opacas umida terras.

II. TRANSLATE Aen. X. 431–438.
Scan the last two lines.

June, 1885.

I. TRANSLATE:—

'Inmemores' que 'mei discenditis' inquit 'Achivi?
Obrutaque est mecum virtutis gratia nostrae?
Ne facite! utque meum non sit sine honore sepulchrum,
Placet Achilleos mactata Polyxena manes.'
Dixit, et inmiti sociis parentibus umbrae,
Rapta sinu matris, quam iam prope sola fovebat,
Fortis et infelix et plus quam femina virgo
Ducitur ad tumulum diroque fit hostia busto.
Quae memor ipsa sui, postquam crudelibus aris
Admota est sensitque sibi fera sacra parari,
Utque Neoptolemum stantem ferrumque tenentem
Inque suo vidit figentem lumina vultu,
'Utere iamdudum generoso sanguine!' dixit
'Nulla mora est. Quin tu iugulo vel pectore telum
Conde meo!' iugulumque simul pectusque retexit.
OVID, Met. XIII. 445–459.

II. TRANSLATE Virg. Aen. XI. 237–254.

What is meant by "caesura"? Point out the principal caesura in lines 245, 248, 254. Give the rule for the quantity of every syllable in l. 251.

September, 1884.

I. TRANSLATE Aen. X. 689–701.

II. TRANSLATE:—

Hic tamen accessit delubris advena nostris:
Caesar in urbe sua deus est quem Marte togaque
Praecipuum non bella magis finita triumphis

Resque domi gestae properataque gloria rerum
In sidus vertere novum stellamque comantem,
Quam sua progenies. Neque enim de Caesaris actis
Ullum est majus opus, quam quod pater extitit hujus.
Scilicet aequoreos plus est domuisse Britannos.
Perque papyriferi septemflua flumina Nili
Victrices egisse rates, Numidasque rebelles
Cinyphiumque Jubam Mithridateisque tumentem
Nominibus Pontum populo adjecisse Quirini,
Et multos meruisse, aliquos egisse triumphos,
Quam tantum genuisse virum? quo praeside rerum
Humano generi, superi, favistis abunde.
Ne foret hic igitur mortali semine cretus,
Ille deus faciendus erat. — OVID, XV. 746–761.

Give instances of caesura in the 2d and 4th feet, and of two kinds of caesura in the 3d foot, out of any lines in the passage from Ovid. State three important rules of prosody, giving instances from either of the above passages. Who are the *hic* and *ille* of the last two lines from Ovid?

June, 1884.

I. TRANSLATE Aen. IX. 176–191.

Divide into feet lines 179–181, and mark the principal caesura in each. What is unusual in the metrical structure of l. 179? Account for the quantity of the *e* in *Aeneae*, l. 177, and *es* in *comes*, l. 179.

II. TRANSLATE : —

Talia dicenti curarum maxima nutrix
Nox intervenit, tenebrisque audacia crevit.
Prima quies aderat, qua curis fessa diurnis
Pectora somnus habet. Thalamos taciturna paternos
Intrat, et heu facinus! vitali nata parentem

Crine suum spoliat, praedaque potita nefanda
Fert secum spolium sceleris, progressaque porta
Per medios hostes — meriti fiducia tanta est —
Pervenit ad regem.   Quem sic adfata paventem est :
' Suasit amor, facinus.   Proles ego regia Nisi
Scylla tibi trado patriaque meosque Penates.'
Ovid, Met. VIII. 81–91.

What two words in the last line have sometimes a different measurement from that used here?

June, 1883.

I. Translate Aen. VIII. 51–65.

[Subject. — The river-god Tiber gives directions to Aeneas.]

Mark the scansion of the first four verses.

II. Translate : —

[Subject. — Description of a pestilence.]

Semi animes errare viis, dum stare valebant,
Adspiceres, flentes alios terraque iacentes,
Lassaque versantes supremo lumina motu,
Membraque pendentis tendunt ad sidera caeli,
Hic, illic, ubi mors deprenderat, exhalantes.
Ovid, Met. VII. 588–592.

Scan the first and last verses, and explain the peculiarity of versification in the first.

SOLID GEOMETRY.

One and a half hours allowed.

September, 1887.

1. Show that through any given line a plane can be drawn perpendicular to a given plane.

In what case can *more than one* plane be so drawn?

2. When only one plane can be drawn through a given line perpendicular to a given plane, let the intersection of the two planes be called the projection of the given line on given plane.

Prove that the angle made by a line with its projection on a plane is less than the angle it makes with any other line of the plane.

3. Prove that two rectangular parallelopipeds having the same base are to each other as their altitudes.

Consider the case where the altitudes are incommensurable.

4. What is meant by the polar triangle of a given spherical triangle? Prove that the angles of a spherical triangle are measured by the supplements of the opposite sides of its polar triangle.

5. The sides of a spherical triangle on a sphere 14 inches in diameter are 20°, 40°, and 50°; find the area of its polar triangle in square inches. (Take $\pi = 3\frac{1}{7}$.)

6. The diameter of a sphere is 14 inches; two planes are passed through its centre, making an angle of 5° with each other: how many cubic inches in the wedge they cut out? (Take $\pi = 3\frac{1}{7}$.)

June, 1887.

1. Prove that if a plane is perpendicular to a line it is perpendicular to every plane containing the line.

2. Prove that a triangular pyramid is one-third of a triangular prism of the same base and altitude.

3. Prove that the sum of the face angles of a solid angle is less than four right angles. What proposition concerning the perimeter of a spherical polygon follows immediately from this theorem?

4. Prove that the sum of the areas of the lateral faces of a pyramid is greater than the area of the base.

5. State and prove the proposition concerning the area of a spherical triangle.

The angles of a spherical triangle are 70°, 80°, 120°, the radius of the sphere is 7 feet; find the area of the triangle in square feet. (Given $\pi = \frac{22}{7}$.)

6. The exterior diameter of a spherical shell is 7 inches, and its weight is one-tenth that of a solid ball made of the same material and having the same diameter. Find the thickness of the shell.

July, 1886.

[In solving problems use for π the approximate value $3\frac{1}{7}$.]

1. Prove that if a straight line is perpendicular to each of two straight lines at their point of intersection, it is perpendicular to the plane of these lines.

2. Prove that the sum of any two face angles of a triedral angle is greater than the third.

3. Prove that if the base of a cone is a circle, every section made by a plane parallel to the base is a circle.

4. Prove that all the points in the circumference of a circle on the surface of a sphere are equally distant from the poles of the circle.

SOLID GEOMETRY. 161

5. Prove that if $A'B'C'$ is the polar triangle of ABC, then, reciprocally, ABC is the polar triangle of $A'B'C'$.

6. One hundred spherical bullets one-half of an inch in diameter are placed in a cylindrical tomato can 4 inches in diameter and 5 inches high. How much water will the can hold besides the bullets?

7. A cone of revolution whose height is 10 inches and the radius of whose base is 5 inches has a round hole an inch in diameter bored through it; what is the volume of the wood removed?

September, 1885.

[In solving problems use for π the approximate value $3\frac{1}{7}$.]

1. When is a straight line said to be perpendicular to a plane? Prove that if a straight line is perpendicular to each of two straight lines at their point of intersection, it is perpendicular to the plane of these lines.

2. Find the locus of the points in space which are equally distant from three given straight lines which lie in a plane and are not all parallel. What would the locus be if the given lines were parallel?

3. Prove that the sum of the four angles of any convex polyedral angle is less than four right angles.

The length of one side of the base of a regular hexagonal pyramid is 4 feet, and the height of the pyramid is 6 feet; find the whole surface of the pyramid.

4. The planes of the faces of a quadrangular spherical pyramid make with each other angles of 80°, 100°, 120°, and 150°; and the length of a lateral edge of the pyramid is 42 feet. Find the area in square feet of the spherical polygon which forms the pyramid's base.

5. Assuming the formula for the lateral area of a cone of

revolution in terms of the radius of the base and the slant height; prove that the lateral area of the frustum of a cone of revolution is equal to πs (r and r') when s is the slant height of the frustum and r and r' the radii of its bases.

6. A cylinder of revolution and a cone of revolution are inscribable in the same sphere. A section of the cylinder through its axis is a square, and a section of the cone through its axis is an equilateral triangle; prove that the volume of the cylinder is a mean proportional between the volume of the sphere and that of the cone.

June, 1885.

[In solving problems use for π the approximate value $3\frac{1}{7}$.]

1. When is a straight line said to be parallel to a plane? Prove that if a straight line is parallel to a plane, any plane perpendicular to the line is perpendicular to the plane also.

2. What is the locus of the points in a given plane which are equally distant from two given points out of the plane?

The distances of two points P, Q, from a given plane are 11 inches and 19 inches respectively, and the distance between the feet of the perpendiculars dropped from P and Q upon the plane is 6 inches. Find the distance from P to Q.

3. Prove that the lateral area of a regular pyramid is equal to the product of the perimeter of its base by one-half its slant height.

Find the volume of a regular pyramid whose slant height is 12 feet and whose base is an equilateral triangle each of whose sides is $5\sqrt{3}$ feet long.

4. Prove that the curve of intersection of two spheres is a circle.

A sphere of radius 13 inches is cut by a plane distant 12 inches from the centre of the sphere: find the area of the section.

SOLID GEOMETRY. 163

5. The area of a certain spherical triangle is equal to one-tenth of the surface of the sphere on which it lies. Two angles of the triangle are 96° and 87°: find the third angle.

If the radius of the sphere is 7 feet, find the length of one of the sides of the triangle polar to the triangle mentioned above.

6. A cylindrical tin pail 7 inches in diameter contains water to the depth of 4 inches. An egg is then immersed in the water and the level of the latter rises to 4.22 inches above the bottom of the pail: find the volume of the egg.

June, 1884.

[In solving problems use for π the approximate value $3\frac{1}{7}$.]

1. Prove that if a straight line is perpendicular to a plane, every plane passed through the line is also perpendicular to that plane.

2. Prove that if a pyramid is cut by a plane parallel to its base, the edges and the altitude are divided proportionally and the section is a polygon similar to the base.

3. A regular hexagon revolves about a line which bisects two opposite sides: what two kinds of surfaces are generated?

Prove that the total areas of similar cylinders of revolution are to each other as the squares of their altitudes.

4. What is the "limit" of a variable quantity? What is the relation between the limits of two variables which are always equal?

Show that the volume of any cone is equal to one-third the product of its base and its altitude.

5. The angles of a certain spherical triangle which lies on a sphere of 14 inches radius are 123°, 60°, 87°, respectively: find the area of the triangle in square feet and prove the

theorem on which your method of computing this area is based.

6. A polyedron is circumscribed about a sphere whose radius is 2 inches: the volume of the polyedron is 60 cubic inches; what is the area of its surface?

7. Prove that the lateral surface of any pyramid is greater than the base.

September, 1883.

1. Prove that if a line is perpendicular to a plane, every plane containing that line is perpendicular to that plane.

2. Prove that if a line is perpendicular to a plane, every line perpendicular to the line is parallel to the plane.

3. Prove that rectangular parallelopipeds with equal bases are to each other as their altitudes, even when the altitudes are incommensurable.

4. Prove that the angle of a spherical triangle equals 180° minus the opposite side of the polar triangle.

5. Prove that the surface of a sphere equals 4 times the area of its great circle.

6. The volume of a right circular cylinder, whose altitude equals the diameter of its base, is 9 cubic feet: what is the volume of the inscribed sphere?

June, 1883.

[Use the value $3\frac{1}{7}$ for π.]

1. Prove that if two planes are perpendicular, a line drawn in one of them perpendicular to the line of intersection of the planes is perpendicular to the other.

2. Prove that if two planes are perpendicular to a third, their line of intersection is perpendicular to the third plane.

SOLID GEOMETRY.

3. Prove that the volume of a triangular prism is one-half the area of one of the lateral faces multiplied by its distance from the opposite lateral edge.

4. Prove that a triangular pyramid is one-third of a triangular prism of the same base and altitude.

5. How do you find the area of a spherical triangle? What units do you use?
The angles of a spherical triangle are 80°, 70°, and 75°; the radius of the sphere is 7 feet. How many square feet in the triangle?

6. The radius of a sphere is 7 feet: what is its volume? What is the volume of the circumscribed cylinder of revolution?

June, 1882.

1. If a line is perpendicular to a plane, every plane containing the line is also perpendicular to the plane. Prove.

2. The sum of two face angles of a triedral angle is greater than the third. Prove. What property of a spherical triangle follows immediately from this?

3. The area of a spherical triangle is equal to its spherical excess. Prove, explaining clearly what units you use.

4. What are the volumes of the following figures: a rectangular parallelopiped whose edges are 2, 4, and 8 feet respectively; a cylinder formed by the revolution of one of the largest faces of the parallelopiped about one of its longest sides; a sphere which the cylinder will just contain; a spherical pyramid cut from the sphere by planes which make the centre at a triedral angle whose diedral angles are 85°, 120°, 155°?

SOLID GEOMETRY.

June, 1881.

1. Define the projection of a point on a plane.
Prove that a straight line makes a less angle with its projection on any plane than with any other line of that plane.

2. Prove that if parallel lines are projected on any plane, the projections are parallel.

3. Prove that a plane passed through two diagonally opposite edges of a parallelopiped divides it into two equivalent triangular prisms.

4. Prove that when two triangles are polar to one another, any angle of one is measured by the supplement of the side opposite it in the other triangle.

5. Prove that the volume of any triangular prism is measured by the area of a lateral face multiplied by one-half the distance from that face of the opposite lateral edge.

September, 1880.

[Make each proof complete; give all the work of No. 6, but leave result in terms of π.]

1. Prove that if a straight line is perpendicular to a plane, every plane containing that line is perpendicular to that plane.

2. Prove that if a straight line and perpendicular are parallel, every plane which is perpendicular to the line is perpendicular to the plane also.

3. Prove that if a pyramid be cut by plane parallel to the base, the edges and altitude are divided proportionately, and the section is a polygon similar to the base.

4. Prove that if two pyramids have equal altitudes and equivalent bases, sections formed by a plane parallel to the bases and at equal distances from them are equivalent.

5. Prove that symmetrical spherical triangles are equivalent.

6. A pyramid with base of same area as a great circle of a given sphere, and with altitude equal to a diameter of the sphere, is cut by a plane which bisects all its lateral edges. Find the volume of the frustum of the pyramid, if the volume of sphere equal 288 π cubic feet.

July, 1880.

1. State how the angle between two planes is measured. Prove that the vertical angles formed by two intersecting planes are equal.

2. Prove that oblique lines drawn from a point to a plane at equal distances from the foot of the perpendicular are equal; and of two oblique lines unequally distant from the foot of the perpendicular, the more remote is the greater.

3. Show how to find a point in a given plane equally distant from three given points in space.

4. Prove that if two semi-circumferences of great circles intersect on the surface of a hemisphere, the sum of the opposite triangles thus formed is equivalent to a lunary surface whose angle is equal to that included by the semi-circumferences.

5. The area of a spherical triangle is measured by its spherical excess. Explain fully what is meant by this statement, and prove the proposition.

6. Prove that the volumes of a right circular cone, a sphere, and a right circular cylinder are proportional to the numbers 1, 2, 3, if the bases of the cone and cylinder are each equal to a great circle of the sphere, and their altitudes are each equal to a diameter of the sphere.

7. Find the volume of the spherical pyramid whose lateral edges are 9 feet each, and whose adjacent faces make angles of 150°, 130°, 100°, and 70°.

LOGARITHMS AND TRIGONOMETRY.

September, 1886.

1. Find, by logarithms, the value of $\sqrt[3]{\dfrac{14.69 \times (\frac{1}{17})^5}{0.0002}}$.

2. Prove that
$$\sin x(1 + \tan x) + \cos x(1 + \operatorname{ctn} x) = \csc x + \sec x.$$

3. Find a formula for finding $\cos \frac{1}{2} C$, in the triangle ABC; given the three sides.

4. Given $\cos (90° + \phi) = m$; find $\operatorname{ctn} (270° + \phi)$.

5. Find all values of x, under $360°$, which satisfy the equation
$$\sin x + 2 \cos x = 0.$$

6. Solve the right-angled triangle whose hypotenuse is 5, the perpendicular from the right angle to the hypotenuse being 2.

7. Two angles of a triangle are $47°$ and $71°$, and the included side is 6. Find the area of the triangle.

September, 1885.

1. Do or do not negative numbers have logarithms? Prove.

2. Find, by logarithms, the value of $\sqrt{\dfrac{0.01 \times (0.2938)^5}{\frac{1}{3}}}$.

3. Given $\sin x = \sqrt{\frac{1}{5}}$; in what quadrants may x lie? Find, by formulas, $\cos x$, $\operatorname{ctn} x$, for each value of x, giving to each function its proper sign.

4. Given $10 \sin^2 x + \operatorname{ctn}^2 x = 10$; find all values of x between $180°$ and $270°$.

5. Prove $\sin (x + y) \sin (x - y) = \cos^2 y - \cos^2 x$.

6. One angle of a triangle is 50°, and one of the two including sides is 15. What is the smallest value the side opposite the angle can have? Supposing this side to increase, for what values will there be two solutions to the triangle?

7. Beginning with expressions for sin $(x+y)$ and cos $(x+y)$, find an expression for tan $(2x)$ in terms of tan x.

8. Prove $\tan \tfrac{1}{2} x = \dfrac{1 - \cos x}{\sin x}$.

June, 1885.

1. In any system of logarithms, prove the relation that exists between the logarithm of a number and the logarithm of the reciprocal of this number.

2. Find, by logarithms, the value of $(0.01209)^{\frac{2}{3}}$.

3. Show by a figure what change takes place, in magnitude and in sign, in the tangent of an angle as the angle increases from 0° to 270°.

4. Given $\sin x \cos x = \tfrac{2}{5}$; find all the values of x under 360°.

5. Prove $\cos 2x = 2 \cos^2 x - 1$.

6. Given $\sin 10° = m$; find $\sec 250°$.

7. The sides of a triangle are 2, 3, and 4. Find the largest angle.

8. Prove $\tan 50° + \ctn 50° = 2 \sec 10°$.

June, 1884.

1. Why is log $\tfrac{1}{2}$ equal to $-\log 2$? Show why 251, 0.251, and 0.00251 have logarithms differing only in the value of the characteristic.

2. Given $16^x = 25$; find by the aid of your table of logarithms the value of x.

3. Solve the trigonometric equation

$$\cos x \operatorname{ctn} x = 1.$$

[Find the value of some function of x by solving the equation, and then the value of x by help of the tables.]

4. Show by the aid of a figure that

$$\csc(180° + \phi) = -\csc \phi.$$

5. Given $\cos^2 a - \sin^2 a = \cos 2a$; obtain formulas for $\sin \frac{\phi}{2}$, $\cos \frac{\phi}{2}$, and $\tan \frac{\phi}{2}$ in terms of $\cos \phi$.

6. Prove the formula $\sin x\,(2\cos x - 1) = 2\sin\frac{x}{2}\cos\frac{3x}{2}$.

7. A pine-tree, 120 feet high, standing on the side of a mountain which is inclined to the horizontal at an angle of 25°, is broken by the wind and not severed, at a distance of 40 feet from the ground. The top falls toward the foot of the mountain. How far from the base of the tree does it strike the ground?

8. Two sides of a triangle are 6.4 feet and 8.3 feet long and make with each other an angle of 42°. Find the other angles and the area.

September, 1883.

[In numerical examples find answers to one more figure than those given in the table.]

1. What is logarithm of 1 in any system? Of the base? Of its reciprocal? For what numbers is the logarithm positive, and for what negative? Give reasons for your answers.

2. How many values of D between 0° and 360° satisfy the equation $\sec D = -\frac{5}{3}$, and in what quadrants do they lie? Draw a figure representing them.

Calculate the sin, cos, tan, cot, and cosec of *both* these values of D: distinguish them as D' and D''.

3. Prove the general formulas

$$\sin \alpha + \sin \beta = 2 \sin \tfrac{1}{2}(\alpha+\beta) \cos \tfrac{1}{2}(\alpha-\beta),$$
$$\sin \alpha - \sin \beta = 2 \cos \tfrac{1}{2}(\alpha+\beta) \sin \tfrac{1}{2}(\alpha-\beta),$$

and prove that in any triangles

$$\frac{a+b}{a-b} = \frac{\tan \tfrac{1}{2}(A+B)}{\tan \tfrac{1}{2}(A-B)}.$$

4. Two straight roads cross a third at the points A and B, and meet each other at C.
$AC = 715.8$ ft., $BC = 1132.4$ ft., the angle which road AC makes with $AB = 34° 27'$. Find the distance AB.

Show by figure that this question has two solutions, and find both.

5. Wishing to find the relative position of two objects, A and B, which stand in a level plain and are separated by an intervening house, I find point C from which both are visible and directly accessible. Then I find $CA = 413$ ft., $CB = 521$ ft. A is just northeast of C, while the direction of B from C is south $65°$ east. Find distance and direction of A from B.

June, 1883.

1. In a system of logarithms of which the base is $a^{\frac{m}{n}}$, find the logarithms of the following numbers: —

$$a^{\frac{m}{n}}; \quad a^{\frac{2m}{n}}; \quad a^{\frac{m^2}{n^2}}; \quad a; \quad a^2; \quad \frac{1}{a}; \quad a^{-\frac{p}{2}}; \quad 1; \quad a^p a^q.$$

2. Find by logarithms the value of $\sqrt[5]{(0.0002)^3}$.

3. A man wishes to find the height of a spire which he sees on the other side of an impassable stream. He observes that the direction of the spire from the spot where he stands is due north; and that a surveyor's telescope, pointed at the apex of the spire, makes an angle of $17° 33'$ with the

plane of the horizon. He then walks due east until he sees the spire in a precisely northwesterly direction; and he finds that the distance between the two points of observation is 432.6 feet.

Compute the height of the spire.

4. The following parts of a triangle are given:—
$$b = 0.03287, \quad c = 0.02702, \quad C = 48° \, 12'.$$
Find the remaining sides and angles and the areas of the *two* triangles that satisfy these conditions, and represent the triangles in a figure.

5. Given the formula
$$\cos 2\theta = \cos^2 \theta - \sin^2 \theta;$$
prove the formulas
$$\sin \tfrac{1}{2} a = \sqrt{\tfrac{1}{2}(1-\cos a)},$$
$$\cos \tfrac{1}{2} a = \sqrt{\tfrac{1}{2}(1+\cos a)},$$
$$\tan (45° + \tfrac{1}{2} a) = \sec a + \tan a.$$

6. Find all the trigonometric functions of 45°, without the use of the tables, by general reasoning.

September, 1882.

1. Prove that the logarithm of a product is equal to the sum of the logarithms of the factors.

2. In a system of logarithms of which the base is 9, what are the logarithms of 3, 27, 9, 1, $\tfrac{1}{27}$, 0?

3. Compute by logarithms
$$\sqrt[3]{\frac{(134.9)^2 \times \sqrt[5]{16}}{\sqrt{10190.04 \times 46.49}}}.$$

4. Prove the formula for the cosine of the sum of two angles.

LOGARITHMS AND TRIGONOMETRY. 173

5. Find, by the tables, the logarithms of the trigonometric functions of 207° 17' (marking the signs).

6. Prove the formulas
$$\frac{\sin \alpha}{\sin \beta} = \sin(\alpha + 2\beta)\csc\beta - 2\cos(\alpha+\beta),$$
$$2\sec 2\theta = \frac{\sec(45° - \theta)}{\cos(45° + \theta)}.$$

7. Given two sides of a triangle equal to 1.0121 and 1.5421, and the included angle equal to 41° 02'; to solve the triangle.

June, 1882.

1. Explain the reason of the rule for finding the *characteristic* (or integral part) of the logarithm of a number.

Show that (according to this rule) the *mantissa* (or fractional part) is always *positive*.

In what cases is the logarithm, as a whole, positive, and in what cases negative?

Thus, state clearly the value of the logarithm of 36270; of 0.003627. What decimal must be added to the latter logarithm to produce the logarithm of 0.01?

2. Find the time required to increase a sum of money a hundred-fold, at *ten* per cent per annum compound interest, payable yearly.

3. Find the formulas for the trigonometric functions of $90° + \alpha$.

4. Find, by the tables, the logarithms of the trigonometric functions of 290° 38' (marking the signs).

5. An observer from a ship saw two headlands. The first bore E.N.E. (*i.e.* 67° 30' from N. towards E.), and the second N.W. by N. (*i.e.* 33° 45' from N. towards W.). After he had sailed 16.25 miles N. by W. (*i.e.* 11° 15' from N. towards W.), the first headland bore due E., and the

second N.W. by W. (*i.e.* 56° 15' from N. towards W.). Find the direction and distance of the second headland from the first.

6. Prove the formulas

$$\frac{\cos \alpha - \cos \beta}{\cos \alpha + \cos \beta} = -\tan \tfrac{1}{2}(\alpha + \beta)\tan \tfrac{1}{2}(\alpha - \beta),$$

$$\sin \theta = \frac{2\tan \tfrac{1}{2}\theta}{1 + \tan^2 \tfrac{1}{2}\theta}.$$

June, 1881.

1. Define a logarithm. What is the logarithm of $\tfrac{1}{2}$ in the system of which 16 is the base? Find the logarithm of 25 in the same system.

2. Compute the value of $\sqrt[5]{\dfrac{(0.012)^3 \times 0.27}{(64)^2 \times 0.00651}}$ by logarithms.

3. Find the functions of 127° 10' from your trigonometric tables.

4. Prove the formula

$$(\cos A - \cos B)^2 + (\sin A - \sin B)^2 = 4\sin^2 \frac{A-B}{2}.$$

5. Two sides of a triangle are 243 feet and 188 feet, and the angle opposite the second side is 42° 20'. Solve the triangle completely.

6. A pine-tree growing on the side of a mountain, which is inclined to the horizontal at an angle of 20°, is broken by the wind, but not severed, at a distance of 40 feet from the ground. The top falls toward the foot of the mountain and strikes the ground 50 feet from the base of the tree; find the height of the tree.

September, 1880.

1. Find logarithm of 50 in the system of which 2 is the base.

2. Sec $(180° + \phi) = a$. Find all other functions of ϕ.

LOGARITHMS AND TRIGONOMETRY. 175

3. Prove that $\cos(\alpha+\beta)\cdot\cos(\alpha-\beta) = \cos^2\alpha - \sin^2\beta$.

4. Prove formula $\sin\tfrac{1}{2}A = \sqrt{\dfrac{(s-b)(s-c)}{bc}}$

5. Given 2 sides of triangle equal 251.2 feet and 146.1, and that angle opposite second side equals 12° 20′. Find other angles.

6. Sides of angle equal 5 feet, 12 feet, and 13 feet. Find the angle opposite the longest side.

7. From two corners (A and B) of the triangular field in which Memorial Hall stands, lines, which make angles of 19° 52′ and 57° 52′ respectively with the side AB, meet directly under the tower of the hall. AB equals 345.1 feet. At A the angle of elevation of the tower is 32° 26′. Find the height of the tower.

8. Compute $\left(\dfrac{(0.507)^2 \times \sqrt[4]{140}}{\sqrt{0.4} \times 67}\right)^{\!\frac{1}{3}}$ by logs.

June, 1880

1. Define a logarithm. Prove the rule for finding the characteristic of a logarithm.

2. How do you obtain the functions of an obtuse angle from an ordinary table of Trigonometric Functions? why?

3. Prove that $\tan(45° - \tfrac{1}{2}\alpha) = \sec\alpha - \tan\alpha$.

4. Deduce the formulas required for solving a triangle when two sides and the included angle are given.

5. Given that two sides of a triangle are $10\tfrac{1}{2}$ ft. and $16\tfrac{1}{4}$ ft., and that the angle opposite the first side is 15°; solve the triangle.

6. Given that the sides of the Delta on which Memorial Hall stands are 265 and 241 yards, and the included angle is 26° 40'; required the length of the end of the Delta.

7. Given $2^x = \frac{56}{89}$; find the value of x by logarithms.

PHYSICAL AND NATURAL SCIENCE.

PHYSICS.

September, 1887.

1. How much work will gravity do upon a kilogram mass during the first quarter-second of its fall from rest? during the second quarter-second? State the unit in which you express the work.

2. Two equal inelastic masses moving in opposite directions, one at the rate of 10 meters a second, the other at the rate of 6 meters per second, collide centrally. What fraction of their original kinetic energy disappears in the collision?

3. If the pressure of the atmosphere were 15 lbs. per square inch, how great a force would be required to separate two Magdeburg hemispheres of 5 inches' diameter, the space within the sphere being a vacuum?

4. A certain quantity of air has a volume of 200 cu. cm. at 40° C. under a pressure of 600 mm. of mercury. What would be its volume at 100° C. under a pressure of 900 mm. of mercury?

5. Write a short discourse upon the law, *Bodies when cold absorb the same kinds of rays that they give out when heated*, showing how the law has been proved by experiment and how its application has led to important discoveries.

PHYSICAL AND NATURAL SCIENCE. 177

6. Give an exact quantitative definition of the conductivity of a substance for heat.

7. What is electric *inductive capacity?* What furnishes the light of the electric spark at the discharge of a Leyden jar? Show to what extent the potential energy of a Leyden jar is affected by doubling the quantity of electricity contained in its charge.

July, 1886.

[In problems 1, 2, and 3 adopt any *units* you please, but tell what ones you adopt.]

1. A body whose mass is m, originally at rest on a smooth horizontal plane, is acted upon by a horizontal force of f units during t seconds. What is its final velocity? How far does it move during the t seconds? Show how much *work* is done upon it during this time.

2. Let the mass, m, of a body and its velocity, v, be such that the product mv is 600. How *long* would this body move against a constant resistance equal to the force of gravity upon a body whose mass is 5? Can you tell how *far* the body would move against this resistance?

3. If the kinetic energy of such a body were 600, and its momentum unknown, how *far* would it move against the given resistance? Can you tell how *long* it would move in this case?

4. Show in what respect the air-thermometer is superior to any liquid thermometer as a scientific instrument. Show in what respects it is less convenient than the mercury thermometer.

5. A certain quantity of air has a volume of 200 cu. cm. at 40° C., under a pressure of 700 mm. of mercury. What would be its volume at 100° C. under a pressure of 800 mm. of mercury?

6. Describe, as fully as you can, two methods which have been used for determining the velocity of light. Explain how the motion of a body may affect the position of the lines in its spectrum. In what cases has such an effect been observed?

7. Give a careful account of Volta's theory of the action in his electric pile and of the criticisms which this theory has encountered.

September, 1885.

1. Give your idea of "mass" and a careful account of the experiments and reasoning by means of which Newton proved that bodies of the same weight are of the same mass.

2. Give as full and accurate an account as you can of the way in which Newton established the law of universal gravitation.

3. A cord passing over a frictionless pulley has a mass of 20 grm. at one end, and 15 grm. at the other end. How long will it take these masses, starting from rest under the influence of gravity, to acquire a velocity of 2 meters per second?

4. Two equal inelastic masses moving in opposite directions, one at the rate of 10 meters a second, the other at the rate of 5 meters a second, collide centrally. What fraction of their original kinetic energy is converted into heat by the collision?

5. Define a "horse-power."

If the temperature in the boiler of an engine is 150° C. and the temperature in the condenser 50° C., what is the largest possible fraction of the heat entering the cylinder that can be utilized in doing work?

6. Write a short discourse upon the law, *Bodies when cold absorb the same kind of rays that they give out when*

heated, showing how the law has been established by experiment and how its application has led to important discoveries.

7. Give a careful account of Volta's theory of the action in his electric pile and the criticisms that have been made upon this theory.

June, 1885.

1. Give your idea of "mass" and a careful account of the experiments and reasoning by means of which Newton proved that bodies of the same weight are also of the same mass.

2. Let the mass of a body in kilograms be m, and let its velocity in meters per second be v. Prove that in virtue of its motion it can do $\frac{mv^2}{19.6}$ kilograameters of work.

3. Define energy and give an account of the doctrine of conservation of energy, with illustrations involving as many varieties of energy as possible.

4. Show why a sound-wave moving with the wind tends to keep close to the earth, while moving against the wind it tends to rise from the earth.

5. Define a "horse-power."
Why could we not, even with a perfect engine, utilize in work all the heat supplied to the cylinder?

6. Define specific heat.
What is Dulong and Petit's law in regard to the connection between specific heat and atomic weight?

7. Explain, as if for a person unacquainted with physics, how the presence of certain substances has been detected in the sun.

8. It being admitted that light is propagated by means of vibrations, what reason have we for believing these to be transverse vibrations?

9. Prove that in the case of any given Leyden jar the potential energy is proportional to the square of the quantity of electricity constituting the charge.

June, 1884.

1. What is the ordinary method of comparing the masses of bodies? What possible method does Stewart describe as applicable where the ordinary method would fail?

2. Give the best account you can of the method by which Newton established the law of universal gravitation.

3. If the pressure of the atmosphere were 15 lbs. per square inch, what force would be required to separate two Magdeburg hemispheres of 4 inches diameter, the space within the sphere being a vacuum?

4. Show how Stewart, by means of the supposed collision of two railway trains, illustrates the law that the kinetic energy of a body is proportional to the square of its velocity.

5. Suppose a body to be vibrating in a straight line backward and forward on either side of its position of rest, toward which it is attracted by a force proportional to its distance from that point: give such proof as you can of the fact that the time of vibration will be independent of the range of vibration.

6. Give an exact numerical definition of the conductivity of a substance for heat.

7. Describe Watt's three main improvements in the steam-engine.

8. Give a brief description of the apparatus by means of which you would compare the intensity of radiation in different parts of the spectrum.

9. State Ohm's law for an electric current, and show that, if the "external" resistance of a circuit is small, the current may be only slightly increased by increasing the number of cells in the battery.

10. From a mechanical point of view, from what depth could coal be raised with profit? Mechanical equivalent of heat is 772 foot pounds. One pound coal gives out 11,000 units of heat in burning.

CHEMISTRY.

Eliot and Storer.

1. Describe experiments by which the composition of water may be determined both analytically and synthetically. What are the grounds for writing the symbol of water H_2O?

2. Describe the preparation of hydrochloric acid gas, and write the reaction by which the process is represented. How many liters of hydrochloric acid gas can be made from ten grams of salt? What is the liquid hydrochloric acid used in the laboratory? What is the action of hydrochloric acid on zinc, and on sodic carbonate? Write the reaction in both cases.

3. What is the common ore of lead? How is the metal obtained from the ore? What is the best solvent for this metal, and what is the substance formed by the solution? How is silver in a lead ore separated from the lead?

4. What is the chief source of alcohol, and what is the nature of the process by which it is formed? Describe the preparation of vinegar and the nature of the chemical process involved.

BOTANY.

[Omit one question.]

1. Name and describe the parts of a typical flower. Which of them are essential?

2. Describe the mode of life of an annual, a biennial, and a perennial plant. Mention two plants of each type.

3. Define the following terms relating to (*a*) the root and (*b*) the stem.

(*a*) Aerial, fibrous, parasitic.
(*b*) Herbaceous, stolon, endogenous, heart-wood.

4. Name the parts of a complete leaf. What are equitant leaves?

5. Show clearly how you would distinguish a cyme from a corymb. What is an umbel, a raceme, a spadix?

6. Describe the various ways in which the parts of a flower may be united and the ways in which the ovules may be placed in the ovary.

7. Describe the structure of the seed. Tell how the seeds of the morning-glory, the bean, the pine, and Indian corn differ from one another.

8. What is a natural system of classification? What are the principal differences between exogens and endogens?

9. What are the principal uses of plants?

PAPERS

OF

YALE UNIVERSITY; SHEFFIELD SCIENTIFIC SCHOOL; COLLEGE OF NEW JERSEY (PRINCETON); COLUMBIA SCHOOL OF MINES.

YALE UNIVERSITY.

June, 1887.

LATIN GRAMMAR.

[Time allowed, 45 minutes.]

1. Compare *malus, nequam, pulcher, similis*. Decline *senex, filia, duo, scribens*. Give the Latin expression for May 10th.

2. Give the perfect and supine of *rapio, crepo, meto, tundo*. What are denominative verbs? Give examples. Inflect *volo* and *eo* in the present and future indicative, and the present and imperfect subjunctive.

3. State what rules are violated in the following sentences and make the necessary corrections : —

   (*a*) *hanc vitam sine libris frui non possumus.*
   (*b*) *ii qui in Capua capiebantur, ignoscendi sunt.*
   (*c*) *me ipsum nunquam satisfacio.*
   (*d*) *quid tibi hoc interest.*

4. Put the following indirect discourse into the direct: *Ei* [Caesari] *Ariovistus respondit*, si quid ipsi a Caesare opus esset sese ad eum venturum fuisse ; sibi mirum videri, quid in sua Gallia, quam bello vicisset, Caesari negotii esset.

CAESAR.

[Time allowed, 30 minutes.]

I. TRANSLATE Bell. Gal. I. 41.

II. TRANSLATE Bell. Gal. III. 18.

III. (*a*) When and by what authority was Caesar in Gaul? (*b*) Describe the Roman legion as it was in Caesar's time, — its size, divisions, officers, and weapons.

CICERO.

[Time allowed, 1 hour.]

I. Explain the meaning of *novus homo*. In what year was Cicero consul? What offices had he previously held? What became of Catiline? How was the punishment of the conspirators the cause of Cicero's banishment? Where was Cicero born? What other distinguished man was born at the same place?

II. TRANSLATE Cat. II. 21.

What kind of a numeral is *quartus?* Give the force of the derivative endings in *turbulentus*, *inertia*, and *proscriptio*. What does *ita* modify?

III. TRANSLATE Cat. IV. 9.

Explain the subjunctives. Give the construction of *mea* (1), *cognitore*, *alteram*. To what classes do the genitives *Caesaris*, *sententiae*, and *negotii* belong?

IV. TRANSLATE Arch. I.

What were the provisions of the law under which Archias claimed Roman citizenship? With which requirement was it difficult to show that he had complied? What is the conclusion of *si quid . . . ingenii ?* What is the construction of *quod* (1)? Why is *sit* subjunctive? Give the principal parts of *infitior* and *confiteor.*

VERGIL, INCLUDING LATIN PROSODY.

[Time allowed, 70 minutes.]

I. Copy and divide into feet the following four verses, marking the caesurae (Aen. IV. 60-64).

Give rules for the quantity of the ultima in *ipsa* (60), *dextra* (60), *Dido* (60), *donis* (63) ; and of the penult in *ora* (62), *spatiatur* (62), and *pecudum* (63). What rule for the quantity of an ultima is not observed in 64? What is *hiatus ?*

VERGIL.

II. TRANSLATE Ecl. III. 32-39.

III. Mode and tense of *ausim* (32)? What is the construction of *id* (35) ? Why are the *vitis* and the *hedera* appropriate decorations for the *pocula ?* What poet did Vergil chiefly imitate in the Eclogues?

IV. TRANSLATE Aen. I. 565-574.

V. (*a*) What is the construction of *vestra* (573)? Give the uncontracted form for *Aeneadum* (565). Account for the mode of *nesciat* (565). (*b*) Explain the meaning of verse 4. What is meant by *Saturnia arva* (569) and what by *Erycis fines* (570)?

VI. TRANSLATE Aen. IV. 416-428.

VII. (*a*) Remark upon the use of the voice in *properari* (416) and of the mode in *colere* (422). (*b*) Give the meaning of the last four verses and explain the references.

OVID AT SIGHT.

[Time allowed, 40 minutes.]

TRANSLATE: —

Aesacon umbrosa furtim peperisse sub Ida
Fertur Alexirhoë, Granico nata bicorni.
Oderat hic urbes, nitidaque remotus ab aula
Secretos montes et inambitiosa colebat
Rura, nec Iliacos coetus nisi rarus adibat.
Non agreste tamen nec inexpugnabile amori
Pectus habens, silvas captatam saepe per omnes.
Aspicit Hesperien patria Cebrenida[1] ripa,
Iniectos umeris siccantem sole capillos.
Visa fugit nymphe, veluti perterrita fulvum
Cerva lupum, longeque lacu deprensa relicto
Accipitrem fluvialis anas. quam Troius heros
Insequitur, celeremque metu celer urguet amore.
Ecce latens herba coluber fugientis adunco
Dente pedem strinxit, virusque in corpore liquit.
Cum vita subpressa fuga est. amplectitur amens
Exanimem, clamatque "piget, piget esse secutum!
Sed non hoc timui, nec erat mihi vincere tanti.
Perdidimus miseram nos te duo: vulnus ab angue,
A me causa data est. ego sum sceleratior illo:
Qui tibi morte mea mortis solacia mittam."
Dixit, et e scopulo, quem rauca subederat unda,
Se dedit in pontum. Tethys miserata cadentem
Molliter excepit, nantemque per aequora pennis
Texit, et optatae non est data copia mortis.

[1] *Cebren*, a river in the Troad.

PROSE LATIN AT SIGHT.

[Time allowed, 45 minutes.]

TRANSLATE : —

Pr. Idus Oct. Athenas venimus, cum sane adversis ventis usi essemus tardeque et incommode navigassemus. De nave exeuntibus nobis Acastus cum litteris praesto fuit uno et vicensimo die, sane strenue. Accepi tuas litteras, quibus intellexi te vereri ne superiores mihi redditae non essent: omnes sunt redditae diligentissimeque a te perscripta sunt omnia; idque mihi gratissimum fuit. Neque sum admiratus hanc epistolam, quam Acastus attulit, brevem fuisse; iam enim me ipsum exspectas sive nos ipsos, qui quidem quam primum ad vos venire cupimus, etsi, in quam rem publicam veniamus, intellego: cognovi enim ex multorum amicorum litteris, quas attulit Acastus, ad arma rem spectare, ut mihi, cum venero, dissimulare non liceat, quid sentiam. Sed, quoniam subeunda fortuna est, eo citius dabimus operam, ut veniamus, quo facilius de tota re deliberemus. Tu velim, quam longissime poteris obviam nobis prodeas. De hereditate Preciana, quae quidem mihi magno dolori est — valde enim illum amavi —, sed hoc velim cures: si auctio ante meum adventum fiet, ut Pomponius aut, si is minus poterit, Camillus nostrum negotium curet. Nos cum salvi venerimus, reliqua per nos agemus; sin tu iam Roma profecta eris, tamen curabis, ut hoc ita fiat. Nos, si di adiuvabant, circiter Idus Novembres in Italia speramus fore.

LATIN COMPOSITION.

[Time allowed, 45 minutes.]

Many advised Hannibal to take the remainder of that day and the following night for rest; but Maharbal thought that there should be no delay. "That you may know," he said, "how great is our victory, within five days you shall feast in the Capitol. Pursue the enemy; I will go ahead with the cavalry that the Romans may know that you have come before they know that you are coming." As Hannibal said that he must take time to deliberate, Maharbal replied: "Hannibal, you know how to conquer: you do not know how to use your conquest." It is believed that that day's delay was the salvation of Rome.

ROMAN HISTORY.

[Time allowed, 30 minutes.]

1. What powers did Octavianus Augustus take to himself? What change did he make in the government of Rome? What changes did Constantine make?

2. The gradual extension of the right of Roman citizenship, the causes of each extension and dates.

3. What were the possessions of Rome at the beginning of the Christian Era? How were they acquired and when?

4. Explain: *praetorian guards; provincia; colonia; tribunus plebis; comitia centuriata.*

5. *Allia, Beneventum, Saguntum, Metaurus, Pharsalia;* where were they? what happened there, and when?

GREEK GRAMMAR AND COMPOSITION.

[Time allowed, 1½ hours. All Greek words to be written with accents.]

I. TRANSLATE INTO GREEK:—

Orontes told Cyrus that if he would give him one thousand cavalry he would utterly destroy the hostile force before them. This seemed a good plan to Cyrus, and he bade Orontes take a company from each leader. When the traitor believed that all was in readiness, he wrote a letter to the king to tell him that he would come with as many horsemen as possible. But the man who received the letter, gave it not to the king, but to Cyrus, who read it and at once arrested Orontes.

II. τῶν δὲ Μένωνος στρατιωτῶν ξύλα σχίζων τις ὡς εἶδε τὸν Κλέαρχον διελαύνοντα, ἵησι τῇ ἀξίνῃ· καὶ οὗτος μὲν αὐτοῦ ἥμαρτεν· ἄλλος δὲ λίθῳ καὶ ἄλλος, εἶτα πολλοί, κραυγῆς γενομένης. ὁ δὲ καταφεύγει εἰς τὸ ἑαυτοῦ στράτευμα, καὶ εὐθὺς παραγγέλλει εἰς τὰ ὅπλα.

a. Give the principal parts of the verbs in the passage. *b.* The synopsis (first form in each mode) of the first four verbs (in the tense used here). *c.* Construction of each nominative, genitive, and dative. *d.* Force of each preposition in the passage. *e.* Inflect τίς, οὗτος, ἀνήρ, ἡδύς, πολύς, (in sing.). *f.* Inflect the imperfect active of ἐρωτάω. *g.* What are the different forms of conditional sentences? *h.* Give examples of hiatus, elision, apocope, assimilation of consonants. *i.* Compare πολύς, σοφός, δίκαιος, μέλας. *j.* What different ways of expressing purpose are used in Greek?

XENOPHON.

[Time allowed, 1 hour.]

I. TRANSLATE Anabasis I. ii, 25 f. as far as πρὶν ἡ γυνὴ αὐτὸν ἔπεισε καὶ πίστεις ἔλαβε.

What is the force of τῶν after ὁρῶν, εἶτα? Construction of τι, ὑπολειφθέντας, τοὺς Ταρσοὺς, οὐδενί, Κύρῳ.

II. TRANSLATE Anabasis II. iii. 5–7.

Give the construction of μάχης, ὁ τολμήσων, ᾧ, εἰκότα, δοκοῖεν, βασιλεῖ, ἅπασιν, διαγγελθῇ. Force of αὐτοῖς. Why is μή (not οὐ) used with πορίσας?

III. TRANSLATE Anabasis III. ii. 11–13.

Give the construction of κινδύνους, ἀγαθοῖς, στόλῳ, πολεμίων. Force of the preposition in ἀναμνήσω, καταθύσειν, ἀποθύουσιν. Force of ὡς (before ἀφανισῦνταν), τὲ (after ἀγαθοῖς), καὶ (before ἐκ). To what events does the speaker refer?

[The following may be substituted for any one of the foregoing passages.]

IV. TRANSLATE Hellenica II. iii. 52 f.

Give the construction of ἐννομώτατα εἶναι, ἐξαλείφειν, ὑμῖν, ὑμῶν, ταῦτα. Who were οἱ ἐν καταλόγῳ? Explain ἐπὶ τὴν Ἑστίαν.

HOMER.

[Time allowed, 1 hour.]

I. TRANSLATE Iliad A 436–450.

Give a metrical scheme for vs. 439, 444, 448, 449, commenting on any peculiarities. Define caesura. Where is the most frequent caesura in Homeric verse? Construction of κατά (436), Ἀπόλλωνι (438), τοῖσιν, μεγάλα (450). What is the tense of βῆσαν (438), τίθει (441), ἱλασόμεσθα (444), ἔστησαν (448)? Comment on the order of words in v. 449, on the derivation of χερνίψαντο, οὐλοχύτας (449), on the attitude of χεῖρας ἀνασλών (450).

II. TRANSLATE Iliad B 149–165.

Enumerate the dialectic peculiarities found in this passage. Explain the use of ὑπό (154), κέν (155), κάδ (160). Construction of νηῶν (152), ἱεμένων (154), εὐχωλήν (158). What were the οὐροί (153), ἔρματα (154)?

III. TRANSLATE Iliad B 657–666.

Comment on βίῃ Ἡρακληείῃ.

GREEK AT SIGHT.

[The following may be substituted for any one of the foregoing passages.]

IV. TRANSLATE Iliad Z 441–455.
Give a metrical scheme of vs. 443, 447, commenting on any peculiarities. Explain the accent of ὡς (443). Construction of πολέμοιο (443), αὐτοῦ (446), Ἑκάβης (451), πολέες (452). Explain the form ἐυμμελίω (449). Comment on ἐλεύθερον ἦμαρ (455).

GREEK AT SIGHT.

[Time allowed, 45 minutes.]

Τῷ δ' ἐπιόντι ἔτει, Λύσανδρος ἀφικόμενος εἰς Ἔφεσον μετεπέμψατο Ἐτεόνικον ἐκ Χίου σὺν ταῖς ναυσί, καὶ τὰς ἄλλας πάσας συνήθροισεν, εἴ πού τις ἦν, καὶ ταύτας τ' ἐπεσκεύαζε καὶ ἄλλας ἐν Ἀντάνδρῳ ἐναυπηγεῖτο. ἐλθὼν δὲ παρὰ Κῦρον χρήματα ᾔτει· ὁ δ' αὐτῷ εἶπεν ὅτι τὰ μὲν παρὰ βασιλέως ἀνηλωμένα εἴη, καὶ ἔτι πλείω πολλῷ, δεικνύων ὅσα ἕκαστος τῶν ναυάρχων ἔχοι, ὅμως δ' ἔδωκε. λαβὼν δὲ ὁ Λύσανδρος τἀργύριον ἐπὶ τὰς τριήρεις τριηράρχους ἐπέστησε καὶ τοῖς ναύταις τὸν ὀφειλόμενον μισθὸν ἀπέδωκε. παρεσκευάζοντο δὲ καὶ οἱ τῶν Ἀθηναίων στρατηγοὶ πρὸς τὸ ναυτικὸν ἐν τῇ Σάμῳ.

Κῦρος δ' ἐπὶ τούτοις μετεπέμψατο Λύσανδρον, ἐπεὶ αὐτῷ παρὰ τοῦ πατρὸς ἧκεν ἄγγελος λέγων ὅτι ἀρρωστῶν ἐκεῖνον καλοίη, ὢν ἐν Θαμνηρίοις τῆς Μηδίας ἐγγὺς Καδουσίων, ἐφ' οὓς ἐστράτευσεν ἀφεστῶτας. ἥκοντα δὲ Λύσανδρον οὐκ εἴα ναυμαχεῖν πρὸς Ἀθηναίους, ἐὰν μὴ π. ολλῷ πλείους ναῦς ἔχῃ· εἶναι γὰρ χρήματα πολλὰ καὶ βασιλεῖ καὶ ἑαυτῷ, ὥστε τούτου ἕνεκεν πολλὰ πληροῦν. παρέδειξε δ' αὐτῷ πάντας τοὺς φόρους τοὺς ἐκ τῶν πόλεων, οἳ αὐτῷ ἴδιοι ἦσαν, καὶ τὰ περιττὰ χρήματα ἔδωκε· καὶ ἀναμνήσας ὡς εἶχε φιλίας πρός τε τὴν τῶν

Λακεδαιμονίων πόλιν καὶ πρὸς Λύσανδρον ἰδίᾳ, ἀνέβαινε παρὰ τὸν πατέρα.

ἐπισκευάζω: repair. ναυπηγέομαι: build ships. ἀναλίσκω: expend.
ἀρρωστέω: to be weak, ill. πληρόω: to fill, man.

GREEK HISTORY.

[Time allowed, 30 minutes.]

1. Enumerate the steps by which the islands of the Aegean Sea become subject to Athens in the fifth century B.C. State what you know of the Confederacy of Delos.

2. Arrange in chronological order *Aristides, Cleon, Isocrates, Lysias, Nicias, Pisistratus, Solon;* and state the most important facts concerning each.

3. State what you know of the mountains and rivers of Greece, describing the location or course of the most important.

4. Locate *Aegospotami, Amyclae, Artemisium, Chaeronea, Plataea, Sphacteria;* and state the event or events for which each is best known (with exact or approximate dates).

ARITHMETIC.

[Time allowed, 1 hour.]

1. Add $\frac{1}{2}$, $\frac{2}{3}$ of $\frac{4}{9}$, and $\frac{7\frac{2}{3}}{8\frac{3}{4}}$.

2. Reduce 1 furlong 25 rods 12 feet and 11 inches to the decimal of a mile.

3. What is the interest on $25 from Nov. 10, 1884, to July 1, 1887, at 5 per cent per annum?

4. Compute the value of $\sqrt{3}-1+\sqrt{6}$ to four decimal places.

5. A cubical block contains 12695.24 cubic inches. Required the length of one side.

6. Reduce 305 milligrams, 218 dekagrams and 7 metric tons to kilograms.

7. How many square rods in a field 300 meters long and $\frac{1}{10}$ of a kilometer wide?

ALGEBRA.

[Time allowed, 1 hour.]

1. Resolve each of the following expressions into three factors:
$$a^4 b + 8 a c^3 b m^6, \qquad 4 c^3 x^2 + 4 c^2 x y + c y^2.$$

2. Divide $\dfrac{a}{a-b} - \dfrac{b}{a+b}$ by $\dfrac{b}{a-b} - \dfrac{a}{a+b}$.

3. Multiply $\left(x - \dfrac{1-\sqrt{3}}{2\sqrt{2}}\right)\left(x - \dfrac{1+\sqrt{3}}{2\sqrt{2}}\right)\left(x + \dfrac{1}{\sqrt{2}}\right)$.

4. Solve $\sqrt{x+40} = 10 - \sqrt{x}$.

5. Solve $mx^2 + mn = 2m\sqrt{nx} + nx^2$.

6. Given $\dfrac{15}{x} : \dfrac{21}{y} :: 3 : 7$, and $x^2 - y^2 = 9$, to find x and y.

7. Expand by the Binomial Theorem, $3b(2x-y)^{\frac{1}{2}}$.

GEOMETRY.

[Time allowed, 1 hour. The candidate may omit any two propositions.]

1. To inscribe a circle in a given triangle, —

2. If a perpendicular is drawn from the vertex of the right angle to the hypotenuse of a right triangle.

(1) The two triangles thus formed are similar to each other, and to the whole triangle;

(2) The perpendicular is a mean proportional between the segments of the hypotenuse;

(3) Each side about the right angle is a mean proportional between the hypotenuse and the adjacent segment.

3. The area of a circle is equal to half the product of its circumference by its radius.

4. Given the radius of a circle as 8 inches; find the circumference of the circle, also the area of a sector of 40° of the circle.

5. If BC is the base of an isosceles triangle, ABC, and BD is drawn perpendicular to AC, the angle DBC is equal to one-half the angle A.

6. AB is any chord, and AC is tangent to a circle at A, CDE a line cutting the circumference in D and E and parallel to AB; show that the triangle ACD is similar to the triangle EAB.

GERMAN.

Es war vor vier Jahren, am Tage der Kirchweih. Du wirst dich gewiß noch erinnern, wie lustig wir damals in dem Garten tanzten, einen Menuett um den andern. Die schönste Tänzerin war deine Schwester Lisette. Doch als wir eben zum Walzer antraten, war sie verschwunden, niemand wußte wohin. Sie blieb fast eine Stunde fort, es erregte Aufsehen. Sie behauptete nachher, von deinem Vater befragt, zu Hause Vorbereitungen fürs Abendessen getroffen zu haben. Allein das war eine Notlüge. Sie ging ganz wo anders hin, und ich weiß, wo sie gewesen ist, denn ich bin ihr nachgeschlichen; sie war nicht zu Hause, wie sie später angab, sondern sie eilte vor die Stadt und verschwand dort in dem Hirtenhäuschen, wo

der Schäfer Balzer wohnt, der sich eines sehr getrübten Leumundes
erfreut und für einen Hundedieb gilt, weil er mit Hundefett handelt.
Wie konnte eine Amtmannstochter, und obendrein im Ballkleide, den
Balzer besuchen? Das dünkte mir sehr verdächtig. Also wartete
ich eine Weile, bis Lisette wieder herauskäme, um sie zur Rede zu
stellen. Aber sie kam nicht. Voll Ungeduld umging ich das Häus=
chen. Die Fenster sind ganz niedrig, und man kann bequem hinein=
schauen, ohne von innen bemerkt zu werden. Ich spähte hinein, und
denke dir, was ich da sah! Auf einem Strohsack lag die zwölfjährige
Tochter des Schäfers und neben dem hilflosen Wesen saß Lisette im
weißen Kleide mit den roten Bändern, und pflegte und beruhigte
das arme Kind. Es hatte tags vorher den Arm gebrochen und sich
den Kopf arg zerfallen, indem es von der Leiter stürzte. Die rohen
Eltern waren trotzdem heute zur Musik gegangen, unbekümmert um
die Leiden der verlassenen Kleinen. Lisette aber hatte den Schäfer
und sein Weib auf dem Tanzplatz gaffend gesehen und beide lange
beobachtet; sie wußte von dem Unfalle des Kindes, sie stellte sich vor,
wie es ungepflegt daheim liege, sie konnte nicht weiter tanzen und
eilte hinaus, zu helfen und zu trösten. Und so sah ich sie durchs
Fenster und konnte mich nicht satt sehen an dem Bilde. Von Kin=
desbeinen hatten wir zusammen gelebt, und doch war es mir, als
hätte ich heute Lisette zum ersten Mal erblickt. Soll ich das Wort
sprechen? Wir hatten uns bisher so nahe gestanden, daß ich sie nur
gern haben, nicht lieben konnte; jetzt stand sie mir so hoch, so fern,
daß ich sie liebte, — seit dieser Stunde! Man lebt sich nicht lang=
sam ein in die Liebe; die Liebe zündet wie der Blitz, oder sie zündet
überhaupt nicht. Ich erzähle jetzt nicht weiter; ich habe nicht Atem
dazu.

FRENCH.

[Time allowed, 1 hour.]

Je suis depuis hier aux Pâturages : c'est le nom de la
ferme, et je ne m'étonne pas qu'on le lui ait donné en voyant

les beaux prés qui l'entourent et les troupeaux qui y paissent. La maison est tout ce qu'il y a de plus simple. Elle est basse et tout entourée des granges et des étables. On y entre par une cour rustique, au centre de laquelle un magnifique saule pleureur abrite une fontaine. J'ai été toute surprise en voyant de l'autre côté un vaste jardin rempli de roses de toutes les nuances et de toutes les espèces. Au delà s'étendent de grandes prairies en pente douce semées d'arbres fruitiers. On ne se douterait pas qu'on est si près d'un village, car on n'aperçoit pas une maison. Sur la gauche, à une lieue environ de la ferme, on voit une grande forêt qu'on me promet de me faire visiter. De l'autre côté, un ravin profond la sépare d'une colline où s'élève une tour en ruines. On dit que c'est le plus beau point de vue du pays.

Hier, madame Simon est venue me chercher elle-même. Mademoiselle Barbe avait fait ma malle avec tant de peines, de soupirs, d'allées et venues, que, lorsqu'elle eut fini, j'étais plus fatiguée que si j'avais fait dix malles moi-même. Ma tante Cornélie m'a donné mystérieusement une petite bourse antique et fanée contenant cinq francs pour le cas où j'aurais quelque dépense à faire. Ma tante Angélique ne m'a fait ni cadeau ni recommandation ; ses adieux ont été froids. Geneviève m'a grondée de ce que je m'en allais ainsi courir le monde ; puis elle m'a embrassée et m'a dit: " Amusez-vous et faites-vous du bien."

Madame Simon m'a fait monter dans la voiture découverte et s'est mise près de moi. On a placé ma petite caisse derrière nous, et nous sommes partis au trot de deux lourds chevaux que conduisait un paysan en blouse bleue. Je me sentais intimidée. Madame Simon ne disait rien. Une fois seulement elle a remonté mon châle qui avait glissé, et m'a demandé si j'étais bien fatiguée. Sa voix est douce et caressante ; j'aime à l'entendre.

CLASSIFIED PAPERS.

LATIN GRAMMAR.

July, 1886.

[In writing Latin words mark the quantity of the penult.]

1. Decline throughout *filia, fructus, vis,* and *vir*.
2. Compare *acer, frugi,* and *malus.* Decline *acer*.
3. Give the mode and tense of each of the following forms, and state to which conjugation each verb belongs: *edam, currebatis, partiar, ameris, quaesierat, rueritis, scistis, tribuamus, sedebitis?*
4. Inflect in the present and future indicative *malo, eo, morior*.
5. *Is tanti eget quanto opus est* — give rules for the oblique cases. Explain why *ignoscor* is not to be written for " I am pardoned." *Hostibus victis Caesar Italiam profectus est* — what principle of syntax is violated here? Illustrate with sentences how present and past conditions contrary to fact are expressed in Latin.
6. Explain the subjunctives in the following passage: *Cum quaereret Caesar, quam ob rem Ariovistus bello non decertaret, hanc reperiebat causam, quod apud Germanos ea consuetudo esset, ut matresfamiliae eorum sortibus declararent, utrum proelium committi ex usu esset necne.*

June, 1885.

[In writing Latin words of more than two syllables mark the quantity of the penult.]

1. Decline in full *dea, frater, liber* (book), *os* (bone).

2. Form the adverbs from *liber, acer, melior.* Compare *similis, nequam, multus.* Decline *melior.*

3. Give the synopsis in the third person singular, indicative and subjunctive, of *sto, jubeo, venio.*

4. Give the present and imperfect subjunctive of *nolo, eo, fio.*

5. In the following sentences give the construction of italicized words; the nominative and genitive, singular, and the gender of all the nouns; the nominative and genitive, singular, in full, of all the adjectives and pronouns; the principal parts of all the verbs, and the reason for the subjunctive mode in each instance:

(a) In his locis *navium parandarum* causa moratur.
(b) Caesar intelligebat qua de causa ea dicerentur.
(c) Id oppidum, ne *cui* esset *usui Romanis*, incenderunt.
(d) Quaesivi *quid* dubitaret proficisci *domum.*

What other expressions might be used instead of *navium parandarum causa?*

June, 1884.

[In writing Latin words, mark the quantity of the penult in those of more than two syllables.]

1. Decline *dies, vis, maior.*

2. Decline each of the personal pronouns.

3. Give the synopsis of the third person plural, indicative, active and passive, of a verb of each of the four regular conjugations.

4. Synopsis of the third person singular, indicative and subjunctive, of *possum, volo.*

5. Rules for accusative and ablative of time.
Use of the modes in indirect discourse.

In the following sentences tell where each word is made, with its construction or agreement; give the nominative and genitive singular and gender of each noun; the nominative and genitive singular in full of each adjective or pronoun; the comparison of each word in the comparative or superlative degree; the principal parts of each verb; and the reason for each instance of the subjunctive mode.

(a) Non cognovi quid fieri possit.
(b) Hoc in aliis minus mirabar.
(c) Si quis domum relinquere velit, poscat.
(d) Cum maxima pars hostium fusa erat, rediit exercitus in castra.

What change of meaning would be made in the last sentence by the substitution of *esset* for *erat*?

June, 1883.

[In writing Latin words, mark the quantity of the penult in those of more than two syllables.]

1. Decline *pars, corpus, domus*.

2. Decline *idem, qui*.

3. Give the synopsis of the third person singular, indicative and subjunctive active, of a verb of each of the four regular conjugations.

4. What are the tenses in common use of the verbs *memini* and *aio* respectively?

5. Under what circumstances can the dative be used to express the agent? When can relative clauses take the subjunctive?

In the following sentences tell where each word is made, with its construction or agreement; give the nominative and genitive singular and gender of each noun; the nominative and genitive singular in full of each adjective or pronoun; the comparison of any word which is in the comparative degree; the principal parts of each verb; and the reason for each instance of the subjunctive mode.

(*a*) Senex ille plus quam voluit perdidit.
(*b*) In fines eorum mittebantur, ut auxilium ferrent.
(*c*) Odi profanum vulgus et arceo.
(*d*) Non vidi quid perfecisset.

What difference of meaning would be made by the substitution of *perfecerit* in the last sentence? By the substitution of *perficeret*?

September, 1882.

[In writing Latin words of more than one syllable, mark the quantity of the penult.]

1. Give the synopsis in the third plural indicative of a verb of each of the four regular conjugations.

2. Decline a noun of the third declension having the nominative plural ending in -*ia*. What is the stem of such a noun?

3. Give the nominative and genitive singular and the gender of the substantives in the following sentences; the nominative and genitive singular of all genders of the adjectives and pronouns; and the principal parts of the verbs and participles. If a noun or verb is defective, or has different meanings in different forms, call attention to the fact.

(*a*) Eodem tempore interfecti sunt hostium duces.
(*b*) Castra in locis iniquis posita.
(*c*) Quis mortuus erat?
(*d*) Abiit, excessit, evasit, erupit.

4. Name, and illustrate by short Latin sentences, the different uses of the genitive case.

5. In what ways does the Latin express the Agent?

6. Use of the modes in indirect discourse.

7. Give some of the circumstances under which a relative clause will take the subjunctive.

CAESAR.

September, 1886.

I. TRANSLATE Bell. Gall. I. 36.

II. TRANSLATE Bell. Gall. II. 11.

III. Give a brief sketch of Caesar's life.

July, 1886.

I. TRANSLATE Bell. Gall. II. 31.

II. Change the speech to the direct form.

III. TRANSLATE Bell. Gall. III. 19.

IV. (a) When, how long, and by what authority was Caesar in Gaul? (b) Mention the leading events of the first three books. (c) Name the size, divisions, and officers of the Roman legion.

September, 1885.

I. TRANSLATE Bell. Gall. II. 6.

II. TRANSLATE Bell. Gall. III. 22.

III. (a) Describe *passus, testudo, legio, vigilia, hora.* (b) Give the time, cause, and results of Caesar's campaigns in Gaul.

June, 1885.

I. Translate Bell. Gall. I. 50.

II. Translate Bell. Gall. III. 24.

III. (*a*) Give a brief outline of Caesar's life. (*b*) When and by what authority was he in Gaul? (*c*) State what you know about the ancient Gauls.

June, 1884.

[Translate any two of the passages.]

I. Bell. Gall. I. 25.   III. Bell. Civ. I. 14.

II. Bell. Gall. IV. 11.   IV. Bell. Civ. II. 4.

September, 1883.

[Translate any two of the passages.]

I. Bell. Gall. I. 50.   III. Bell. Civ. I. 42.

II. Bell. Gall. III. 19.   IV. Bell. Civ. II. 42.

July, 1883.

[Write a brief life of Julius Caesar. Translate any two of the following passages.]

I. Bell. Gall. I. 46.   III. Bell. Civ. I. 14.

II. Bell. Gall. III. 28.   IV. Bell. Civ. II. 19.

CICERO.

July, 1886.

I. Translate Cat. I. 13.

II. (*a*) Give the etymology of *Stator*. Why was Jupiter at first so called? Why does Cicero say *vere* nominamus? (*b*) To what classes do the genitive *urbis*, *urbis*, *civium*, and *patriae* belong? (*c*) Give the construction of *urbs* and *Romulo*. (*d*) *arcebis* — what use of the tense?

III. TRANSLATE Cat. IV. 5.'

IV. (*a*) What business was before the senate when this oration was delivered? What was the *lex Sempronia*, and why was it so called? Who was the *lator?* (*b*) What was a *supplicatio?*

V. TRANSLATE Arch. 10.

VI. (*a*) Explain the mode of *inveneris*, and the mode and tense of *obruisset*. (*b*) Locate *Sigeum*. How came Alexander to be there? Supply the verb with *et vere*. (*c*) Name some of the teachers of Cicero. Give some account of his banishment. When did he write his philosophical works?

June, 1885.

I. (*a*) Give the principal verb in the first sentence (*cum summis . . . integram deferrem*) of the following passage. After this write the successive dependent verbs in the order of their dependence, in each case giving the connecting word, whether conjunction or relative, and the verbs which it connects. What name is given to a sentence composed thus of a principal clause and dependent clauses? How does the Latin language differ from the English in regard to the employment of such sentences?

(*b*) TRANSLATE In Catilinam III. 3.

II. (*a*) TRANSLATE In Catilinam IV. 1.

(*b*) What was the *forum* (line 5), and in what part of the city was it? What place is meant by *campus* (line 6), and what popular assembly was held there as implied by the words *consularibus auspiciis?* What is the subject discussed by the orator in this oration, and what course does he advocate? What other Latin writer besides Cicero has treated in detail of the Catilinarian conspiracy?

III. (*a*) TRANSLATE In Catilinam I. 7.

(*b*) Give the etymology of *mehercule*. Explain the mode of *metuerent*. Explain the case of *aspectu*. Where is *mallem* made, and what is its derivation?

June, 1884.

I. TRANSLATE Pro Archia, VI.

II. (*a*) State briefly what you know on the following points about the life and times of Cicero: The time and place of Cicero's birth. His education and his career in politics until he reached the consulship. The nominal and the real reason for his exile. The manner of his death. How he bore the sorrows and disappointments which fell to his lot. Whether we have any specimens of his extemporaneous oratory. The nature of his literary works other than his speeches. His date compared with that of the other great Latin writers, like Caesar, Vergil, Livy, Ovid, and Horace.

(*b*) Account for the subjunctives *suasissem*, *obiecissem*, and *iacerent*. What is the genitive plural of *mortis*, of *voces*, of *mentem?* State the general principle which applies to each case. What is the ablative singular of *omnia*, and what of *proponens?* State the general principle which applies to each case. The genitive singular of words like *exsilium* is in some texts written *exsilii*, and in others *exsili;* which was probably Cicero's method? What is the construction of *parvi?* What kind of a pronoun is *mihi?* Form the following words, giving in each case the stem word and the termination with its meaning: *adulescentia, dimicatio, vetustas, scriptor.*

III. In Catilinam II. 11.
IV. Pro Lege Manilia, XIII.
V. Pro M. Marcello, IX.

June, 1883.

[Any two passages may be omitted.]

I. (*a*) TRANSLATE In L. Catilinam Prima, XI.

(*b*) Give a brief sketch of Cicero's life up to the time of the delivery of this oration. What political offices had he successively held, as suggested by the words *per omnis honorum gradus?* What in general were the duties of these officers, and at what age did he reach the consulship, as suggested by the words *tam mature ad summum imperium?*

II. (*a*) TRANSLATE Pro Archia, III.

(*b*) *Mario consule et Catulo* — about what time was this? *Res ad scribendum maximas* — mention some of them.

(*c*) Explain the expression *cum praetextatus . . . Archias esset.* What does it imply as to the age of Archias at the time when he came to Rome? Why is Quintus Metellus called *ille Numidicus?* Give the present of *nactus est.* Explain the subjunctives in the passage.

III. (*a*) TRANSLATE Pro M. Marcello, VI.

(*b*) What part of speech is *nostri*, and how is this determined? From what kind of a verb does the *sc* show *extimescentem* to be? What figure of speech in *Martis vis?* Why is *quin* employed here rather, for example, than *quominus?* What does *ut* connect, *quin*, *si*, and *quoniam?* Explain the uses of the subjunctive mode in the passage.

IV. (*a*) TRANSLATE Pro Lege Manilia, XXIII.

(*b*) Explain the uses of subjunctive mode in the passage. What other ways of expressing a prohibition than the one employed in *nolite dubitare?* What other constructions after verbs of rejoicing than the accusative with the infinitive, as in *quem . . . venisse gaudeant?*

(*c*) State briefly the subject of this oration and the circumstances under which it was delivered.

September, 1882.

I. TRANSLATE Pro Archia, III.

(*a*) *Mario consule et Catulo* — about what time was this? *Res ad scribendum maximas* — mention some of them.

(*b*) Explain the expression *cum praetextatus . . . Archias esset.* What does it imply as to the age of Archias at the time when he came to Rome? Why is Quintus Metellus called *ille Numidicus?*

(*c*) Give the present of *nactus est.* Explain the subjunctives *posset,* and *esset,* and the genitive *ingenii.*

II. TRANSLATE In Catilinam Tertia, IX.

(*a*) Give the derivation of the words *caedes, incendia, interitum, hodierno,* and *conjurati.*

(*b*) Explain the subjunctives *neget* and *esset responsum.* What answer is implied by the interrogative particle *nonne?* What other particles does the Latin use to introduce simple direct questions, and what answers do they respectively imply?

[Any two of the following passages may be omitted.]

III. TRANSLATE In Catilinam Quarta, VII.

(*a*) Give the origin of the expression *Patres conscripti.* What is the difference in use between *libertinus* and *libertus?* What is meant by *fortunam civitatis?*

(b) Explain the ablatives *loco* and *conditione* and the subjunctives *sit* and *cupiat*. What part of speech is *defendendam*? Could the gerund be substituted and how would the Latin differ if it were employed?

IV. TRANSLATE Pro Ligario, VII.

(a) Give the construction of *utrum*, of the clause *Ligarium . . . venire*, and of *senatui*.

(b) State briefly the circumstances under which the oration was delivered.

V. TRANSLATE Pro Marcello, V.

(a) Who is meant by *ille?* What is the construction of *pacis?* What is the derivation of *prudens?*

(b) Describe the toga. With whom did Cicero side in the civil war?

6 LATIN PROSODY, VERGIL, AND OVID.

July, 1886.

LATIN PROSODY.

Copy and divide into feet the following verses, marking the caesurae:

AEN. I. 697-700.

Give rules for the quantity of the ultima in *venit, aurea, Aeneas, strato*, and of the *penult* in *Aeneas*.

What is the most common verse *caesura* in this kind of metre?

VERGIL.

I. TRANSLATE Aen. II. 776-784.

II. (a) Give the construction of *quid* (776), *tantum* (776), *dolori* (776), *tibi* (780), *Hesperiam* (781). Why the plural in *exsilia* (780)? (b) Who is the *dulcis conjunx* (777)?— the *regia conjunx* (783)? Why is *Thybris* called *Lydius?* (c) How is the definite prophecy given to Aeneas in 781 inconsistent with the story of his subsequent attempts at settlement?

III. TRANSLATE Aen. V. 799–811.

IV. (a) Why is the adjective *Saturnius* (799) applied to *domitor maris?* *Cytherea* (800) — who is addressed? Explain the reference in *unde genus ducis* (801). (b) What kind of a derivative is *Pelides* (808)? What endings are employed to form such derivatives?

V. TRANSLATE Ecl. I. 64–72.

VI. (a) What is the construction of *Afros* (64)? What do the four localities of verses 64–66 represent? How long had the Romans possessed any definite knowledge of Britain? (b) What was Vergil's birthplace? To what personal experience is reference made in 70?

OVID.

[Eurydice has died from the bite of a snake, and Orpheus in the lower world is begging that she may be restored to him.]

" O positi sub terra mumina nundi,
in quem recidimus, quicquid mortale creamur;
si licet, et falsi positis ambagibus oris
vera loqui sinitis, non huc, ut opaca viderem
Tartara, descendi, nec uti villosa colubris
terna Medusaei vincirem guttura monstri.
causa viae conjunx, in quam calcata venenum
vipera diffudit, crescentesque abstulit annos.
posse pati volui, nec me temptasse negabo:
vicit Amor.   Supera deus hic bene notus in ora est: 10
an sit et hic, dubito, sed et hic tamen auguror esse.
famaque si veteris non est mentita rapinae,

vos quoque junxit Amor. Per ego haec loca plena timoris,
per Chaos hoc ingens, vastique silentia regni,
Eurydices, oro, properata retexite fata.
quod si fata negant veniam pro conjuge, certum est
nolle redire mihi: leto gaudete duorum."
Talia dicentem nervosque ad verba moventem
exsangues flebant animae; nec Tantalus undam
captavit refugam stupuitque Ixionis orbis, 20
nec carpsere jecur volucres, urnisque vacarunt
Belides,[1] inque tuo sedisti, Sisyphe, saxo.
tunc primum lacrimis victarum carmine fama est
Eumenidum maduisse genas. Nec regia conjunx
sustinet oranti, nec qui regit ima, negare.

Explain briefly verse 12. What was the offence of Tantalus? The reference in *nec carpsere jecur volucres* (v. 21). How does Vergil describe this (Aen. vi.)?

June, 1885.
LATIN PROSODY.

I. Copy and divide into feet Aen. 752-756, marking the caesurae.

Give rules for the length of *is* in *navigiis*, *i* final in *exigui*, *a* in *interea*, and the second syllable in *robora* and *Aeneas*. Define (*a*) masculine caesura, (*b*) feminine caesura. Illustrate the use of one or both of these, if possible, from the preceding passage.

VERGIL.

II. TRANSLATE Aen. II. 657-668.

Genitor (657) refers to whom? Explain the case of *animo* (660), *ore* (658), *hoc* (664). What is the subject of *erat* (664), and *juvat* (661)? By what clause is *hoc* (664)

---
[1] *Belides = Danaides.*

explained? What is the usual construction with *sperare?* What part of speech is *quod* (664)? Give the circumstances connecting this passage with the main thread of the story. At what point in his wanderings is Aeneas first introduced to the reader of the Aeneid?

III. TRANSLATE Aen. V. 724–735.

To whom do *nate* and *mihi* (724) refer? Locate Avernus. Explain the reference in *qui classibus ignem depulit*, 726–7. What is the subject of Book V. of the Aeneid?

3. TRANSLATE Ecl. VI. 1–12.

Who is symbolized by *Tityrus?* Comment upon *Syracosio* (1), *Cynthius* (3). Explain briefly in your own language the first eight lines. Who was *Varus* (10), and how was he connected with *Vergil?*

OVID.

IV. TRANSLATE:—

1. Viribus inferior — quis enim par esset Atlanti
viribus? — 'At quoniam parvi tibi gratia nostra est,
accipe munus,' ait; laevaque a parte Medusae
ipse retroversus squalentia prodidit ora.
quantus erat, mons factus Atlas: nam barba comaeque
in silvas abeunt, juga sunt humerique manusque;
quod caput ante fuit, summo est in monte cacumen;
ossa lapis fiunt. Tum partes auctus in omnes
crevit in immensum — sic di statuistis — et omne
cum tot sideribus caelum requievit in illo.

2. Dis tribus ille focos totidem de cespite ponit,
laevum Mercurio, dextrum tibi, bellica Virgo;
ara Jovis media est: mactatur vacca Minervae,
alipedi vitulus, taurus tibi, summe deorum.
protinus Andromedan et tanti praemia facti

indotata rapit. Taedas Hymenaeus Amorque
praecutiunt; largis satiantur odoribus ignes,
sertaque dependent tectis, et ubique lyraeque
tibiaque et cantus, animi felicia laeti
argumenta, sonant. Reseratis aurea valvis
atria tota patent, pulchroque instructa paratu
Cepheni proceres ineunt convivia regis.
 Postquam epulis functi generosi munere Bacchi
diffudere animos, cultusque genusque locorum
quaerit Lyncides, moresque animumque virorum ;
qui simul edocuit, ' Nunc, O fortissime,' dixit
' fare precor, Perseu, quanta virtute, quibusque
artibus abstuleris crinita draconibus ora.'

reserare = unclose.   *Cephenus* = Ethiopian.
diffundere = relax.   *crinita draconibus* = with snaky locks.

June, 1884.

LATIN PROSODY.

I. Copy Aen. 446–449, and divide them into feet, marking the *caesurae*.

What figures of prosody in the 447–448?

Rules for the quantity of *o* in *Iunoni*, *o* in *cardo*, *is* in *donis*.

VERGIL.

II. TRANSLATE Aen. I. 483–493.

Why the change of tense in *raptaverat*—*vendebat?* Account for the form *Hectora*. Comment upon *tendentem manus*—*Eoas acies*—*lunatis peltis*. What kind of an ablative is *peltis?* *Se* (488)—refers to whom? *Principibus Achivis*—name some of them. Who was Memnon? and on which side was he at Troy?

III. TRANSLATE Ecl. IV. 50-59.

Give the myth of Orpheus. How is *Orpheus* declined? What do *bucolic* and *eclogue* mean etymologically?

[Omit any two of the following passages.]

IV. TRANSLATE Geor. II. 449-457.

Nec tiliae leves aut torno rasile buxum
non formam accipiunt ferroque cavantur acuto;
nec non et torrentem undam levis innatat alnus,
missa Pado; nec non et apes examina condunt
corticibusque cavis vitiosaeque ilicis alveo.
quid memorandum aeque Baccheia dona tulerunt?
Bacchus et ad culpam causas dedit: ille furentis
Centauros leto domuit, Rhoetumque Pholumque
et magno Hylaeum Lapithis cratere minantem.

To what do verses 8 and 9 refer? What subjects are treated in the first two books of the Georgics?

V. TRANSLATE Aen. VIII. 184-192.

Explain the reference in *tanti numinis*. Relate the story of Cacus and of his encounter with Hercules.

OVID.

VI. TRANSLATE Met. VII. 29-36.

' At nisi opem tulero, taurorum adflabitur ore,
concurretque suae segetis tellure creatis
hostibus, aut avido dabitur fera praeda draconi.
hoc ego si patiar, tum me de tigride natam,
tum ferrum et scopulos gestare in corde fatebor.
cur non et specto pereuntem, oculosque videndo
conscelero? cur non tauros exhortor in illum,
terrigenasque feros, insopitumque draconem?

Give briefly the story of the Argonauts. When, where, and at what age did Ovid die?

June, 1883.
PROSODY.

I. Describe the following verse by giving its full metrical name:

Quippe etiam festis quaedam exercere diebus.

Divide it into feet, marking the quantity of each syllable and the place of the caesura. What figure of prosody does this verse illustrate? Show wherein. Mark the quantity of the final syllables in *possis, audi, bonus, dummodo, bos, illuc.*

VERGIL.

II. TRANSLATE Aen. VI. 56–65.

Explain the reference in 57. What were the Syrtes? How had Aeneas made this voyage *"duce te"?*

III. TRANSLATE Ecl. VI. 64–73.

How is *Aonas* declined? Who is meant by *Ascraeo seni?* The construction of *crines.*

[Omit any two of the following passages.]

IV. TRANSLATE Aen. VII. 523–530.

What had Alecto done to bring on this conflict between the Trojans and the Latins?

V. TRANSLATE Geor. II. 61–68.

    Scilicet omnibus est labor impendendus, et omnes
Cogendae in sulcum ac multa mercede domandae.
Sede truncis oleae melius, propagine vites
Respondent, solido Paphiae de robore myrtus;
Plantis et durae coryli nascuntur et ingens
Fraxinus Herculeaeque arbos umbrosa coronae
Chaoniique patris glandes; etiam ardua palma
Nascitur et casus abies visura marinos.

At whose request did Vergil write the Georgics? The main subject to Book II.

OVID.

VI. TRANSLATE Met. I. 244-252.

Dicta Jovis pars voce probant stimulosque frementi
Adiciunt, alii partes assensibus implent.
Est tamen humani generis jactura dolori
Omnibus, et, quae sit terrae mortalibus orbae
Forma futura, rogant; quis sit laturus in aras
Tura? ferisne paret populandas tradere terras?
Talia quaerentes, sibi enim fore cetera curae,
Rex superum trepidare vetat, subolemque priori
Dissimilem populo promittit origine mira.

Explain the meaning of the first two verses. How, according to this myth, was the earth repeopled?

LATIN AT SIGHT.

July, 1886.

TRANSLATE : —

Hic ait sc ille, iudices, regnum meum ferre non posse. quod tandem, Torquate, regnum? consulatus, credo, mei; in quo ego imperavi nihil et contra patribus conscriptis et bonis omnibus parui; quo in magistratu non institutum est videlicet a me regnum, sed repressum. an tum in tanto imperio tantaque potestate non dicis me fuisse regem, nunc privatum regnare dicis? quo tandem nomine? 'quod in quos testimonia dixisti,' inquit 'damnati sunt; quem defendis, sperat se absolutum iri.' hic tibi ego de testimoniis meis hoc respondeo: si falsum dixerim, te in eosdem dixisse; sin verum, non esse hoc regnare, cum verum iuratus dicas, probare. de huius spe tantum dico, nullas a me opes P. Sullam, nullam potentiam, nihil denique praeter fidem defensionis exspectare. ' nisi tu' inquit 'causam recepisses, numquam mihi restitisset, sed indicta causa profugisset.' si iam hoc tibi concedam, Q. Hortensium, tanta gravitate hominem, si, hos talis viros non suo stare iudicio, sed meo; si hoc tibi dem, quod credi non potest, nisi ego huic adessem, hos adfuturos non fuisse, uter tandem rex est, isne, cui innocentes homines non resistunt, an is, qui calamitosos non deserit? at hic etiam, id quod tibi necesse minime fuit, facetus esse voluisti, cum Tarquinium et Numam et me tertium peregrinum regem esse dixisti. mitto iam de rege quaerere; illud quaero, peregrinum cur me esse dixeris: nam si ita sum, non tam est admirandum regem esse me, quoniam, ut tu ais, etiam peregrini reges Romae fuerunt, quam consulem Romae fuisse peregrinum. 'hoc dico,' inquit ' te esse ex municipio.' fateor, et addo etiam ex eo municipio, unde iterum iam salus huic urbi imperioque missa est. sed scire ex te pervelim quam ob rem qui ex municipiis veniant peregrina tibi esse videantur.

quo nomine, on what account.
cum verum iuratus dicas, probare, when you speak the truth under oath, to prove it.
indicta causa, without pleading his cause.

June, 1885.

TRANSLATE : —

I. Deorum immortalium iudicia solent in scholis proferre de morte, nec vero ea fingere ipsi, sed Herodoto auctore aliisque pluribus. primum Argivae sacerdotis Cleobis et Biton filii praedicantur. nota fabula est: cum enim illam ad sollemne et statum sacrificium curru vehi ius esset, satis longe ab oppido ad fanum, morarenturque iumenta, tum iuvenes ii, quos modo nominavi, veste posita corpora oleo perunxerunt, ad iugum accesserunt. ita sacerdos advecta in fanum, cum currus esset ductus a filiis, precata a dea dicitur,

ut illis praemium daret pro pietate quod maximum homini
dari posset a deo; post cpulatos cum matre adulescentis
somno se dedisse, mane inventos esse mortuos. adfertur
etiam de Sileno fabella quaedam, qui cum a Mida captus
esset, hoc ei muneris pro sua missione dedisse scribitur:
docuisse regem non nasci homini longe optimum esse,
proximum autem quam primum mori.

II. Caesar nulla ratione ad pugnam elici posse Pompeium
existimans hanc sibi commodissiman belli rationem iudicavit,
uti castra ex eo loco moveret semperque esset in itineribus,
haec spectans, ut movendis castris pluribusque adeundis
locis commodiore re frumentaria uteretur, simulque in itinere
ut aliquam occasionem dimicandi nancisceretur et insolitum
ad laborem Pompei exercitum cotidianis itineribus defati-
garet. his constitutis rebus signo iam profectionis dato
tabernaculisque detensis animadversum est paulo ante extra
cotidianam consuetudinem longius a vallo esse aciem Pompei
progressam, ut non iniquo loco posse dimicari videretur.

June, 1884.

Num te, quum haec pro salute rei publicae tanta gessisses,
fortunae tuae, num amplitudinis, num claritatis, num gloriae
poenitebat? Unde igitur subito tanta ista mutatio? Non
possum adduci ut suspicer te pecunia captum. Licet quod
cuique libet loquatur. Credere non est necesse. Nihil enim
umquam in te sordidum, nihil humile cognovi. Illud magis
vereor, ne ignorans verum iter gloriae gloriosum putes plus
te unum posse quam omnes et metui a civibus tuis. Quod
si ita putas, totam ignoras viam gloriae. Carum esse civem,
bene de re publica mereri, laudari, coli, diligi gloriosum est:
metui vero et in odio esse invidiosum, detestabile, imbecil-
lum. Quod videmus etiam in fabula ille ipsi, qui *Oderint,
dum metuant*, dixerit, perniciosum fuisse. Utinam, M. An-

toni, avum tuum meminisses! de quo tamen audisti multa ex me eaque saepissime. Putasne illum immortalitatem mereri voluisse, ut propter armorum habendorum licentiam metueretur! Illa erat vita, illa secunda fortuna libertate esse parem ceteris, principem dignitate. Itaque, ut omittam res avi tui prosperas, acerbissimum eius supremum diem malim quam L. Cinnae dominatum, a quo ille crudelissime est interfectus.

Sed quid oratione te flectam? Si enim exitus C. Caesaris efficere non potest ut malis carus esse quam metui, nihil cuiusquam proficiet nec valebit oratio. Quem qui beatum fuisse putant, miseri ipsi sunt. Beatus est nemo, qui ea lege vivit, ut non modo impune, sed etiam cum summa interfectoris gloria interfici possit. Qua re flecte te, quaeso, et maiores tuos respice atque ita guberna rem publicam, ut natum esse te cives tui gaudeant: sine quo nec beatus neo clarus nec tutus quisquam esse omnino potest.

June, 1883.

TRANSLATE:—

Haec interposui, patres conscripti, non tam ut pro me dicerem, quam ut quosdam nimis ieiuno animo et angusto monerem, id quod semper ipse fecissem, uti excellentium civium virtutem imitatione dignam, non invidia putarent. utinam quidem illi principes viverent, qui me post meum consulatum, cum eis ipse cederem, principem non inviti videbant! hoc vero tempore in tanta inopia constantium et fortium consularium quo me dolore adfici creditis, cum alios male sentire, alios nihil omnino curare videam, alios parum constanter in suscepta causa permanere sententiamque suam non semper utilitate rei publicae, sed tum spe tum timore moderari? quod si quis de contentione principatus laborat, quae nulla esse debet, stultissime facit, si vitiis cum virtute contendit; ut enim cursu cursus, sic in viris fortibus virtus virtute superatur. tu, si ego de re publica optime sentiam, ut me vincas, ipse pessime senties? aut, si ad me bonorum concursum fieri videbis, ad te improbos invitabis? nollem, primum rei publicae causa, deinde etiam dignitatis tuae. sed si principatus ageretur, quem numquam expetivi, quid tandem mihi esset optatius? ego enim malis sententiis vinci non possum, bonis forsitan possim et libenter.

LATIN COMPOSITION.

September, 1886.

TRANSLATE : —

I. When Epaminondas had conquered the Lacedæmonians and saw that he was dying of a wound, he asked whether his shield was safe. When his weeping friends answered that it was safe, he asked if the enemy were routed. After hearing that question also answered as he wished, he ordered the spear, with which he was transfixed, to be drawn out. And so, after shedding much blood, he died in joy and victory.

II. (*a*) If he returns from the country to-morrow, I hope that all of you will see him at my house Sept. 30th, at about 9 o'clock P.M. (*b*) Though she is not yet fifteen years old, it is said that she is a foot taller than her mother. (*c*) Cato the elder said he had so lived that he thought he had not been born in vain.[1]

July, 1886.

TRANSLATE : —

The general spoke thus : — " The enemy that you have so long been seeking is now only two miles away : prepare then to conquer or to die. I will send messengers to inform me

[1] Translate both directly and indirectly.

of their numbers and the position of their camp. After I have done this, I must entrust the rest to you. Remember that your country depends upon you. If you conquer, you will enjoy peace, freedom, and glory; if you are defeated, you will be treated as slaves. Ask yourselves whether you prefer a glorious death, or a shameful flight." At these words the soldiers cast aside fear, forgot their complaints, and promised one another to conquer or to die.

September, 1885.

TRANSLATE : —

After this King Porsena made war against the Latins, and his army was beaten, and fled to Rome; and the Romans received them kindly, and took care of those who were wounded, and sent them back safe to Porsena. For this the king gave back to the Romans all the rest of their hostages whom he had still with him, and also certain lands. And so Tarquinius, seeing that there was no more hope of aid from King Porsena, left Clusium and went to Tusculum; for Octavius, the chief of the Tusculans, had married his daughter, and he hoped that the Latins would restore him to Rome, for their cities were many, and when he had been king he had favored them rather than the Romans.

June, 1885.

TRANSLATE : —

When the ambassadors of the Samnites had brought to Curius a great weight of gold and asked him to be willing to use it, he laughed, and said: "Tell the Samnites that I would rather rule the rich than myself be rich; carry home that gift, and remember that I can neither be conquered in battle nor corrupted by money."

Do you not see how, in Homer, Nestor very often speaks of his own virtues? It was not necessary for him to fear that, while telling the truth about himself, he might seem proud or to talk too much; for, as Homer says, from his tongue flowed speech sweeter than honey. The famous leader of the Greeks prayed that he might have ten men, not like Ajax, but like Nestor, and if that should happen he did not doubt that Troy would soon fall.

June, 1884.

TRANSLATE: —

When all was ready, Lucius went to the forum with armed men, and seated himself on the throne where the king was wont to judge the people. And when the king was told that Lucius was sitting on his throne, he hastened to the forum, and when he saw Lucius he asked him why he dared sit in the royal seat. Lucius replied that it was his father's throne and that he had more right there than Servius. Then he seized the old man and threw him to the ground, and called the senators together as if he was already king. Soon Servius arose and began to go home, but he was seized and slain by friends of Lucius, who left him covered with blood in the middle of the street.

September, 1883.

TRANSLATE: —

Who has not heard the story of King Canute? One day he was sitting on the sea-shore, surrounded by his courtiers (*optimates*), and watching the rising tide (*aestus*). One of the courtiers said that nothing could resist the king's commands. At first he seemed not to hear, and only commanded the waves not to rise beyond a certain mark. Still the water rose higher and higher, and at last touched the king's feet. Then he turned to his courtiers, who were wondering why he sat so unmoved, and made them see that the waves would not obey him, and asked them to confess that God alone is omnipotent.

June, 1883.

TRANSLATE:—

Labienus, one of Caesar's lieutenants, desiring to fight against the Gauls before the arrival of the Germans, who he knew would come to aid them, pretended want-of-confidence (*diffidentia*), and, placing his camp on the other bank, proclaimed (*edico*) a departure for the next day. The Gauls, believing that he was flying, began to cross the river which was between; but Labienus, leading his army around, cut them to pieces in the midst of the difficulties of crossing the river.

ROMAN HISTORY.
July, 1886.

1. Describe the circumstances under which the tribunate was established.

2. When and where did the principal military events in the war between the Caesarians and Pompeians occur?

3. Sketch briefly the career of Pompeius.

4. What persons composed the Second Triumvirate? In what essential points did the Second Triumvirate differ from the First?

5. When and for what reasons was the right of citizenship given to the provinces?

6. What radical changes in the government were made by Diocletian?

June, 1885.

1. Give an account of the second Punic war (with dates).

2. Explain *tribunus plebis, censor, dictator, imperator*.

3. How were the provinces governed under the Republic, and how under the Empire?

4. What were the causes of the social war, and what the results?

5. When and where did the following events take place: the defeat of Varus; the first Roman naval victory; the decisive victory over Pyrrhus; the death of Brutus and Cassius; the conquest of the first Roman province?

June, 1883.

1. What evils did the Gracchi attempt to reform? What was the difference between the plans of T. Gracchus and C. Gracchus? Why did they fail?

2. What were the limits of the Roman Empire at the death of Augustus?

3. Where were *Actium*, *Metaurus*, *Zama*, *Pharsalia*, *Cynoscephalae?* What happened at those places, and when?

4. Explain *Tribunus*, *Provincia*, *Censor*, *Decemvir*, *Dictator*.

5. Name in order of time the foreign enemies that Rome fought on Italian soil.

June, 1884.

1. How did Rome subdue the rest of Italy? Name the conquests in their chronological order and, where you can, give dates.

2. How and by whom were Consuls elected? For how long a term? Were they re-eligible? What employment was usually given them when their term was ended?

3. The first Triumvirate: When was it formed? Who were the members of it? What became of each?

4. Where were *Actium, Cannae, Cynoscephalae, Pharsalus,* the *Allia?* When were battles fought at these places? Who were the victors, and who the vanquished in each case?

5. When did Constantine the Great live? What important changes did he make in the Empire?

GREEK GRAMMAR.

July, 1886.

[All Greek words to be written with accents.]

1. Decline throughout Πέρσης, ἅλς, τίς, and, in the singular, the comparative of ταχύς.

2. Give the principal parts of βάλλω, μένω, τρέφω, φεύγω.

3. Inflect the first aorist middle indicative of ποιέω.

4. Analyze the forms φανῶσι, σχοῖεν, γεγαμηκέναι, stating where each is found.

5. What two meanings may ὁ ἄνθρωπος have, and what is the article called in each case?

6. What two meanings may ὁ φόβος τῶν πολεμίων have, and what is the genitive called in each case?

7. What two meanings may οἶδα ἀκούων have, and what is the participle called in each case?

June, 1885.

[All Greek words to be written with accents.]

1. Give the construction (telling where each word is made and why) of every underscored word in the following : —

'Αλλ' ὤφελε μὲν Κῦρος ζῆν· ἐπεὶ δὲ τετελεύτηκεν, ἀπαγγέλλετε 'Αριαίῳ ὅτι ἡμεῖς νικῶμέν τε βασιλέα καὶ ὡς ὁρᾶτε οὐδεὶς ἔτι ἡμῖν μάχεται, καὶ εἰ μὴ ὑμεῖς ἤλθετε, ἐπορευόμεθα ἂν ἐπὶ βασιλέα. ἐπαγγελλόμεθα δὲ Ἀριαίῳ ἐὰν ἐνθάδε ἔλθῃ, εἰς τὸν θρόνον τὸν βασίλειον καθιεῖν αὐτόν· τῶν γὰρ μάχῃ νικώντων καὶ τὸ ἄρχειν ἐστί.

2. Inflect in the singular σύ and οὐδείς, in the plural ὅς.

3. Give the principal parts of πείθω, τίθημι, λείπω, φαίνω, φέρω, ἔρχομαι.

4. Give a synopsis (first form in each mode) of the future active and second aorist passive of στέλλω.

5. What are the principal uses of the optative mode?

6. Give examples of crasis, apocope, elision.

June, 1884.

[All Greek words to be written with accents.]

1. Define and give examples of metathesis, synizesis, hiatus.

2. What consonants may end a Greek word? What becomes of the other consonants which at the end of a stem would naturally end a word? ν, ρ, ς.

3. When is a syllable long by position?

4. Inflect throughout πολίτης, βασιλεύς, ἡδύς, λελυκώς.

5. Give the rules for the comparison of adjectives?

6. Inflect the simple relative pronoun in the singular.

7. Inflect τιμάω in the present and imperfect indicative active, giving the contract forms.

8. Give the principal parts of λύω, τιμάω, φαίνω, λαμβάνω, δείκνυμι, λείπω.

9. State the principles of augment.

10. What construction corresponds to the Latin ablative absolute, with what differences?

11. State the principles of indirect discourse.

June, 1883.

[All Greek words to be written with accents.]

1. Decline throughout ὀργή, χείρ, τεῖχος, δύναμις; also ὅστις.

2. Analyze λυθῶμεν.

3. What uses of the *genitive* are illustrated in the following examples: πολλοὶ τῶν Ἀθηναίων, — νόμισμα ἀργύρου, — ὁ φόβος τῶν πολεμίων, — τριῶν ἡμερῶν ὁδός.

4. Explain, with Greek examples, the terms *proclitic*, *potential optative*, *verbal adjective*.

5. Give the comparative and superlative of μέλας, μέγας, πολύς.

6. Write the synopsis (*i.e.* first form of every mode) of the perfect middle of λύω, the first aorist active of στέλλω, the second aorist passive of φαίνω.

7. Where found and from what presents are εἷλον, ἠλλάχθην, ἐγρήγορα?

8. State the difference in meaning between μὴ τοῦτο ποιήσῃς and μὴ τοῦτο ποιήσειας, between ἔστην and ἔστησα.

9. Name the classes into which verbs are divided according to the form of the present stem, with an example under each.

GREEK COMPOSITION.
July, 1886.

TRANSLATE: —

When urged[1] to join the expedition against the king, Xenophon asked Socrates what he ought to do. And Socrates answered, If you should go to the oracle[2] at Delphi, Apollo would advise³ you. So Xenophon went and asked, To what god ought I to sacrifice, in order that I may make the journey most successfully? But when he had returned, Socrates blamed⁴ him because he had not first asked whether it was better to go or stay at home.

Would that I were not poor.⁵ I know that he is not a bad man. Let us go, that he may not see us.

¹ κελεύω.   ² μαντεῖον.   ³ συμβουλεύω.   ⁴ αἰτιάομαι.   ⁵ πένης.

June, 1885.
[All Greek words to be written with accents.]

TRANSLATE:—

The old priest came to the camp of the Greeks with many gifts, in order that he might persuade the king to restore to him his beloved daughter. The soldiers, indeed, honored the old man, but the king was angry and sent him home, saying: "If I see thee here a second time I shall put thee to death." This frightened him and he went away in silence, but prayed to the gods, who heard him and sent calamities upon the camp.

June, 1884.
[All Greek words to be written with accents.]

1. The Greeks fought bravely at Salamis. They sank many of the Persian ships and put the rest to flight. Xerxes and his army marched away in haste by land.

2. It is evident that both Greeks and barbarians believe that the gods know all things which are said and done and thought.

3. When Diogenes was asked where in Greece he had seen good men, he said that he had seen boys in Lacedaemon, but men nowhere.

4. Prometheus stole fire from heaven in order to give it to men.

ANABASIS.

June, 1883.
[All Greek words to be written with accents.]

TRANSLATE : —

1. The citizens chose Kyros (to be) general out of many (candidates), (one) of whom was the brother of Kyros. After not many days this brother, commanding in-the-absence-of-Kyros,[1] won a great victory, but the praise for the victory was given to Kyros as being general. The brother therefore said, "One (man) sows,[2] another reaps-the-harvest."[3]

2. But if any one sees a better (plan), let him speak.

3. Whenever any one wished to make-war with the king, he used-to-praise them.

4. I fear that he may take (me) and inflict punishment on me.

[1] genitive absolute with participle. [2] σπείρω. [3] καρποῦμαι.

ANABASIS.

July, 1886.

I. TRANSLATE An. I. 3. 1–3.

Give the construction (saying where each word is made and why it is in this case) of (a) ἡμέρας, (b) τοῦ πρόσω, (c) τοιάδε, (d) πράγμασιν, (e) ἄλλα, (f) ἐμοί. (g) Distinguish ἐπὶ βασιλέα, πρὸς βασιλέα, παρὰ βασιλέα. (h) What is the force of the tense of ἔβαλλον? (i) Comment on the use of μή. (j) What is the technical meaning of φεύγοντα. Explain the etymology of δαρεικούς.

II. TRANSLATE An. II. 4. 2, 3.

(a) What is the difference between the English and Greek idioms in ἔνδηλοι ἦσαν? Explain the uses of the modes in

(b) ἀπολέσαι, (c) ποιήσαιτο, (d) ᾖ, (e) στρατεύειν, (f) διεσπάρθαι, (g) ἁλισθῇ. What is the subject of (h) ἔλεγον, (i) ἔστιν?

III. TRANSLATE An. III. 4. 1, 2.

Give the construction of (a) διαβαίνουσιν, (b) αὐτοῖς, (c) τοσούτους, (d) Τισσαφέρνην. What is the force of the tenses of (e) ἐπιθοῖντο, διαβαίνουσιν, ποιῆσαι.

[The following passage may be substituted for any one of the preceding.]

IV. TRANSLATE Xen. Hell. II. 3. 48.

"ἐγὼ δ', ὦ Κριτία, ἐκείνοις μὲν ἀεί ποτε πολεμῶ τοῖς οὐ πρόσθεν οἰομένοις καλὴν ἂν δημοκρατίαν εἶναι, πρὶν καὶ οἱ δοῦλοι, καὶ οἱ δι' ἀπορίαν δραχμῆς ἂν ἀποδόμενοι τὴν πόλιν, δραχμῆς μετέχοιεν· καὶ τοῖσδέ γ' αὖ ἀεὶ
5 ἐναντίος εἰμί, οἳ οὐκ οἴονται καλὴν ἂν ἐγγενέσθαι ὀλιγαρχίαν πρὶν εἰς τὸ ὑπ' ὀλίγων τυραννεῖσθαι τὴν πόλιν καταστήσειαν. τὸ μέντοι σὺν τοῖς δυναμένοις, καὶ μεθ' ἵππων καὶ μετ' ἀσπίδων ὠφελεῖν διὰ τούτων τὴν πολιτείαν, πρόσθεν ἄριστον ἡγούμην εἶναι, καὶ νῦν οὐ μετα-
10 βάλλομαι. εἰ δ' ἔχεις εἰπεῖν, ὦ Κριτία, ὅπου ἐγὼ ξὺν τοῖς δημοτικοῖς ἢ τυραννικοῖς τοὺς καλούς τε κἀγαθοὺς ἀποστερεῖν πολιτείας ἐπεχείρησα, λέγε."

(a) Tell what you know about Kritias. Give the construction of (b) οἰομένοις (2), (c) δραχμῆς (3), (d) δραχμῆς 3, 4, (e) καταστήσειαν (6), (f) πολιτείας (10). (g) What is the force of ἄν (2)? (h) Write καὶ οἱ ... πόλιν (3) as a relative clause.

June, 1885.

I. TRANSLATE Xen. An. I. 5. 17 f.

What river is mentioned here? — Construction of αὐτῷ, μαστῶν, πλοίοις, θεῖον. Explain the tense of ὑποχωρῆσαι. Force of ὡς with βασιλεύσοντι.

II. TRANSLATE Xen. An. II. 2. 1 f.

Who was Ariaeus? Why had messengers been sent to him? Construction of φαίη, αὐτοῦ, νυκτός. Force of ἄν before ἀνασχέσθαι. What is the conclusion of εἰ βούλεσθε συναπιέναι? What is supplied with εἰ δὲ μή?

III. TRANSLATE Xen. An. III. 2. 7 f.

On what occasion was this speech made? Construction of νικᾶν, καλλίστων, λόγου. Force of καί before στρατηγούς. Subject of πεπόνθασιν.

IV. TRANSLATE Herod. VI. 112.

[The following may be substituted for either of the preceding passages.]

ὡς δέ σφι διετέτακτο καὶ τὰ σφάγια ἐγίνετο καλά, ἐνθαῦτα ὡς ἀπείθησαν οἱ Ἀθηναῖοι, δρόμῳ ἵεντο ἐς τοὺς βαρβάρους, οἱ δὲ Πέρσαι ὁρέοντες δρόμῳ ἐπιόντας, παρεσκευάζοντο ὡς δεξόμενοι· μανίην δέ τοῖσι Ἀθη-
5 ναίοισι ἐπέφερον καὶ πάγχυ ὀλεθρίην, ὁρέοντες αὐτοὺς ὀλίγους, καὶ τούτους δρόμῳ ἐπειγομένους, οὔτε ἵππου ὑπαρχούσης σφι οὔτε τοξευμάτων. ταῦτα μέν νυν οἱ βάρβαροι κατείκαζον· Ἀθηναῖοι δὲ ἐπεί τε ἀθρόοι προσέμιξαν τοῖσι βαρβάροισι, ἐμάχοντο ἀξίως λόγου,
10 πρῶτοι μὲν γὰρ Ἑλλήνων πάντων τῶν ἡμεῖς ἴδμεν δρόμῳ ἐς πολεμίους ἐχρήσαντο, πρῶτοι δὲ ἀνέσχοντο ἐσθῆτά τε Μηδικὴν ὁρέοντες καί τοὺς ἄνδρας ταύτην ἐσθημένους.

Give the corresponding Attic forms for ἐνθαῦτα, ἀπείθησαν (2), ὁρέοντες (3), τῶν (9), ἴδμεν (9). Construction of δρόμῳ (2), τοξευμάτων (6), τῶν (9), ταύτην (11). How many generals did the Athenians have at Marathon? Who commanded at the battle? Why was not the battle fought earlier?

June, 1884.

I. TRANSLATE Xen. An. I. 3. 15 f.

Construction of ἐμέ, στρατηγίαν, ἀνδρί, εἴη, ᾧ. What other case might have been used for Κύρου ποιουμένου? What was the occasion of this discussion?

II. TRANSLATE Xen. An. II. 6. 1 f.

Who were the στρατηγοί here mentioned? How does the use of ὡς differ from that of εἰς? What other prepositions might have been used with similar meaning? Why is the article not used with βασιλέα? What was the war mentioned in the fourth line? From what state did Clearchus come?

III. TRANSLATE Xen. An. III. 2. 9.

Why is the article used with θεόν? Construction of ἡμῶν. Explain the transferred meaning of οἰωνός. Force of the prepositions in συνεπεύξασθαι. What was a παιάν (ἐπαιώνισαν)?

IV. TRANSLATE Xen. An. IV. 3. 3 f.

Construction of ἡμέρᾳ, ἱππέων, Ὀρόντου, ταύτῃ. Describe the γέρρα. What does the preposition in διαβαίνειν imply as to the depth of Greek rivers?

[Either of the following may be substituted for either of the preceding passages.]

V. TRANSLATE Xen. Hell. II. 3. 52.

ἀκούσας ταῦτα ὁ Θηραμένης ἀνεπήδησεν ἐπὶ τὴν
Ἑστίαν, καὶ εἶπεν· "'Εγὼ δ', ἔφη, ὦ ἄνδρες, ἱκετεύω
τὰ πάντων ἐννομώτατα, μὴ ἐπὶ Κριτίᾳ εἶναι ἐξαλείφειν
μήτε ἐμὲ μήτε ὑμῶν ὃν ἂν βούληται, ἀλλ' ὅνπερ νόμον
5 οὗτοι ἔγραψαν περὶ τῶν ἐν τῷ καταλόγῳ, κατὰ τοῦτον
καὶ ὑμῖν καὶ ἐμοὶ τὴν κρίσιν εἶναι. καὶ τοῦτο μὲν, ἔφη,
μὰ τοὺς θεοὺς οὐκ ἀγνοῶ ὅτι οὐδέν μοι ἀρκέσει ὅδε ὁ

βωμός· ἀλλὰ βούλομαι καὶ τοῦτο ἐπιδεῖξαι ὅτι οὗτοι
οὐ μόνον εἰσὶ περὶ ἀνθρώπους ἀδικώτατοι, ἀλλὰ καὶ
10 περὶ θεοὺς ἀσεβέστατοι. ὑμῶν μέντοι, ἔφη, ὦ ἄνδρες
καλοὶ κἀγαθοὶ, θαυμάζω εἰ μὴ βοηθήσετε ὑμῖν αὐτοῖς,
καὶ ταῦτα γιγνώσκοντες ὅτι οὐδὲν τὸ ἐμὸν ὄνομα εὐεξα-
λειπτότερον ἢ τὸ ὑμῶν ἑκάστου."

Give a brief account of the scene from which this passage
is taken. Give a sketch of the history of Theramenes.
Construction of ἐννομώτατα (2), εἶναι, ἐξαλείφειν (2), νόμον (3),
τοῦτο (4), ὑμῶν (7), ταῦτα (8).

VI. TRANSLATE Plato, Phaedo 105 c.

"Ταῦτα μὲν τοίνυν προθυμηθησόμεθα, ἔφη, οὕτω
ποιεῖν· θάπτωμεν δέ σε τίνα τρόπον;" "Ὅπως ἄν, ἔφη,
βούλησθε, ἐάνπερ γε λάβητέ με, καὶ μὴ ἐκφύγω ὑμᾶς."
γελάσας δὲ ἅμα ἡσυχῇ καὶ πρὸς ἡμᾶς ἀποβλέψας,
5 εἶπεν· "Οὐ πείθω, ἔφη, ὦ ἄνδρες, Κρίτωνα, ὡς ἐγώ
εἰμι οὗτος ὁ Σωκράτης ὁ νυνὶ διαλεγόμενος καὶ διατάτ-
των ἕκαστον τῶν λεγομένων, ἀλλ' οἴεταί με ἐκεῖνον
εἶναι, ὃν ὄψεται ὀλίγον ὕστερον νεκρόν καὶ ἐρωτᾷ δὴ
πῶς με θάπτῃ. ὅτι δὲ ἐγὼ πάλαι πολὺν λόγον πεποίη-
10 μαι, ὡς, ἐπειδὰν πίω τὸ φάρμακον, οὐκέτι ὑμῖν παρα-
μενῶ ἀλλ' οἰχήσομαι ἀπιὼν εἰς μακάρων δή τινας εὐδαι-
μονίας, ταυτά μοι δοκῶ αὐτῷ ἄλλως λέγειν, παραμυθού-
λενος ἅμα μὲν ὑμᾶς, ἅμα δ' ἐμαυτόν."

What is the apodosis to ἐάν περ λάβητε (2)? Construction of νεκρόν (5), ὑμῖν (7), αὐτῷ (8), ἐμαυτόν (9). Explain
the mode of θάπτῃ (6). What is known of Crito?

VII. TRANSLATE Herod. VII. 219.

Τοῖσι δὲ ἐν Θερμοπύλῃσι ἐοῦσι Ἑλλήνων πρῶτον μὲν
ὁ μάντις Μεγιστίης ἐσιδὼν ἐς τὰ ἱρά, ἔφρασε τὸν μέλ-
λοντα ἔσεσθαι ἅμα ἠοῖ σφι θάνατον. ἐπὶ δὲ καὶ αὐτό-

μόλις ἦσαν οἱ ἐξαγγείλαντες τῶν Περσέων τὴν περίοδον. 5 οὗτοι μὲν ἔτι νυκτὸς ἐσήμηναν, τρίτοι δὲ οἱ ἡμεροσκόποι καταδραμόντες ἀπὸ τῶν ἄκρων, ἤδη διαφαινούσης ἡμέρης. ἐνθαῦτα ἐβουλεύοντο οἱ ''Ελληνες, καὶ σφεων ἐσχίζοντο αἱ γνῶμαι· οἱ μὲν γὰρ οὐκ ἔων τὴν τάξιν ἐκλιπεῖν, οἱ δὲ ἀντέτεινον. μετὰ δὲ τοῦτο διακριθέντες, 10 οἱ μὲν ἀπαλλάσσοντο καὶ διασκεδασθέντες κατὰ πόλις ἕκαστοι ἐτράποντο, οἱ δὲ αὐτῶν ἅμα Λεωνίδῃ μένειν αὐτοῦ παρεσκευάδατο.

Give the Attic forms for ἐοῦσι (1), ἐνθαῦτα (5), πόλις, ἐτράποντο (7), παρεσκευάδατο (8). Construction of ἐπί (2), νυκτός (3). What was the περίοδος of 3?

June, 1883.

[Any two of the passages may be omitted.]

I. TRANSLATE Xen. An. I. 7. 3.

Construction of ἀνθρώπων, συμμάχους, ὧν. To what does τοῦτο refer? Meaning of the preposition in προσέλαβον. Explain the difference between the two uses of ὅπως in the passage.

II. TRANSLATE Xen. An. II. 5. 32 f.

Construction of πολλῷ, αὐτῶν. Peculiarity of form in ἠμφεγνόουν. Use of the mode in ἐντυγχάνοιεν. What would ἐποίουν be in indirect discourse? What is referred to in πάντα τὰ γεγενημένα?

III. TRANSLATE Xen. An. III. 2. 2 f.

Construction of ἄνδρας, τοὺς ἐχθρούς. What part of speech is πρός here? Point out the attributive and circumstantial participles. With what does ἄν belong?

IV. TRANSLATE Xen. An. IV. 7. 15 f.

Construction of ξύηλην, πήχεων. With what does ἄν belong? In what respects did the Greek spear differ from this one? How long, in time and distance, was the return march from Kunaxa to the sea?

V. TRANSLATE Xen. Hell. II. 3.

ἃ δ' αὖ εἶπεν, ὡς ἐγώ εἰμι οἶος ἀεί ποτε μεταβάλλεσθαι, κατανοήσατε καὶ ταῦτα τὴν μὲν γὰρ τῶν τετρακοσίων πολιτείαν καὶ αὐτὸς δήπου ὁ δῆμος ἐψηφίσατο, διδασκόμενος ὡς οἱ Λακεδαιμόνιοι πάσῃ πολιτείᾳ μᾶλλον ἂν ἢ δημοκρατίᾳ πιστεύσειαν. ἐπεὶ δέ γε ἐκεῖνοι μὲν οὐδὲν ἀνίεσαν, οἱ δὲ ἀμφὶ Ἀριστοτέλην καὶ Μελάνθιον καὶ Ἀρίσταρχον, στρατηγοῦντες, φανεροὶ ἐγένοντο ἐπὶ τῷ χώματι ἔρυμα τειχίζοντες, ἐς ὃ ἐβούλοντο τοὺς πολεμίους δεξάμενοι ὑφ' αὑτοῖς καὶ τοῖς ἑτέροις τὴν πόλιν ποιήσασθαι, — εἰ ταῦτ' αἰσθόμενος ἐγὼ διεκώλυσα, τοῦτ' ἐστι προδότην εἶναι τῶν φίλων;

Explain the reference in τῶν τετρακοσίων. When did the event occur? Where was this χῶμα? What form of conditional sentence is seen in the last clause? What nickname was given to the speaker, expressing the idea οἶος μεταβάλλεσθαι?

VI. TRANSLATE Xen. Mem. I. 1.

βουλεύσας γάρ ποτε καὶ τὸν βουλευτικὸν ὅρκον ὀμόσας, ἐν ᾧ ἦν κατὰ τοὺς νόμους βουλεύσειν, ἐπιστάτης ἐν τῷ δήμῳ γενόμενος, ἐπιθυμήσαντος τοῦ δήμου παρὰ τοὺς νόμους ἐννέα στρατηγοὺς μιᾷ ψήφῳ τοὺς ἀμφὶ Θράσυλλον καὶ Ἐρασινίδην ἀποκτεῖναι πάντας, οὐκ ἠθέλησεν ἐπιψηφίσαι, ὀργιζομένου μὲν αὐτῷ τοῦ δήμου, πολλῶν δὲ καὶ δυνατῶν ἀπειλούντων· ἀλλὰ περὶ πλείονος ἐποιήσατο εὐορκεῖν ἢ χαρίσασθαι τῷ δήμῳ παρὰ τὸ δίκαιον καὶ φυλάξασθαι τοὺς ἀπειλοῦντας.

What sort of accusative is ὅρκον? In what year and after what battle did this event take place? What was the illegality in the proposed vote? From what officers was the ἐπιστάτης selected and how often?

HOMER.

July, 1886.

I. TRANSLATE Il. A 135–151.

(a) Turn 137 into an Attic sentence. Give the Attic forms for (b) τεόν, (c) Ὀδυσῆος, (d) ἀγείρομεν, (e) θείομεν, (f) ἱλάσσεαι, (g) ἐλθέμεναι. (h) What is the conclusion to the condition of 135? Explain the mode of (i) ἔλωμαι 137, (j) ἱλάσσεαι 147, (k) πείθηται, v. 16. (l) To what does ταῦτα 149 refer? Give the construction (telling where each noun is made and why it is in that case) of (m) ἄν 143, (n) ἀρχός 144, (o) πρόφρων 150, (p) ὁδόν 151. (q) What is the force of αὐτήν 143? State what you know of (r) Ἰδομενεύς and (s) Αἴας. (t) Who is ἑκάεργον 147? What similar epithets are applied to him?

II. TRANSLATE Il. B 295–309.

(a) Give a metrical scheme (marking the long and short syllables and the cæsural pauses) for vs. 299–301. Give the construction of (b) ἡμῖν 295, (c) τῷ 296. Explain the forms (d) μιμνόντεσσι 296, (e) ἀσχαλάαν 297. (f) Where was Aulis? (g) How did the Homeric δράκων differ from a snake? (h) What vowels are not elided in Homer?

June, 1885.

I. TRANSLATE Il. A 415–427.

Give the corresponding Attic forms for ὄφελες, νηυσίν, αἴ κε, Αἰθιοπῆας, ποτί, δῶ. Construction of δήν 416, τῷ 418, χθιζός 424, δωδεκάτῃ 425. With what is νῦν 417 contrasted? What is elided from μήνι' 422? Why has Οὔλυμπόνδε 425 two accents?

II. TRANSLATE Il. B 235–249.

Give a scheme to show the scansion of vs. 237–239, explaining all metrical irregularities. Construction of οἱ 238, ἕο, μέγα 239, Ἀχιλῆι, φρεσίν 241. Explain the accent of κάκ' 235. What is elided from χ' 238? How is this shown? Force of καί 239. What is the antecedent of ὅσσοι 249? Explain the use of the preposition in ὑπὸ Ἴλιον 249.

[The following passage may be substituted for either of the preceding.]

III. TRANSLATE Il. Z 390–403.

Ἡ ῥα γυνὴ ταμίη, ὁ δ' ἀπέσσυτο δώματος Ἕκτωρ
τὴν αὐτὴν ὁδὸν αὖτις ἐϋκτιμένας κατ' ἀγυιάς.
εὖτε πύλας ἵκανε διερχόμενος μέγα ἄστυ,
Σκαιάς — τῇ γὰρ ἔμελλε διεξίμεναι πεδίονδε —
5 ἔνθ' ἄλοχος πολύδωρος ἐναντίη ἦλθε θέουσα
Ἀνδρομάχη, θυγάτηρ μεγαλήτορος Ἠετίωνος,
Ἠετίων ὃς ἔναιεν ὑπὸ Πλάκῳ ὑληέσσῃ,
Θήβῃ Ὑποπλακίῃ, Κιλίκεσσ' ἄνδρεσσιν ἀνάσσων·
τοῦπερ δὴ θυγάτηρ ἔχεθ' Ἕκτορι χαλκοκορυστῇ.
10 ἥ οἱ ἔπειτ' ἤντησ', ἅμα δ' ἀμφίπολος κίεν αὐτῇ
παῖδ' ἐπὶ κόλπῳ ἔχουσ' ἀταλάφρονα, νήπιον αὔτως,
Ἑκτορίδην ἀγαπητόν, ἀλίγκιον ἀστέρι καλῷ,
τόν ῥ' Ἕκτωρ καλέεσκε Σκαμάνδριον, αὐτὰρ οἱ ἄλλοι
Ἀστυάνακτ'· οἶος γὰρ ἐρύετο Ἴλιον Ἕκτωρ.

Give a scheme to show the scansion of vs. 1–3. Construction of ὁδόν (2), πύλας (3), τῇ (4), ἐναντίη (5), Ἠετίων (7), ἄνδρεσσιν (8). Is τὴν αὐτὴν ὁδόν (2) exactly equivalent to the same Attic expression? What other cities named Thebes were known to the ancients. Analyze διεξίμεναι (4).

Explain why Hector's son receives the names mentioned in 14 f.

June, 1884.

I. TRANSLATE Il. A 240-249.

Make a list of the forms peculiar to the Homeric dialect in this passage, adding in each case the Attic prose form. Construction of υἶας 240. What is elided in ὅτ' 244? Why is ὥς 245 accented? Construction of τοῖσι 247 and μέλιστος 249.

II. TRANSLATE Il. B 179-187.

Mark on your writing-paper the metrical feet of 181 and 185, giving the rule in every case of variation from natural quantity. Construction of ἀπό 183, 'Ατρείδεω 185, οἱ 186. With what is αὐτός 185 contrasted?

III. TRANSLATE Il. Γ 276-286.

What is the Latin equivalent of Ζεῦ πάτερ κύδιστε μέγιστε 276? Explain the number of τίνυσθον and of ὅτις 279. With what is εἰ μέν 281 contrasted? What other name is used for 'Αλέξανδρος 281? Which of the two seems to be the Greek name? Why should the single combat be between Menelaus and Alexander? What effect did it have on the course of the war? Construction of ἀποδοῦναι 285.

[The following may be substituted for either of the preceding passages.]

IV. TRANSLATE Il. Z 304-313.

" Πότνι' 'Αθηναίη, ἐρυσίπτολι, δῖα θεάων,
ἆξον δὴ ἔγχος Διομήδεος, ἠδὲ καὶ αὐτόν
πρηνέα δὸς πεσέειν Σκαιῶν προπάροιθε πυλάων,
5 ὄφρα τοι αὐτίκα νῦν δυοκαίδεκα βοῦς ἐνὶ νηῷ,
ἤνις ἠκίστας ἱερεύσομεν, αἴ κ' ἐλεήσῃς
ἄστυ τε καὶ Τρώων ἀλόχους καὶ νήπια τέκνα."
"Ὣς ἔφατ' εὐχομένη, ἀνένευε δὲ Παλλὰς 'Αθήνη.

ὣς αἱ μέν ῥ᾽ εὔχοντο Διὸς κούρῃ μεγάλοιο,
10 Ἕκτωρ δὲ πρὸς δώματ᾽ Ἀλεξάνδροιο βεβήκει.

Construction of θεάων (2), πρηνέα (4). Give the Attic forms for ἱερεύσομεν, αἴ κε (6). What is the force of the preposition in ἀνένευε (8)? What preposition has the opposite force? Illustrate from the first book of the Iliad. Who are αἱ μέν (9)?

June, 1883.

I. TRANSLATE Il. I. 320–330.

Make a list of the forms peculiar to the Homeric dialect in this passage, adding in each case the Attic prose form. What different uses of τώ are seen in lines 321 and 327? Construction of χειρός 323. Use of the mode in ἀγέμεν 323 and ἕλωμαι 324. Explain the use of δέ after ἐγώ in 324.

II. TRANSLATE Il. II. 455–458, 469–473.

Mark on your writing-paper the metrical feet of 471 and 472, giving the rule in every case of variation from natural quantity. Construction of τῶν 457, οὐρανόν 458. What Latin words show the same stem with ὕλην 455, εἰαρινῇ 471, γλάγος 471? What words contain the point of comparison in 469–473?

III. TRANSLATE Il. III. 428–436.

Give the full forms without elision of αὐτόθ᾽ 428, εὖχε᾽ 430, τάχ᾽ 436. Where are προκάλεσσαι 432 and δαμήῃς 436 found? What two constructions are possible for δουρί 436? Give the general rule for the accent of verbs, and point out the exceptions in this passage.

GREEK AT SIGHT.

July, 1886.

TRANSLATE: —

οἱ δὲ στρατιῶται τότε μὲν δειπνήσαντες καὶ φυλακὰς καταστησάμενοι καὶ συσκευασάμενοι πάντα ἃ ἔδει ἐκοιμήθησαν. ἡνίκα δ' ἦν ἐν μέσῳ νυκτῶν, ἐσήμηνε τῷ κέρατί. Κῦρος δ' εἰπὼν τῷ Χρυσάντᾳ ὅτι ἐπὶ τῇ ὁδῷ ὑπομενοίη ἐν τῷ πρόσθεν τοῦ στρατεύματος ἐξῄει λαβὼν τοὺς ἀμφ' αὑτὸν ὑπηρέτας· βραχεῖ δὲ χρόνῳ ὕστερον Χρυσάντας παρῆν ἄγων τοὺς θωρακοφόρους. τούτῳ μὲν ὁ Κῦρος δοὺς ἡγεμόνας τῆς ὁδοῦ πορεύεσθαι ἐκέλευεν ἡσύχως· οὐ γάρ πω ἐν ὁδῷ πάντες ἦσαν· αὐτὸς δὲ ἑστηκὼς ἐν τῇ ὁδῷ τὸν μὲν προσιόντα προυπέμπετο ἐν τάξει, ἐπὶ δὲ τὸν ὑστερίζοντα ἔπεμπε καλῶν. ἐπεὶ δὲ πάντες ἐν ὁδῷ ἦσαν, πρὸς μὲν Χρυσάνταν ἱππέας ἔπεμψεν ἐροῦντας ὅτι ἐν ὁδῷ ἤδη πάντες· ἄγε οὖν ἤδη θᾶττον. αὐτὸς δὲ παρελαύνων τὸν ἵππον εἰς τὸ πρόσθεν ἥσυχος κατεθεᾶτο τὰς τάξεις. καὶ οὓς μὲν ἴδοι εὐτάκτως καὶ σιωπῇ ἰόντας, προσελαύνων αὐτοῖς τίνες τε εἶεν ἠρώτα καὶ ἐπεὶ πύθοιτο ἐπῄνει· εἰ δέ τινας θορυβουμένους αἴσθοιτο, τὸ αἴτιον τούτου σκοπῶν κατασβεννύναι τὴν ταραχὴν ἐπειρᾶτο.

ἐπεὶ δὲ ἡμέρα ἐγένετο, τοὺς μὲν Καδουσίων ἱππέας, ὅτι αὐτῶν καὶ οἱ πεζοὶ ἐπορεύοντο ἔσχατοι, παρὰ τούτοις κατέλιπεν, ὡς μηδ' οὗτοι ψιλοὶ ἱππέων ἴοιεν· τοὺς δ' ἄλλους εἰς τὸ πρόσθεν παρελαύνειν ἐκέλευσεν, ὅτι καὶ οἱ πολέμιοι ἐν τῷ πρόσθεν ἦσαν, ὅπως εἴ τί που ἐναντιοῖτο αὐτῷ, ἀπαντῴη ἔχων τὴν ἰσχὺν ἐν τάξει καὶ μάχοιτο εἴ τέ τί που φεῦγον ὀφθείη, ὡς ἐξ ἑτοιμοτάτου διώκοι.

[σβέννυμι: quench, put an end to.]

June, 1885.

TRANSLATE : —

Ἐπειδὴ δὲ ἡμέρα ἐγένετο, εὐθὺς ἐπὶ Σάρδεις ἦγε Κῦρος. ὡς δ' ἐγένετο πρὸς τῷ τείχει τῷ ἐν Σάρδεσι τάς τε μηχανὰς ἀνίστη ὡς προσβαλὼν πρὸς τὸ τεῖχος καὶ κλίμακας[1] παρεσκευάζετο. ταῦτα δὲ ποιῶν κατὰ τὰ ἀποτομώτατα[2] δοκοῦντα εἶναι τοῦ Σαρδιανῶν ἐρύματος, τῆς ἐπιούσης νυκτὸς ἀναβιβάζει Χαλδαίους τε καὶ Πέρσας. ἡγήσατο δ' αὐτοῖς ἀνὴρ Πέρσης, δοῦλος γεγενημένος τῶν ἐν τῇ ἀκροπόλει τινὸς φρουρῶν καὶ καταμεμαθηκὼς κατάβασιν εἰς τὸν ποταμὸν καὶ ἀνάβασιν τὴν αὐτήν. ὡς δ' ἐγένετο τοῦτο δῆλον ὅτι εἴχετο τὰ ἄκρα, πάντες δὴ ἔφευγον οἱ Λυδοὶ ἀπὸ τῶν τειχῶν ὅποι ἐδύνατο ἕκαστος τῆς πόλεως. Κῦρος δὲ ἅμα τῇ ἡμέρᾳ εἰσῄει εἰς τὴν πόλιν.

[1] scaling-ladders. [2] most precipitous.

June, 1884.

TRANSLATE : —

Οἱ μὲν δὴ εὐξάμενοι τοῖς θεοῖς ἀπῇσαν πρὸς τὰς τάξεις· τῷ δὲ Κύρῳ καὶ τοῖς ἀμφ' αὐτὸν προσήνεγκαν οἱ θεράποντες ἐμπιεῖν καὶ φαγεῖν ἔτι οὖσιν ἀμφὶ τὰ ἱερά. ὁ δὲ Κῦρος ὥσπερ εἶχεν ἑστηκὼς ἠρίστα καὶ μετεδίδου ἀεὶ τῷ μάλιστα δεομένῳ· καὶ σπείσας καὶ εὐξάμενος ἔπιε, καὶ οἱ ἄλλοι δὲ οἱ περὶ αὐτὸν οὕτως ἐποίουν. μετὰ δὲ ταῦτα αἰτησάμενος Δία πατρῷον ἡγεμόνα εἶναι καὶ σύμμαχον, ἀνέβαινεν ἐπὶ τὸν ἵππον καὶ τοὺς ἀμφ' αὐτὸν ἐκέλευσεν. ὡπλισμένοι δὲ πάντες οἱ περὶ τὸν Κῦρον τοῖς αὐτοῖς Κύρῳ ὅπλοις, χιτῶσι φοινικοῖς, θώραξι χαλκοῖς, κράνεσι χαλκοῖς, μαχαίραις, παλτῷ ἑνὶ ἕκαστος· οἱ δὲ ἵπποι προμετωπιδίοις καὶ προστερνιδίοις καὶ παραμηριδίοις χαλκοῖς· τὰ δὲ αὐτὰ ταῦτα παραμηρίδια ἦν τῷ ἀνδρί.

'June, 1883.

TRANSLATE :—

Μετὰ δὲ ταῦτα ἀναστὰς εἶπε Ξενοφῶν· Ὦ ἄνδρες στρατιῶται, τὴν μὲν πορείαν, ὡς ἔοικε, δῆλον ὅτι πεζῇ ποιητέον· οὐ γὰρ ἔστι πλοῖα· ἀνάγκη δὲ πορεύεσθαι ἤδη· οὐ γὰρ ἔστι μένουσι τὰ ἐπιτήδεια. ἡμεῖς οὖν, ἔφη, θυσόμεθα· ὑμᾶς δὲ δεῖ παρασκευάζεσθαι ὡς μαχουμένους εἴ ποτε καὶ ἄλλοτε· οἱ γὰρ πολέμιοι ἀνατεθαρρήκασιν. ἐκ τούτου ἐθύοντο οἱ στρατηγοί· θυομένοις δὲ ἐπὶ τῇ ἀφόδῳ[1] οὐκ ἐγίγνετο τὰ ἱερά. ταύτην μὲν οὖν τὴν ἡμέραν ἐπαύσαντο. καί τινες ἐτόλμων λέγειν ὡς ὁ Ξενοφῶν βουλόμενος τὸ χωρίον οἰκίσαι[2] πέπεικε[3] τὸν μάντιν λέγειν ὡς τὰ ἱερὰ οὐ γίγνεται ἐπὶ ἀφόδῳ. ἐντεῦθεν κηρύξας τῇ αὔριον παρεῖναι ἐπὶ τὴν θυσίαν τὸν βουλόμενον, ἔθυε· καὶ ἐνταῦθα παρῆσαν πολλοί. θυομένῳ δὲ πάλιν εἰς τρὶς ἐπὶ τῇ ἀφόδῳ οὐκ ἐγίγνετο τὰ ἱερά. ἐκ τούτου χαλεπῶς εἶχον οἱ στρατιῶται· καὶ γὰρ τὰ ἐπιτήδεια ἀπέλιπεν ἃ ἔχοντες ἦλθον, καὶ ἀγορὰ οὐδεμία παρῆν.

[1] departure. [2] to settle in. [3] πείθω.

GREEK HISTORY.

July, 1886.

1. Locate the following places, and mention for what each was famous (adding the date, if the case admits) : Chaeronea, Delphi, Leuctra, Sybaris, Thermopylae.

2. Sketch the history of the Confederacy of Delos, with dates.

3. Sketch the relations between Persia and Greece during the fifth and fourth centuries B.C.

GREEK HISTORY. 243

June, 1885.

1. State what you know of the governments of Athens and of Sparta at the time of the outbreak of the Peloponnesian war. What changes of government took place in Greece between the Homeric and the historic periods?

2. Where were Artemisium, Delphi, Euripus, Mycenae? How far was Athens from the sea? How far was Thebes from the sea?

3. What bonds of national unity existed in Greece? What were the most marked differences in character and tastes between the Athenians and the Spartans?

4. Arrange in chronological order: Alexander the Great, Aristotle, Miltiades, Pericles, Plato, Socrates.

5. By how many years did Cyrus the Great precede the younger Cyrus? What was the relationship between them? What claim had the younger Cyrus to the throne?

June, 1884.

1. Form a chronological table of the principal events in the history of Athens.

2. What were the chief Greek colonies west of Greece? How were any of them concerned in the history of Greece proper?

3. Give the dates, opposed parties, and immediate consequences of the battles of Chaeronea, Leuctra, and Salamis.

4. What were the principal causes and consequences of the Peloponnesian war? When and under whose leadership was it begun? When and from what cause was it ended?

June, 1883.

1. Give some account of Kleisthenes; of Xenophon.

2. Tell what you know about Greek colonies: *e.g.* what

was their relation to the mother city? to what countries were the earlier ones sent? why were most of them on insular or seaboard sites? how were they generally distributed according to tribe-connection? what great advantages resulted to Greece from them? how did they affect the peoples about them? name some of the most important.

3. Tell the story of the Athenian expedition against Syrakuse.

ARITHMETIC.
September, 1886.

1. Divide $3\frac{2}{3} - 1\frac{1}{3}$ by $\frac{5}{8}$ of $\left(\dfrac{7\frac{1}{4}}{\frac{2}{3}} + \frac{1}{2}\right)$.

2. If I sell coffee at $2s.\ 3d.$ per pound, and gain 35 per cent, what did I give per pound?

3. What is the difference between the true discount and that taken by banks on $1500 due one year hence without grace? The rate of discount in both cases is 5 per cent.

4. If 8 oz. of bread can be bought for 10 cents when corn is $1.00 per bushel, what weight of it may be bought for 18 cents when the price is $1.12 per bushel?

5. The area of a circle is 5 square rods. What is the length in feet of one side of a square which contains the same area?

6. The volume of a sphere is 0.056 cubic yards. What is the length in inches of the side of a cube containing the same volume?

METRIC SYSTEM.

7. What fractional part of $\frac{1}{24}$ of the avoirdupois ton is 12 kilograms, the ounce being equal to 28.35 grams?

ARITHMETIC. 245

8. The stere contains 1.308 cubic yards. How many meters in the side of the cube in example 6?

June, 1886.

1. Add $\frac{2}{7}$ of $\dfrac{5\frac{1}{3}}{\frac{1}{8}}$ to $\frac{5}{8}$ of $(4\frac{1}{3} - 2\frac{7}{8})$

2. A square field contains 0.8346 of an acre. What is the length of one side in feet?

3. If 8 horses consume $3\frac{1}{2}$ tons of hay in 30 days, how long will $4\frac{9}{10}$ tons last 10 horses and 15 cows, each cow consuming $\frac{3}{4}$ as much as a horse?

4. A merchant bought flour for $1000 cash and sold the same immediately for $1200 on 6 months' credit, for which he received a note. If he should get the note discounted at a bank at 5 per cent, what will be the gain on the flour?

5. A block in the form of a perfect cube contains 12,516 cubic inches. How many square yards of paper are required to cover it?

METRIC SYSTEM.

6. In problem 2 find the length of one side of the field in meters, the hectar being equal to 2.4711 acres.

7. In problem 5 find the weight of the block in kilograms, assuming the weight of a cubic inch of the material to be 2 ounces, and that a tonneau weighs 2204.6 lbs.

September, 1885.

1. Subtract $\frac{1}{8}$ of $\frac{9}{10}$ from $\dfrac{8\frac{2}{3} + 2\frac{1}{4}}{4\frac{1}{2}}$.

2. By selling potatoes at $62\frac{1}{2}$ cents per bushel, 10 per cent was lost; at how much should they be sold to gain 25 per cent?

3. There is a rectangular lot of ground 64.8 rods long and 36.05 rods wide, and a square lot of the same area; which will require the more feet of fencing, and how much?

4. Sold a hundred bushels of wheat, which cost $150, at 50 cents a peck, taking in payment a six months' note, which was discounted immediately at the bank, at 6 per cent. What was the profit?

5. Find the fourth term: $\sqrt[3]{4.913} : 0.0016 :: 48,000 :$

6. A vessel is three decimeters long, 20 centimeters wide, and 100 millimeters deep; how many liters of water will it contain? How many grams? How many cubic inches? How many pounds?

June, 1885

1. Reduce $\dfrac{\frac{4}{7} \text{ of } \frac{3}{8}}{5\frac{1}{4} - 5\frac{51}{56}}$ to the simplest form.

2. Divide 0.0144 by 4800; multiply the quotient by 6.004, and extract the square root of the product.

3. What annual income would a man receive from $9850 invested in railroad stocks costing 109 and paying 5 per cent dividend?

4. If a six-cent loaf weighs 8 ounces when wheat is $1.25 per bushel, how much bread may be bought for 50 cents when wheat is $1.00 per bushel?

5. Extract the cube root of 8365.427.

6. The water contained in a vessel 2 decimeters long, 30 centimeters wide, and 300 millimeters deep, would weigh how many kilograms? would measure how many cubic inches? how many gallons?

June, 1884.

1. How many hektars in a strip of land 62 decimeters broad and 1.7 hektometers long?

ARITHMETIC.

2. A cubical cistern is 6 meters in each dimension. If 1.725 hektoliters of water can flow out per minute, how much must flow in per minute to fill it in an hour?

3. What is the present worth of $1609.30 due in 10 months and 24 days, when money is worth 5 per cent?

4. A rectangular field contains 110 acres; $37\frac{1}{2}$ per cent of the length is 381.183 yards. What is the breadth in rods?

5. Divide $\dfrac{\frac{629}{17}\text{ of }\sqrt{94\frac{3}{49}}}{\dfrac{215}{5\frac{3}{8}}}$ by $\sqrt[3]{67419143}$.

September, 1883.

1. Divide the difference between $25\frac{6}{8}$ and $7\frac{7}{12}$ by $\frac{1}{10}$ of the square root of $2756\frac{1}{4}$.

2. Find the greatest common divisor and the least common multiple of 128, 148, and 168.

3. What is the value of a piece of ground $16\frac{7}{11}$ rods long and $27\frac{1}{8}$ yards wide at $1s.\ 4d.$ per square foot?

4. If $4\frac{1}{2}$ per cent Government bonds sell at 116, what sum of money invested in them will yield an interest of $1.00 per day?

5. If 1 meter = $39\frac{2}{8}$ inches, and 1 gallon contains 277.274 cubic inches, what part of a liter is $\frac{2}{5}$ of a quart?

June, 1883.

1. Divide 82.1 by 41; 8.21 by 0.41; and 0.821 by 410. Carry the result in each case to four decimal places.

2. Find the value to three decimal places of
$$\sqrt{(0.146)^2 + (0.063)^2}.$$

3. Divide $\dfrac{3\frac{3}{8} + \frac{6}{5} + \frac{1}{12}}{\frac{2}{3}\text{ of }5\frac{7}{8}} \times \dfrac{1}{\frac{1}{4}}$ by $\dfrac{133}{141}$.

4. Some sugar is adulterated as follows:

$\frac{3}{10}$ is worth 8 cents per pound,
$\frac{4}{8}$ is worth 10 cents per pound,
$\frac{2}{15}$ is worth 12 cents per pound,

and the remainder, 33 lbs., is sand. What is the mixture worth per pound?

5. Bank stock which sells at 170 pays an annual dividend of $12\frac{1}{2}$ per cent. What rate of interest does a buyer receive?

6. Find the depth in meters of a cubical cistern which has a capacity of 30,000 liters. Give the result to three decimal places.

ALGEBRA.

September, 1886.

1. Divide $\dfrac{x^4 - y^4}{x^2 - 2xy + y^2}$ by $\dfrac{x^2 + xy}{x - y}$.

2. Multiply $a^{\frac{5}{3}} - a^2 b^{\frac{1}{3}} + a^{\frac{5}{3}} b^{\frac{2}{3}} - ab + a^{\frac{1}{3}} b^{\frac{4}{3}} - b^{\frac{5}{3}}$ by $a^{\frac{1}{3}} + b^{\frac{1}{3}}$.

3. Free the fraction $\dfrac{1 - a^{-2} - y^2}{1 - x^{-3} y^{-2} + x^{-2}}$ from negative exponents.

4. Find x from $\dfrac{7x + 9}{4} - \left(x - \dfrac{2x - 1}{9}\right) = 7$.

5. Find $x, y,$ and z from $\begin{cases} a = y + z, \\ b = x + z, \\ c = x + y. \end{cases}$

6. Multiply $x - 5 + 2\sqrt{-1}$ by $x - 5 - 2\sqrt{-1}$.

7. Make the denominator of the following fraction rational:

$$\dfrac{\sqrt{x} - \sqrt{x + y}}{\sqrt{x} + \sqrt{x + y}}$$

ALGEBRA.

8. Solve the equation $\dfrac{1}{x-1} + \dfrac{2}{x-2} = \dfrac{4}{3}$.

9. If $a:b = c:d$, prove by the principles of proportion that
$$\dfrac{a+b+c+d}{a+b-c-d} = \dfrac{a-b+c-d}{a-b-c+d}.$$

10. In a geometrical progression having given, first term, ratio, and sum of series, write formula for last term.

11. Expand to four terms $(a+x)^{-\frac{1}{4}}$.

June, 1886.

1. Divide $\dfrac{c-b}{c+b} - \dfrac{c^3-b^3}{c^3+b^3}$ by $\dfrac{c+b}{c-b} + \dfrac{c^2+b^2}{c^2-b^2}$.

2. Divide $x^2y^{-\frac{2}{3}} - 2 + x^{-2}y^{\frac{4}{3}}$ by $x^{\frac{1}{2}}y^{-\frac{1}{3}} - x^{-\frac{1}{2}}y^{\frac{1}{3}}$.

3. Multiply $\sqrt{-a} + c\sqrt[3]{b}$ by $\sqrt{-a} - c\sqrt[3]{b}$.

4. In $\dfrac{1}{\sqrt{3}-1}$ make the denominator rational, and compute the value of the expression to three places of decimals.

5. Given $a + x = \sqrt{a^2 + x\sqrt{b^2+x^2}}$ to find x.

6. Solve the equations $\begin{cases} x + y = 12, \\ x^2 + y^2 = 74. \end{cases}$

7. If $A:B = C:D$, prove by the principles of proportion that $A^2 - B^2 : B^2 = C^2 - D^2 : D^2$.

8. Find the sum of the infinite series $\frac{1}{5} + \frac{1}{25} + \frac{1}{125} +$ etc.

9. Expand to four terms by the binomial theorem $\dfrac{1}{\sqrt{1+x^2}}$

September, 1885.

1. Reduce $\dfrac{\dfrac{a^2}{b^3}+\dfrac{1}{a}}{\dfrac{a}{b}-\dfrac{1}{b}+\dfrac{1}{a}}$ to a simple fraction.

2. Find the greatest common divisor of $x^4 - 6x^2 - 8x - 3$ and $4x^3 - 12x - 8$.

3. Given $\sqrt{13+x} + \sqrt{13-x} = 6$ to find x.

4. Given $x^4 - 21x^2 = 100$ to find four values for x.

5. Find the value of $a^{\frac{2}{3}} + a^{\frac{1}{3}}b^{\frac{1}{3}} + b^{\frac{2}{3}}$ when $a = 8$ and $b = 64$.

6. Given $\begin{cases} x+y = a \\ x^2 - y^2 = b^2 \end{cases}$ to find x and y.

7. Given $(x^2 - ax) : \sqrt{x} :: \sqrt{x} : x$ to find values of x.

8. Expand $\dfrac{1}{(2a-3)^{\frac{1}{2}}}$ into a series.

9. Compute the value of the continued fraction

$$12 + \cfrac{1}{1 + \cfrac{1}{2 + \cfrac{1}{3}}}.$$

June, 1885.

1. Given $\dfrac{5x+2}{3} - \left(3 - \dfrac{3x-1}{2}\right) = \dfrac{3x+19}{2} - \left(\dfrac{x+1}{6} + 3\right)$ to find x.

2. Multiply $\dfrac{b-y}{a^3+y^3}$, $\dfrac{ca+cy}{b^2-by}$, $\dfrac{b^6+y^6}{b^2+y^2}$ and $\dfrac{b}{c}$.

3. Multiply $x - \tfrac{1}{2}(1 - \sqrt{-3})$ by $x - \tfrac{1}{2}(1 + \sqrt{-3})$.

ALGEBRA.

4. Divide $x^2 y^{-\frac{2}{3}} - 2 + x^{-2} y^{\frac{2}{3}}$ by $x^{\frac{1}{2}} y^{-\frac{1}{3}} - x^{-\frac{1}{2}} y^{\frac{1}{3}}$.

5. Given $91 x^2 - 2x = 45$ to find both values of x.

6. Given $\dfrac{7}{\sqrt{x}} + \dfrac{4}{\sqrt{y}} = 4$,

$\dfrac{1}{\sqrt{x}} + \dfrac{2}{\sqrt{y}} = 1$ to find x and y.

7. Expand by the Binomial Theorem to five terms $(1+a)^{xy}$.

8. In Arithmetical Progression, given $d =$ the common difference, $a =$ the first term, and $s =$ the sum of series; derive the formula for $l =$ the last term.

9. If $\dfrac{\sqrt{a-bx}+\sqrt{c-mx}}{\sqrt{a-bx}+\sqrt{nx-d}} = \dfrac{\sqrt{a-bx}-\sqrt{c-mx}}{\sqrt{a-bx}-\sqrt{nx-d}}$, prove by using the principles of proportion that $\dfrac{c-mx}{nx-d} = 1$.

June, 1884.

1. Reduce the following fractions to their lowest terms:

$\dfrac{a^2 c + abc + b^2 c}{a^4 + a^2 b^2 + b^4}$; $\dfrac{b^2 + 4 y^2}{b^6 + 64 y^6}$.

2. Reduce $\dfrac{x+1}{x-1}\sqrt{\dfrac{x-1}{x+1}}$ to its simplest form.

3. Solve the equations

$x + y = \dfrac{2(a^2 + b^2)}{a^2 - b^2}$;

$x - y = \dfrac{4ab}{a^2 - b^2}$.

4. Multiply

$x - \sqrt{5} + 1 - \sqrt{-10 - 2\sqrt{5}}$ by $x - \sqrt{5} + 1 + \sqrt{-10 - 2\sqrt{5}}$.

5. Find the number whose cube root is one-fifth of its square root.

ALGEBRA.

6. Find x from the equation
$$\sqrt{1+x-x^2} - 2(1+x-x^2) = \tfrac{1}{8}.$$

7. A and B can do a piece of work together in 8 days. A works alone 4 days, and then both finish it in 5 days more. In what time could each have done it alone?

8. A traveller has a journey of 132 miles to perform. He goes 27 miles the first day, 24 the second, and so on, travelling 3 miles less each day than the day before. In how many days will he complete the journey?

9. The ratio of the circumference of a circle to its diameter is 3.141592. Find by continued fractions three approximate values.

10. Expand by the method of undetermined coefficients to four terms $\sqrt{a-x^2}$.

September, 1883.

1. Divide $\dfrac{c-b}{c+b} - \dfrac{c^2-b^2}{c^2+b^2}$ by $\dfrac{c+b}{c-b} + \dfrac{c^2+b^2}{c^2-b^2}$.

2. Find the value of $\dfrac{1}{\sqrt{3}+1}$ to three decimal places.

3. Given $\sqrt{x^{\tfrac{3}{5}}} = 2\sqrt{2}$ to find x.

4. Find the $-\tfrac{3}{4}$th power of $256\, x^{\tfrac{2}{3}} y^{-\tfrac{2}{3}}$.

5. A grocer has two sorts of tea, one worth a cents per pound, the other b cents per pound. How many pounds of each sort must be taken to make a mixture of m pounds worth c cents a pound?

6. Reduce $\dfrac{a^{m-\tfrac{1}{2}}}{b^{m+\tfrac{1}{2}}} \div \dfrac{a^{m+\tfrac{1}{2}}}{b^{m-\tfrac{1}{2}}}$ to the simplest form.

7. Solve the equation
$$4\sqrt[4]{x} + \sqrt{x} = 21.$$

ALGEBRA.

8. Find the cube root of
$$x^6 - 6x^5 + 3x^4 + 28x^3 - 9x^2 - 54x - 27.$$

9. In the proportion $\dfrac{a^2 - b^2}{b^2} = \dfrac{c^2 - d^2}{d^2}$ prove that $\dfrac{a}{b} = \dfrac{c}{d}$.

10. Insert three arithmetical means between -9 and 18.

11. Write down the eighth term of $(a-b)^{12}$.

June, 1883.

1. Reduce the following expression to its simplest form:
$$\frac{1}{x(x-a)(x-b)} + \frac{1}{a(a-x)(a-b)} + \frac{1}{b(b-x)(b-a)}.$$

2. Resolve $y^9 - b^9$ into three factors.

3. Change $xy^{-2} - 2x^{\frac{1}{2}}y^{-1}z^{-\frac{1}{2}} + z^{-1}$ to an expression which will contain no negative exponents.

4. If $\dfrac{a+b+c+d}{a+b-c-d} = \dfrac{a-b+c-d}{a-b-c+d}$, prove by the principles of proportion that $\dfrac{a}{b} = \dfrac{c}{d}$.

5. Find the value of $2a\sqrt{(1+x^2)}$ when $x = \tfrac{1}{2}\left(\sqrt{\dfrac{a}{b}} - \sqrt{\dfrac{b}{a}}\right).$

6. Given $(7 - 4\sqrt{3})x^2 + (2 - \sqrt{3})x = 2$ to find x.

7. The sum of two numbers is 16, and the sum of their reciprocals is $\tfrac{1}{3}$; what are the numbers?

8. Compute the value of the continued fraction
$$\cfrac{1}{2 + \cfrac{1}{1 + \cfrac{1}{4 + \cfrac{1}{5}}}}.$$

9. Convert $\dfrac{1}{\sqrt{(1+x^2)}}$ into an infinite series by the Method of Intermediate Coefficients, or by the Binomial Theorem.

10. Insert three geometrical means between $\tfrac{1}{2}$ and 128.

GEOMETRY
September, 1886.

1. If two triangles have two angles of the one equal to two angles of the other, each to each, and one side equal to one side, namely, either the sides adjacent to the equal angles, or sides which are opposite to equal angles in each, then shall the other sides be equal, each to each, and also the third angle of the one equal to the third angle of the other.

2. To draw a straight line at right angles to a given straight line, from a given point in the same.

(Show clearly in the figure the method of construction.)

3. An inscribed angle is measured by one-half of the arc intercepted between its sides.

4. The sides, AB, AD, of a quadrilateral $ABCD$ are equal, and the diagonal AC bisects the angle BAD: show that the sides CB and CD are equal, and that the diagonal AC bisects the angle BCD.

5. Construct a triangle, having given the base, one of the angles at the base, and the sum of the sides.

July, 1886.

1. If a side of any triangle be produced, the exterior angle is equal to the two interior and opposite angles;

GEOMETRY.

and the three interior angles of every triangle are together equal to two right angles.

2. (Problem.) To describe a square on a given straight line.

(Show clearly in the figure the methods by which the constructions are made.)

3. An angle formed by a tangent and a chord is measured by one-half the intercepted arc.

4. If the angle C of a triangle is equal to the sum of the angles A and B, the side AB is equal to twice the straight line joining C to the middle point of AB.

5. Find a point in a given straight line such that its distances from two given points may be equal.

PRELIMINARY.

[Candidates offering the whole of Plane Geometry, may take *three* out of *five* of the regular paper, one of the three being either 4 or 5, with the following:]

(A) Two triangles are similar when they are mutually equiangular.

(B) The circumferences of two circles are to each other as their radii, and their areas are as the squares of their radii.

September, 1885.

1. If two triangles have two sides of the one equal to two sides of the other, but their bases unequal, the angle contained by the sides of the one which has the greater base shall be greater than the angle contained by the sides equal to them of the other.

2. The straight lines which join the extremities of two equal and parallel straight lines toward the same parts are themselves equal and parallel.

3. Find a point in a given straight line which shall be equally distant from two given points. (Bisect the line joining the given points.) Show clearly by auxiliary lines the methods by which the figure is constructed.

4. If one angle of a triangle is equal to the sum of the other two, the triangle can be divided into two isosceles triangles.

5. The three bisectors of the three angles of a triangle meet in the same point.

6. An angle inscribed in a semicircle is a right angle.

June, 1885.

1. If two triangles have two sides, and the angle included by them of the one respectively equal to two sides and the angle included by them of the other, the triangles shall be equal.

2. Describe a parallelogram that shall be equal to a given triangle, and have one of its angles equal to a given rectilineal angle. Show clearly in the figure the methods by which the parts are constructed.

3. If a straight line be draw through A, one of the angular points of a square cutting one of the opposite sides, and meeting the other produced at F, show that AF is greater than the diagonal of the square.

4. Construct a triangle, having given the base AB, one of the angles at the base A, and the sum of the sides AC. (Join B and C, and through B draw a line parallel to AC.)

5. Two parallel straight lines cutting a circle intercept equal arcs on the circumference.

6. Two similar polygons may be decomposed into the same number of triangles similar each to each.

GEOMETRY.

June, 1884.

1. To bisect a given rectilineal angle; that is, to divide it into two equal angles.

2. In any right-angled triangle, the square which is described on the side subtending the right angle is equal to the squares described on the sides which contain the right angle.

3. If two isosceles triangles are on the same base, the straight line joining their vertices, or that straight line produced, will bisect the base at right angles.

4. AB and AC are any two straight lines meeting at A: through any point P draw a straight line meeting them at E and F, such that AE may be equal to AF.

June, 1883.

[Candidates who offer Euclid may take 1, 2, and 5. Other candidates may take 1, 3, 4, and 5.]

1. At a given point in a given straight line to construct an angle equal to a given angle.

2. If a straight line be bisected and produced to any point, the rectangle contained by the whole line thus produced, and the part of it produced, together with the square on half the line bisected, is equal to the square on the straight line which is made up of the half and the part produced.

3. The diagonals of a parallelogram bisect each other.

4. To construct a triangle equivalent to a given polygon.

5. If the straight lines bisecting the angles, at the base of an isosceles triangle, be produced to meet, they will contain an angle equal to an exterior angle of the triangle.

FRENCH.
July, 1886.

Quoique la tête des écureuils (squirrel) soit large, leur petit museau est très fin ; leurs yeux sont saillants et noirs, et leur physionomie douce et piquante tout à la fois. Je repris le chemin de la maison en compagnie de mon nouvel ami, pensant à ma petite famille qui serait charmée d'entendre le récit de cet incident de voyage. Mon retour chez mes amis fut un véritable événement pour les enfants ; tous accoururent, et on décida à l'unanimité qu'il fallait se hâter de trouver un logement au gentil petit animal. Nous n'avions pas de cage avec une roue, cette classique habitation de tous les écureuils civilisés ; mais tant de gens se mirent en campagne, qu'on découvrit bientôt au fond du grenier la vieille niche d'un défunt petit chien. Paul, l'aîné, garçon fort adroit, enleva la planche du fond de la niche pour y substituer des barreaux en fil de fer, et là dedans on introduisit le pauvre captif. Il fit son entrée dans sa nouvelle demeure au milieu des sauts, des cris de joie et des battements de mains ; car on ne doutait pas qu'il ne se trouvât là parfaitement heureux ; mais il en fut tout autrement. On eut beau lui apporter toutes sortes de friandises, et mettre en réquisition tous les fruits de la saison, remplir son assiette de l'eau la plus limpide ; il ne touchait presque à rien, et restait toute la journée blotti dans un coin. Les enfants, tout affligés de la tristesse de leur petit ami, ne sachant plus qu'imaginer pour lui faire du bien ou du plaisir, se dirent entre eux : "Il ne faut pas lui faire de la peine ; il paraît qu'il aime mieux être sur les arbres que dans notre petite maison ; conduisons-le dans le bois, peut-être retrouvera-t-il sa maman." On le porta donc en procession à l'entrée du bois ; on lui attacha un petit ruban rouge à la patte, et après que tour à tour nous lui eûmes passé la main sur le dos en signe d'adieu, on le déposa sur la branche où je l'avais trouvé. Aussitôt il sembla reprendre la vivacité naturelle aux écureuils, se mit à grimper vers le sommet de l'arbre et au bout d'un moment il disparut tout à fait.

Plusieurs jours de suite nous allâmes en vain nous promener de ce côté du bois; je ne saurais dire combien mes jeunes camarades perdirent de temps à tenir le nez en l'air, espérant toujours l'apercevoir sur quelque branche, mais ce fut inutilement.

Un jour, de grand matin, le domestique ouvrant la porte du salon trouve sur la terrasse un écureuil. Il s'avance avec précaution; mais il n'eut pas de peine à s'en emparer, car il était demi-mort de faim et de froid. Cet événement fut bientôt connu de toute la maison. En l'apprenant les enfants sautèrent à bas du lit et furent bien vite habillés. Ils accoururent tous et il ne leur fut pas difficile de reconnaître leur ancien favori, à un fragment de ruban encore attaché à sa patte, mais ils furent tout consterneés de le retrouver si maigre. On aurait bien voulu savoir ce qui lui était arrivé depuis son départ jusqu'à son retour; mais à quoi bon l'interroger? il ne pouvait pas repondre. Je crois que s'il avait su parler il aurait dit: "Je suis bien malheureux depuis que je vous ai quitteès; je n'ai rien mangé, je n'ai pas trouvé la moitié d'une noisette, je n'ai plus de famille, je meurs de faim; ayez pitié de moi!" S'il ne dit pas tout cela, on le devina; surtout lorsqu'en le regardant de près, on s'aperçut . . . qu'il était aveugle! Peu de temps après il mourut.

July, 1885.

TRANSLATE into good English:

Il y a bien peu de souverains dont on dût écrire une histoire particulière. En vain la malignité où la flatterie s'est exercée sur presque tous les princes; il n'y en a qu'un très-petit nombre dont la mémoire se conserve, et ce nombre serait encore plus petit si l'on ne se souvenait que de ceux qui ont été justes.

Les princes qui ont le plus de droit à l'immortalité sont ceux qui ont fait quelque bien aux hommes : par une raison contraire on garde le souvenir des mauvais princes, comme on se souvient des inondations des incendies, et des pestes.

Entre les tyrans et les bons rois sont les conquérants, mais plus apprechants des premiers ; ceux-ci ont une réputation éclatante ; on est avide de connaître les moindres particularités de leur vie : telle est la misérable faiblesse des hommes, qu'ils regardent avec admiration ceux qui ont fait du mal d'une manière brillante, et qu'ils parleront souvent plus volontiers du destructeur d'un empire que de celui qui l'a fondé.

Pour tous les autres princes qui n'ont été illustres ni en paix ni en guerre et qui n'ont été connus ni par de grands vices ni par de grandes vertus ; comme leur vie ne fournit aucun exemple ni à imiter ni à fuir, elle n'est pas digne qu'on s'en souvienne.

Il y a un vulgaire parmi les princes comme parmi les autres hommes ; cependant la fureur d'écrire est venue au point, qu'à peine un souverain cesse de vivre, que le public est inondé de volumes sous le nom de mémoires, d'histoire de sa vie, d'anecdotes de sa cour. Par là les livres se multiplient de telle sorte qu'un homme qui vivrait cent ans, et qui les emploierait à lire, n'aurait pas le temps de parcourir ce qui s'est imprimé sur l'histoire seule, depuis deux siècles, en Europe.

Qu'un prince entreprenne une guerre ; que sa cour soit troublée d'intrigues ; qu'il achète l'amitie d'un de ses voisins, et qu'il vende la sienne à un autre ; qu'il fasse enfin la paix avec ses ennemis, après quelques victoires et quelques défaites, ses sujets, pensent être dans l'epoque la plus singulière depuis la création. Qu'arrive-t-il? ce prince meurt: on prend après lui des mesures toutes différentes; on oublie et les intrigues de sa cour, et ses ministres, et ses généraux, et ses guerres, et lui-même.

Depuis le temps que les princes chrétiens tâchent de se tromper les uns les autres, et font des guerres et des alliances, on a signé des milliers de traités et donné autant de batailles; les belles ou infâmes actions sont innombrables. Quand toute cette foule d'événements et de détails se présente devant la postérité, ils sont presque tous anéantis les uns par les autres; les seuls qui restent sont ceux qui ont produit de grandes révolutions, ou ceux qui, ayant été décrits par quelque écrivain excellent, se sauvent de la foule comme des portraits d'hommes obscurs peints par de grands maîtres.

GERMAN.

July, 1886.

TRANSLATE into idiomatic English:—

Es war an einem Sonntag Nachmittag, und ich näherte mich bereits dem Dorfe, das nur noch durch einen kleinen Spaziergang von der Universitätsstadt getrennt ist. Auf einem Fußpfade stieg ich vom Walde einen Abhang hinab und gelangte an ein einsam stehendes Haus, das einige hundert Schritte weit vor dem Dorfe lag, im Ganzen etwas über eine halbe Stunde von der Stadt entfernt. Es war ein altes hölzernes Haus, dessen Balken durch ein Gemisch von Lehm und Kalk zusammenhingen. Man hätte es eine Hütte nennen können, wenn es nicht ein oberes Stockwerk gehabt hätte. Vorn hing das Dach mit breitem Schirme weit herab und bildete, von mehreren Balken gestützt, eine Veranda, die es angenehm beschattete, und unmittelbar an diese Veranda schloß sich ein kleiner Garten mit alten Bäumen und gut bearbeiteten Beeten, in denen allerlei Küchen=

pflanzen wuchsen. Wie alt und arm auch das Material des Hauses
war, so machte es doch einen warmen und gemüthlichen Eindruck.
Es war in allen seinen Theilen sehr reinlich gehalten, und der Gartne
daran war mit vieler Liebe und Sorgfalt gepflegt. Ich konnte alles
bequem überschauen, da der Fußpfad an der einen Seite des niedrigen
Gartenzaunes in einiger Höhe dahin lief, so daß ich von einer ge=
wissen Stelle durch die hintere Thür auch in das Innere zu blicken
vermochte. Etwas müde, wie ich von der Wanderung war, blieb ich
um so lieber stehen, um diese Idylle etwas länger zu betrachten, als
aus dem ärmlichen Hause ein schönes Konzert zweier Violinen erscholl,
von denen die erste mit großer Meisterschaft gehandhabt wurde. Um
das Bild zu vollenden, saß unter der Veranda eine schöne Frau von
ungefähr dreißig Jahren, welche im Gegensatz zu der höchst ländlichen
Umgebung städtische Tracht trug, und zwei hübsche Kinder, die sich
im Garten herumtrieben, von Zeit zu Zeit, wenn sie zu laut wurden,
zu beruhigen suchte.

Das Konzert ging zu Ende, und gleich darauf erschien ein kleiner
Junge mit einer Violine in der Hand unter der Veranda, um sich von
seiner Mutter für seine Leistungen loben zu lassen. Die Frau strei=
chelte ihm die rothen Backen auf das Zärtlichste und ertheilte ihm,
wie mir aus ihren Geberden hervorging, reichliche Lobsprüche. In=
dessen erschien auch ein Mann in der Thüre, der ebenfalls eine Vio=
line in der Hand hatte und in diese Lobsprüche mit einzustimmen
schien. Der Knabe war ganz glücklich, setzte die Violine wieder an
und forderte den Vater bringend auf, ein Gleiches zu thun. Die
Mutter stimmte mit ein, und die beiden Musiker begannen nunmehr
unter der Veranda das Konzert auf's Neue. Die Kinder, die sich
im Garten herumgetrieben hatten, stellten sich jetzt ruhig vor die bei=
den Spielenden hin, legten die Hände auf den Rücken und hörten
aufmerksam zu. Es war eine schöne Gruppe und eine schöne Szene.
Die Gruppe der musizirenden und horchenden Familie stand mir fast
im Schatten; nur der blonde Kopf der Mutter, die an einer der
Säulen saß, wurde von einem Sonnenstrahle erreicht, und war wie
von einem Nimbus umgeben. Nichts war zu hören, als hie und da
in den Bäumen Vogelsang und der Klang der beiden Violinen.

June, 1885.

TRANSLATE into good English: —

In dem Dorf, wo unser Vater wohnte, ist auch die Sitte,[1] daß die Frauen und die Mädchen in den Winterabenden zum Spinnen sich zusammensetzen. Die jungen Burschen kommen dann auch und erzählen Mancherlei. So kam es eines Abends, daß man von Gespenstern[2] und Erscheinungen sprach, und die jungen Burschen erzählten von einem alten Krämer,[3] der schon vor zehn Jahren gestorben sei, aber im Grab keine Ruhe finde. Jede Nacht werfe er die Erde von sich ab, steige aus dem Grab und schleiche langsam, wie er im Leben gethan, nach seinem Laden. Viele behaupteten, ihn gesehen zu haben, und die Mädchen und Weiber fingen an sich zu fürchten. Meine Schwester aber, ein Mädchen von sechzehn Jahren, wollte klüger sein als die Andern, und sagte: „Das glaube ich alles nicht; wer einmal todt ist, kommt nicht wieder!" Da sagte einer von den jungen Leuten: „Wenn Du dies glaubst, so wirst Du Dich auch nicht vor ihm fürchten. Wage es einmal, gehe hin auf den Kirchhof, brich von einem Grab eine Blume und bringe sie uns, so wollen wir glauben, daß Du Dich vor dem Krämer nicht fürchtest!"

Meine Schwester schämte sich, von den Andern verlacht zu werden, darum sagte sie: „Oh! das ist mir ein Leichtes: was wollt Ihr denn für eine Blume?"

„Es blüht im ganzen Dorf keine weiße Rose, als dort; darum bring uns einen Strauß von diesen," antwortete eine ihrer Freundinnen. Sie stand auf und ging, aber die Frauen schüttelten den Kopf und sagten: „Wenn es nur gut abläuft!" Meine Schwester ging dem Kirchhof zu; der Mond schien hell, und sie fing an zu schaudern, als es zwölf Uhr schlug und sie die Kirchhofpforte öffnete.

Jetzt war sie da; zitternd kniete sie nieder und knickte[4] die Blumen ab. Da glaubte sie ganz in der Nähe ein Geräusch zu vernehmen; sie sah sich um: zwei Schritte von ihr flog die Erde von einem Grab hinweg, und langsam richtete sich eine Gestalt daraus empor. Es war ein alter, bleicher Mann mit einer weißen Schlafmütze auf dem

Kopf. Meine Schwester erschrak; als aber der im Grabe mit
näselnder Stimme anfing zu sprechen: „Guten Abend, Jungfer;⁵
woher so spät?" da raffte⁶ sie sich auf, sprang über die Gräber hin
nach jenem Hause, erzählte beinahe atemlos, was sie gesehen, und
wurde so schwach, daß man sie nach Hause tragen mußte. Nach drei
Tagen starb sie an einem hitzigen Fieber. Die Rosen zu ihrem
Totenkranz hatte sie sich selbst gebrochen.

¹ custom.   ² ghosts.   ³ peddler.   ⁴ broke.   ⁴ young woman.
⁴ jumped up.

SHEFFIELD SCIENTIFIC SCHOOL OF YALE UNIVERSITY.

ARITHMETIC.

July, 1887.

1. Find the factors, the greatest common divisor, and the least common multiple of 240, 560, and 616.

2. Find in its simplest form the value of $\dfrac{11\frac{2}{3}}{12\frac{3}{5}} \div \dfrac{5}{9}$.

3. (*a*) Reduce 0.625 to as simple a common fraction as possible. (*b*) Reduce $\frac{3}{16}$ and $\frac{1}{13}$ to decimals. What important difference do you observe between these two requirements?

4. If a slab of marble 8 ft. long, 3 ft. wide, and 3 in. thick weighs 1050 lbs., how much will another slab of the same marble weigh which is 6 ft. long, 2 ft. wide, and 2 in. thick?

5. How long must $350 be at simple interest at 6 per cent per annum to amount to $404.25?

6. Extract the square root of 0.3375 to three places.

7. Express approximately 10 meters in feet; 10 kilometers in miles; the cubic meter in liters; the gram in grains; the kilogram in pounds avoirdupois.

September, 1887.

1. Reduce $\frac{945}{1485}$ to its lowest terms.

2. Find the least common multiple of 945 and 1485.

3. Divide 0.000064 by 0.008.

4. The longitude of Boston is 71° 3' 30" W. That of San Francisco is 122° 25' 40.76" W. When it is noon at Boston, what is the local time of day at San Francisco?

5. If you give your note for $500 payable in 60 days, to a bank discounting at 6 per cent per annum, what amount ought you to receive for it?

6. A broker receives $7537.50 to invest in stocks at $75 per share and cover his brokerage at $\frac{1}{2}$ per cent. How many shares should he purchase?

7. Extract the square root of 0.1528 to three places.

PLANE GEOMETRY.

July, 1887.

[NOTE. — State at the head of your paper what text-book you have studied on the subject and to what extent.]

1. If one angle of a triangle be greater than another, the side opposite the greater angle will exceed that opposite the lesser angle.

2. When two chords of a circle intersect each other, each angle formed by them is measured by half the sum of the arcs intercepted by its sides and the sides of its vertically opposite angle.

3. Find a mean proportional between two given straight lines.

4. Draw two concentric circles such that the chords of the outer circle which touch the inner one may be equal to the diameter of the inner circle. (Prove your construction.)

5. Compare the area inclosed between the circumferences of the two circles of the preceding problem with the area of either of the circles.

SOLID AND SPHERICAL GEOMETRY.

July, 1887.

[Note. — State at the head of your paper what text-book you have studied on the subject and to what extent.]

1. Define a plane, and prove that two planes intersect each other in a straight line, if at all.

2. If two planes are respectively perpendicular to two intersecting lines, their line of intersection is perpendicular to the plane of the line.

3. If a pyramid be cut by a plane parallel to its base, then (*a*) the edges and the altitude are divided proportionately, and (*b*) the section is similar to the base.

4. Write expressions for the volume of a cone and the volume of a sphere, and indicate briefly the methods by which you have been taught to derive them.

5. The radius of a sphere is bisected by a plane at right angles to it. What is the ratio of the two parts into which the plane divides the surface of the sphere? Give the proposition on which you base your answer.

GEOMETRY.

September, 1887.

[Note. — State at the head of your paper what text-book you have studied on the subject and to what extent.]

1. The sum of the three interior angles of a triangle is equal to two right angles.

2. If the opposite sides of a quadrilateral are equal to each other, it is a parallelogram.

3. Draw a common tangent to two given circles and prove your construction.

4. The sum of the squares upon the two diagonals of a parallelogram is equal to the sum of the squares upon the four sides.

5. If from a point without a circle a secant and a tangent be drawn, the rectangle of the whole secant and the part of it without the circle is equal to the square of the tangent.

6. Straight lines perpendicular to the same plane are parallel to each other.

7. To draw a circumference of a great circle through any two given points on the surface of a sphere.

8. Find the ratio of the surfaces and that of the volumes of a sphere and a circumscribed cylinder.

ALGEBRA TO QUADRATICS.

July, 1887.

[NOTE. — State at the head of your paper what text-books you have studied on the subject and to what extent.]

1. Resolve the following expressions into factors: $x^3 - 8$; $x^3 + 8$; $b^2 - (c-d)^2$; $a^4 - 16\,b^4$; $x^{2m} + \tfrac{1}{2}x^m + \tfrac{1}{16}$.

2. Find the value in its simplest form of
$$\frac{a+c}{(a-b)(x-a)} - \frac{(b+c)}{(a-b)(x-b)}.$$

3. Given $x - \dfrac{x-2}{3} = \dfrac{x+23}{4} - \dfrac{10+x}{5}$, to find x.

4. Given $\dfrac{1}{3x} + \dfrac{1}{5y} = \dfrac{2}{9}$ and $\dfrac{1}{5x} + \dfrac{1}{3y} = \dfrac{1}{4}$, to find x and y.

5. Expand $(a^2 - 2b)^3$ by the binomial formula.

6. Simplify the following expressions:
(1) $(a^m)^n$.
(2) $\dfrac{a^0}{b^{-m}}$.
(3) $(-a)^{2n}(-a)^{2n+1}$
 [n entire].
(4) $\sqrt{a^{2m}}$.
(5) $\sqrt{108} + \sqrt{75} - \sqrt{27}$.
(6) $5^{\frac{3}{2}} + 3 \cdot 5^{\frac{1}{2}}$.
(7) $(2^{\frac{2}{3}} \cdot 2^{\frac{1}{2}})^{\frac{6}{7}}$.

ALGEBRA FROM QUADRATICS.
July, 1887.

[NOTE.—State at the head of your paper what text-book you have studied on the subject and to what extent.]

1. Given $12x^2 + x - 1 = 0$, to find the values of x.

2. Find the roots of $(x+1)(x-2)(x^2 - 6x + 9) = 0$.

3. Given $(ax - b)^2 + 4a(ax - b) = \frac{9}{4}a^2$, to find the values of x.

4. Find two numbers such that their product, sum and the difference of their squares shall be equal to each other.

5. How many different signals may be made with 12 different flags, by hoisting 4 at a time above each other?

6. Develop $\dfrac{1+2x}{3+4x}$ into a series of ascending powers of x by the method of undetermined coefficients.

ALGEBRA.
September, 1887.

[NOTE.—State at the head of your paper what text-book you have studied on the subject and to what extent.]

1. Simply $\left(\dfrac{x^2}{y^2} - 1\right)\left(\dfrac{x}{x-1}\right) + \dfrac{x^3}{y^3} - 1\right)\left(\dfrac{x^2 + xy}{x^2 + xy + y^2} - 1\right)$.

2. Given $\dfrac{5}{x+1} - \dfrac{3}{y-1} = -\dfrac{1}{6}$ and $\dfrac{3}{x+1} - \dfrac{1}{y-1} = \dfrac{1}{30}$, to find x and y.

3. Prove that $\left(\dfrac{a}{2+b}\right)^2 > ab$.

4. Simplify the following expressions:

(1) $\left(a^{\frac{m}{2}} b^{\frac{n}{3}}\right)^6$. (2) $\dfrac{2\sqrt{ab^2 c^3 d^4}}{e^{-2}}$. (3) $\dfrac{x^{\frac{2}{3}} - 4}{x^{\frac{1}{3}} - 2}$.

(4) $\sqrt[3]{2a} \times \sqrt{4b}$. (5) $\sqrt[9]{125}$.

(6) $(\sqrt{x} + \sqrt{y})(\sqrt{x} - \sqrt{y})$.

5. Solve the equation $a(x^2 - x) + b(x^2 + x) = \dfrac{ab}{a+b}$.

6. Find all the roots of $x^3 - x^2 - x + 1 = 0$.

7. Solve $\dfrac{\sqrt{1+a}}{\sqrt{x-a} + \sqrt{ax-1}} = \dfrac{1}{\sqrt{x-1}}$.

8. Derive a formula for the sum of the terms of a geometrical progression.

9. How many different amounts can be made up from five different coins.

10. Develop $\dfrac{1-x}{1-2x+x^2}$ into a series of ascending powers of x, by the method of undetermined coefficients.

TRIGONOMETRY.

July, 1887.

[NOTE. — State at the head of your paper what text-book you have studied on the subject and to what extent.]

1. Define the term *radian*. Express an angle of 60° in radians. What is the measure of an angle of $\frac{3}{4}\pi$ radians in degrees?

2. Make a table of the values of the trigonometric functions for the angles $\frac{\pi}{2}$, π, $\frac{3}{2}\pi$, 2π.

3. Show that $\sin(\frac{3}{2}\pi \pm \phi) = -\cos\phi$,
and that $\cot(2\pi - a) = -\cot a$.

4. Deduce the formulas $\sin a = \dfrac{\tan a}{\sqrt{1 + \tan^2 a}}$,

$$\sec a = \dfrac{1}{\sqrt{1 - \sin^2 a}}.$$

Explain the proper sign of the denominator in each case when a is a positive angle of the third quadrant.

5. Deduce a formula to express $\tan a$ in terms of $\tan \frac{1}{2}a$.

6. Find with the help of the tables all angles between 0° and 540° whose cotangent is $-\sqrt[3]{2.34}$.

7. Compute A by the formula $\tan \frac{1}{2}A = \sqrt{\dfrac{(s-b)(s-c)}{s(s-a)}}$, where $s = \frac{1}{2}(a+b+c)$, when $a = 1554$, $b = 1555.2$, $c = 1556.4$. What is the use of this formula in Trigonometry?

September, 1887.

[NOTE.—State what text-book you have studied on the subject and to what extent.]

1. Describe the changes which take place in the sine, cosine, and tangent of an angle, as the angle varies from 0 to 2π.

2. Show that $\cot(\pi + a) = \cot a$;
also that $\csc(\pi + a) = -\csc a$.

3. Express the sine of an angle in terms of the cosine; the tangent in terms of the sine and cosine. Express, also, three of the six trigonometrical functions as reciprocals of three others.

4. Name all positive angles between 0 and 4π whose tangent is -1. How many other angles have this tangent?

5. Derive an expression for $\operatorname{cosec} a$ in terms of $\tan a$.

6. Deduce the formula
$$\cos x - \cos y = -2 \sin \tfrac{1}{2}(x+y) \sin \tfrac{1}{2}(x-y).$$

7. Compute A and B by the formula,
$$\tan\tfrac{1}{2}(A-B) = \frac{a-b}{a+b}\tan\tfrac{1}{2}(A+B),$$
having given $A+B = 120°$, $a = 3467.5$, $b = 3456.7$. Of what use is this formula in Trigonometry?

ENGLISH GRAMMAR.
June, 1887.

[State what text-book you have studied.]

1. Parse the words in the following sentence: —

This person was the man whose conduct brought shame to all his countrymen.

2. Inflect the present and preterite tenses of the verb *to be*.

3. State the distinction between the old (or strong) and the weak (or new) conjugation of the English verb, and illustrate by three examples of each.

CAESAR.
June, 1887

I. TRANSLATE as literally as possible: —

1. Caesari quum id nuntiatum esset, eos per provinciam nostram iter *facere* conari, maturat ab urbe *proficisci*, et,

quam maximis potest itineribus, in Galliam ulteriorem contendit et ad Genevam pervenit. *Provinciae toti* quam maximum potest militum numerum imperat (erat omnino in Gallia ulteriore legio una) ; pontem, qui erat ad Genevam, jubet rescindi.

2. Horum adventu tanta rerum commutatio est facta, ut nostri, etiam qui *vulneribus* confecti procubuissent, *scutis* innixi proelium redintegrarent; tum calones, perterritos hostes conspicati, etiam inermes *armatis* occurrerent ; equites vero, ut turpitudinem fugae virtute delerent, omnibus in locis pugnae se legionariis militibus praeferrent.

3. *Pugnatum* est diu atque acriter, quum Sontiates superioribus *victoriis* freti in sua virtute totius Aquitaniae salutem positam putarent, nostri autem, *quid* sine imperatore et sine reliquis legionibus, adolescentulo duce, efficere possent, perspici cuperent: tandem confecti vulneribus hostes terga vertere.

4. Ita mobilitatem equitum, stabilitatem peditum in proeliis *praestant*, ac tantum usu quotidiano et exercitatione *efficiunt*, uti in declivi ac praecipiti loco incitatos equos *sustinere*, et brevi moderari ac *flectere*, et per temonem *percurrere*, et in jugo insistere et se inde in currus citissime recipere *consuerint*.

5. Tandem dat Cotta permotus manus ; *superat* sententia Sabini. Pronuntiatur prima luce ituros ; *consumitur* vigiliis reliqua pars noctis, quum sua quisque miles circumspiceret, quid secum portare posset, quid ex instrumento hibernorum relinquere *cogeretur*. Omnia excogitantur, quare nec sine periculo *maneatur* et languore militum et vigiliis periculum *augeatur*.

6. Quum superaverunt, animalia capta immolant; reliquas res in unum locum *conferunt*. Multis in civitatibus harum rerum exstructos tumulos locis consecratis conspicari licet;

neque saepe *accidit*, ut, neglecta quispiam religione, aut capta apud se occultare aut posita tollere *auderet;* gravissimumque ei rei supplicium cum cruciatu constitutum est.

II. GRAMMATICAL QUESTIONS, supplementary to the paper on Latin Grammar : —

1. State the construction of all italicized words in passages 1, 2, and 3.

2. Give the principal parts of all italicized words in passages 4, 5, and 6.

3. Quote in full from the above text an example of indirect statement and rewrite it so as to make it direct.

September, 1887.

I. TRANSLATE as literally as possible : —

1. Hic pagus unus, quum *domo* exisset patrum nostrorum *memoria*, Lucium Cassium *consulem* interfecerat et ejus exercitum sub jugum miserat. Ita, sive casu, sive consilio deorum immortalium, *quae* pars civitatis Helvetiae insignem calamitatem *populo* Romano intulerat, ea princeps poenas persolvit.

2. De numero eorum omnia se habere *explorata* Remi dicebant, propterea quod *propinquitatibus* affinitatibusque conjuncti, quantam quisque multitudinem in communi Belgarum concilio ad id bellum pollicitus sit, cognoverint. *Plurimum* inter eos Bellovacos et *virtute* et auctoritate et hominum numero valere; hos posse conficere armata milia centum.

3. Ad *quarum* initium silvarum quum Caesar pervenisset castraque munire instituisset, neque hostis interim visus esset, dispersis in opere nostris, subito ex omnibus partibus silvae evolaverunt et in *nostros* impetum fecerunt. Nostri celeriter arma ceperunt eosque in silvas repulerunt, et compluribus interfectis, longius impeditioribus *locis* secuti paucos ex suis deperdiderunt.

4. "*Desilite*," inquit, "commilitones, nisi vultis aquilam hostibus *prodere:* ego certe meum rei publicae atque imperatori officium *praestitero.*" Hoc quum magna voce dixisset, se ex navi *projecit* atque in hostes aquilam ferre *coepit.* Tum nostri cohortati inter se, ne tantum dedecus admitteretur, universi ex navi desiluerunt.

5. Itaque ex legionibus fabros *deligit* et ex continenti alios *arcessi* jubet; Labieno *scribit*, ut quam plurimas posset, iis legionibus quae sunt apud cum, naves *instituat.* Ipse, etsi res erat multae operae ac laboris, tamen commodissimum esse statuit omnes naves subduci et cum castris una munitione *conjungi.*

6. XXIX. Caesar, postquam per Ubios exploratores *comperit* Suevos sese in silvas recepisse, inopiam frumenti *veritus*, constituit non *progredi* longius; sed ne omnino metum reditus sui barbaris *tolleret* atque ut eorum auxilia *tardaret*, reducto exercitu, partem ultimam pontis *rescindit.*

II. GRAMMATICAL QUESTIONS, supplementary to the paper on Latin Grammar:—

1. State the construction of all italicized words in passages 1, 2, and 3.

2. Give the principal parts of all italicized words in passages 4, 5, and 6.

3. Quote in full from the above text an example of indirect statement and rewrite it so as to make it direct.

LATIN.
[Exercises and Grammar.]
June, 1887.

I. TRANSLATE INTO LATIN:—

1. The Belgae[1] inhabit[2] one[3] part[4] of Gaul.

2. One part of Gaul is inhabited by the Belgae.

3. Those, who inhabit the third[5] part of Gaul, were called[6] Celts.[7]

4. Caesar says (that) the Celts inhabit the third part of Gaul.

5. Rewrite sentence 4, and substitute direct for indirect statement.

6. Caesar said (that) the Gauls inhabited the third part of Gaul.

7. Rewrite sentence 6, and substitute direct for indirect statement.

8. Caesar says (that) the Helvetians[8] surpass[9] the-rest-of-the[10] Gauls[11] in bravery.[12]

9. Caesar said (that) the Helvetians surpassed the other Gauls in bravery.

10. Rewrite sentence 9, and substitute direct for indirect statement.

II. LATIN GRAMMAR.

1. Decline *urbs, iter, ulterior, castra.*

2. Decline *id, ego, aliquis.*

3. Compare *ulterior, parvus, dives.*

4. Write the synopsis, active and passive, of *monēre* and *audīre.*

5. Enumerate all the uses you know of the genitive case.

[1] Belgae (*pl.*).
[2] incolĕre.
[3] unus.
[4] pars.
[5] tertius.
[6] appellāre.
[7] Celtae (*pl.*).
[8] Helvetius.
[9] Praecedĕre — [*governs accusative*].
[10] reliqui (*pl.*).
[11] Gallus.
[12] virtus.

LATIN.

September, 1887.

I. TRANSLATE INTO LATIN:—

1. The ancient[1] Germans[2] used-to-value[3] highly[4] the advice[5] of women[6].

2. The advice of women used-to-be-valued highly by the ancient Germans.

3. The Germans do not value advice highly.

4. Advice is not valued highly by the Germans.

5. Tacitus[7] says[8] the Germans value advice highly.

6. Rewrite sentence 5 and substitute direct for indirect statement.

7. Tacitus says the ancient Germans valued highly the advice of women.

8. Tacitus said the ancient Germans valued highly the advice of women.

9. The Germans never[9] despised[10] the answers of women.

10. It is declared (that) the Germans never despised the answers of women.

II. LATIN GRAMMAR.

1. Decline *domus, consul, exercitus*.

2. Decline *hic, qui, ea*.

3. Compare *juvenis, pessimus, major*.

4. Write the synopsis, active and passive, of *docēre (docui, doctum)*, and *capĕre (cepi, captum)*.

5. Enumerate all the uses you know of the dative case.

[1] vetus.
[2] Germani.
[3] aestimare.
[4] magni.
[5] consilium.
[6] femina.
[7] Tacitus.
[8] dicĕre.
[9] nunquam.
[10] spernere (sprevi, spretum).

HISTORY OF THE UNITED STATES.
July, 1887.

1. Give the dates of the following events: Raleigh's first colony, the persecutions for witchcraft at Salem, Braddock's defeat, the Stamp Act, the presidential terms of Jefferson, John Quincy Adams, Polk, and Johnson.

2. Give an account of the London and Plymouth companies.

3. What treaty ended the Revolutionary War, and what were its terms?

4. Give an account of the Hartford Convention.

5. What were the principles of Free Soil party, and who were its presidential candidates in 1848?

6. Describe the plan of reconstruction as carried out by Congress after the Civil War.

[N. B.—The dates are to be given with every question.]

September, 1887.

1. Give an account of the settlement and government of North and South Carolina.

2. Describe the first Continental Congress, and the acts of Great Britain that brought it about.

3. Give the leading events of Washington's administration.

4. What was the doctrine of State Sovereignty, and on what occasions has it been asserted in our history?

5. Who were the presidential candidates in 1860, and what parties did they represent?

6. Give the dates of the beginning and end of the three principal wars of the United States during the past 100 years.

[N. B.—The dates are to be given with every question.]

GEOGRAPHY.

July, 1887.

1. Bound the State of Missouri, give the position of its greatest city, and name two rivers in the State or on its borders.

2. Where does the river Rhine rise, what direction does it run, where does it empty, and what countries does it run through or touch, in their order, from its head to its mouth?

3. Describe the Gulf of Mexico, what countries touch it, what are the chief rivers which empty into it, what are its chief seaports.

4. Where are the following cities: Atlanta, Geneva, Havre, Hamburgh, Helena, Honolulu?

5. Bound Brazil, what is its form of government, describe two rivers in it, and give the names and positions of two cities in it.

6. What is the torrid zone, and how many English miles wide is it?

7. What are the East Indian Islands? Give the names of such of them as you can, with the position and description of each.

September, 1887.

1. Bound the State of Pennsylvania, what mountains cross the State, what is the largest city in the State west of the mountains and how is it situated, and what is the largest city in the State east of the mountains, and how is it situated?

2. Where does the river Danube rise, what direction does it run, where does it empty, and what countries does it run through or touch, in their order, from its head to its mouth?

3. Describe the Bay of Bengal, what countries touch it, what are the chief rivers which empty into it, and what are its chief seaports?

4. Where are the following cities: Auckland, Madrid, Mobile, Moscow, Chattanooga, Naples?

5. Bound Spain, what is its form of government, name some river in it, and give the name and situation of some city in it.

6. What is the North Frigid (or North Polar) zone, and how many English miles wide is it?

7. Where are the West Indian Islands, give the names of such of them as you can, with the position and description of each.

COLLEGE OF NEW JERSEY, PRINCETON.

ACADEMIC DEPARTMENT.

June, 1887.

ENGLISH.

I.

ENGLISH GRAMMAR.

1. Define the following terms — grammar, clause, adjunct, antecedent, participle, syntax, etymology.

2. State why the *place* of the word in the sentence is so important in English. Compare English and Latin in this respect.

3. State some of the more important rules of Spelling and Punctuation.

4. Give examples of verbal and abstract nouns; of relative, possessive, and adjective pronouns; of participial, pronominal, and numeral adjectives, and compare the adjectives — evil, far, hind, fore.

5. Write the plurals for the following nouns, and give reasons for the respective forms — sky, valley, motto, wharf, penny, summons, father-in-law, man-servant, attorney-general, index, thesis, seraph.

6. Mention the different classes of English Verbs and give the chief parts of — befall, blow, clothe, cost, prove, shear, slit, wed. Give a synopsis of the verb — Be.

7. State the uses of the different moods and tenses and indicate the *parts of speech* of the respective words and phrases in italics.

> *Such as* I have.
> *Whoever* he *himself* was.
> *One* and *another*.
> The *English* flag.
> There were *four* present.
> *Provided* he will do it.
> He is *that* he claims to be.
> I must *needs* do it.

8. Explain the grammatical correctness of the expressions in italics.

> The Notary *Public's* house.
> It was *they* who went.
> Of two evils, choose the *lesser*.
> Each one *has his* faults.
> The bridge is *building*.

9. Give the grammatical analysis of the following quotation.

> " Up from the meadows rich with corn,
> Clear in the cool September morn;
> The clustered spires of Frederick stand,
> Green-walled by the hills of Maryland."
> WHITTIER.

II.

UNITED STATES HISTORY.

1. Give a brief account of the explorations and discoveries from 1492–1607.

2. State some facts as to the following events in the Colonial Period: —

Settlement of Virginia.
Voyage and Settlement of the Pilgrims.
Founding of Harvard College.

3. Mention the thirteen original colonies and the origin of their respective names.

4. In the Revolutionary Period, explain the following acts and events: —
The Navigation Act.
Invasion of Canada.
Taking of Ticonderoga.
Adoption of the Constitution.
Battle of Saratoga.

5. Compare Jefferson's first and second administrations.

6. Mention those Presidents whose respective terms of office have been over four years.

7. Give date and place of some of the more important battles of the Civil War.

8. Mention the respective dates of the following: —
Repeal of the Stamp Act.
Execution of André.
Ratification of Articles of Confederation.
Ratification of the Constitution.
Death of Washington.
War with Mexico.
Emancipation Proclamation.
Impeachment of Andrew Johnson.

9. Give a brief account of the geographical growth of the country and of its industrial and educational progress.

III.

A short essay may be written on any one of the following themes: —

Sir Walter Scott as an Author.
Personal character of Scott.
Sketch of Life of Benjamin Franklin.
Franklin's Scientific Work.

[N. B.—Applicants will state what authors they have studied in United States History and English Grammar.]

GREEK.

[N.B.—State at the head of your paper what Greek you have studied, how long, and at what school; and if the examination is a partial one, the subjects you offer. Write Greek with the accents.]

GRAMMAR.

[For all candidates, except such as have previously passed Grammar in full.]

1. State the gender and inflect the singular of νῆσος, τεῖχος, δόξα; the plural of ἀνήρ, πούς, μείζων.

2. Compare αἰσχρός, ἡδύς, and form adverbs from them in each degree of comparison.

Give adverbs for *twice, four times, often.*

3. Give principal parts of διδάσκω, τάττω, μανθάνω, ὁράω.

Inflect the first aorist indicative middle of σκέπτομαι; the perfect indicative passive of τάττω.

Give the imperative (second singular only), the infinitive, and the participle (nominative masculine) corresponding to these forms in tense and voice: ἤγαγον, ἤχθην, οἶδα, φημί, ἐάω, ἐθυσάμην, δέδογμαι.

4. What case is used for the time at which? for the time within which? What is the case for the crime with verbs of judicial action? What case or cases belong with ἕπομαι, πίμπλημι, κατάρχω, διδάσκω, μεταδίδωμι? with πρό, ἅμα, ἕνεκα, σύν, διά?

5. *If he heard, he obeyed; if he had heard, he would have obeyed:* how do these differ, and by what moods and tenses is each to be expressed?

ANABASIS.

[N.B.—Passages B and C are for those taking preliminary examination in three books. All others do A only; but if you cannot, then do both B and C.]

A.

Ἐντεῦθεν ἔπεμψαν τῆς νυκτὸς Δημοκράτην Τεμενίτην, ἄνδρας δόντες, ἐπὶ τὰ ὄρη ἔνθα ἔφασαν οἱ ἀποσκεδαννύμενοι καθορᾶν τὰ πυρά· οὗτος γὰρ ἐδόκει καὶ πρότερον πολλὰ ἤδη ἀληθεῦσαι τοιαῦτα, τὰ ὄντα τε ὡς ὄντα καὶ τὰ μὴ ὄντα ὡς οὐκ ὄντα. πορευθεὶς δὲ τὰ μὲν πυρὰ οὐκ ἔφη ἰδεῖν, ἄνδρα δὲ συλλαβὼν ἧκεν ἄγων ἔχοντα τόξον Περσικὸν καὶ παρέτραν καὶ σάγαριν οἵανπερ καὶ αἱ Ἀμαζόνες ἔχουσιν. ἐρωτώμενος δὲ ποδαπὸς εἴη, Πέρσης μὲν ἔφη εἶναι, πορεύεσθαι δ' ἀπὸ τοῦ Τηριβάζου στρατεύματος, ὅπως ἐπιτήδεια λάβοι. οἱ δὲ ἠρώτων αὐτὸν τὸ στράτευμα ὁπόσον τε εἴη καὶ ἐπὶ τίνι συνειλεγμένον. ὁ δὲ εἶπεν ὅτι Τηρίβαζος εἴη ἔχων τήν τε ἑαυτοῦ δύναμιν καὶ μισθοφόρους Χάλυβας καὶ Τάοχους· παρεσκευάσθαι δὲ αὐτὸν ἔφη ὡς ἐπὶ τῇ ὑπερβολῇ τοῦ ὄρους ἐν τοῖς στενοῖς, ᾗπερ μοναχῇ εἴη πορεία, ἐνταῦθα ἐπιθησόμενον τοῖς Ἕλλησιν. -

Give reason for mood of εἴη (line 7), λάβοι. Where is ἠρώτων παρεσκευάσθα? Force of participle ἐπιθησόμενον?

[Omit B and C, if you have done the preceding. (See note.)]

B.

Σωτηρίδας δὲ ὁ Σικυώνιος εἶπεν· Οὐκ ἐξ ἴσου, ὦ Ξενοφῶν, ἐσμέν· σὺ μὲν γὰρ ἐφ' ἵππου ὀχῇ, ἐγὼ δὲ χαλεπῶς κάμνω τὴν ἀσπίδα φέρων. καὶ ὃς ἀκούσας ταῦτα, καταπηδήσας ἀπὸ τοῦ ἵππου, ὠθεῖται αὐτὸν ἐκ τῆς τάξεως, καὶ τὴν ἀσπίδα ἀφελόμενος ὡς ἐδύνατο τάχιστα ἔχων ἐπορεύετο. ἐτύγχανε δὲ καὶ θώρακα ἔχων τὸν ἱππικόν· ὥστε ἐπιέζετο. καὶ τοῖς μὲν ἔμπροσθεν ὑπάγειν παρεκελεύετο, τοῖς δὲ ὄπισθεν παριέναι μόλις ἑπομένοις. οἱ δ' ἄλλοι στρατιῶται παίουσι καὶ βάλλουσι καὶ λοιδοροῦσι τὸν Σωτηρίδαν, ἔστε ἠνάγκασαν λαβόντα τὴν ἀσπίδα πορεύεσθαι. ὁ δὲ ἀναβάς, ἕως μὲν βάσιμα ἦν, ἐπὶ τοῦ ἵππου ἦγεν· ἐπεὶ δὲ ἄβατα ἦν, καταλιπὼν τὸν ἵππον ἔσπευδε πεζῇ.

ἀφελόμενος : from what, and force of the participle? ἠνάγκησαν, καταλιπὼν ; from what, and where made?

C.

Πορευόμενοι δὲ ἀφίκοντο εἰς κώμας ὅθεν ἀπέδειξαν οἱ ἡγεμόνες λαμβάνειν τὰ ἐπιτήδεια. ἐνῆν δὲ σῖτος καὶ οἶνος φοινίκων πολὺς καὶ ὄξος ἑψητὸν ἀπὸ τῶν αὐτῶν. αὐταὶ δὲ αἱ βάλανοι τῶν φοινίκων, οἵας μὲν ἐν τοῖς Ἕλλησιν ἔστιν ἰδεῖν, τοῖς οἰκέταις ἀπέκειντο· αἱ δὲ τοῖς δεσπόταις ἀποκείμεναι ἦσαν ἀπόλεκτοι, θαυμάσιαι τὸ κάλλος καὶ τὸ μέγεθος· ἡ δὲ ὄψις ἠλέκτρου οὐδὲν διέφερεν· τὰς δέ τινας καὶ ξηραίνοντες τραγήματα ἀπετίθεσαν. καὶ ἦν καὶ παρὰ πότον ἡδὺ μέν, κεφαλαλγὲς δέ.

ἀπέκειντο : from what, and where made? Derive κεφαλαλγὲς.

HOMER.

[Nestor counsels Agamemnon.]

ἀλλά, ἄναξ, αὐτός τ' ἐῢ μήδεο, πείθεό τ' ἄλλῳ·
οὔτοι ἀπόβλητον ἔπος ἔσσεται ὅττι κεν εἴπω·
κρῖν' ἄνδρας κατὰ φῦλα, κατὰ φρήτρας, Ἀγάμεμνον,
ὡς φρήτρη φρήτρηφιν ἀρήγῃ, φῦλα δὲ φύλοις.
εἰ δέ κεν ὣς ἔρξῃς, καί τοι πείθωνται Ἀχαιοί,

GREEK.

γνώσῃ ἔπειθ', ὅς θ' ἡγεμόνων κακός, ὅς τέ νυ λαῶν,
ἠδ' ὅς κ' ἐσθλὸς ἔῃσι· κατὰ σφέας γὰρ μαχέονται·
γνώσεαι δ', ἢ καὶ θεσπεσίῃ πόλιν οὐκ ἀλαπάξεις,
ἢ ἀνδρῶν κακότητι καὶ ἀφραδίῃ πολέμοιο.

[Odysseus arrives at Chryse.]

Αὐτὰρ Ὀδυσσεὺς
ἐς Χρύσην ἵκανεν, ἄγων ἱερὴν ἑκατόμβην.
οἱ δ' ὅτε δὴ λιμένος πολυβενθέος ἐντὸς ἵκοντο,
ἱστία μὲν στείλαντο, θέσαν δ' ἐν νηῒ μελαίνῃ·
ἱστὸν δ' ἱστοδόκῃ πέλασαν, προτόνοισιν ὑφέντες,
καρπαλίμως· τὴν δ' εἰς ὅρμον προέρυσσαν ἐρετμοῖς.
ἐκ δ' εὐνὰς ἔβαλον, κατὰ δὲ πρυμνήσι' ἔδησαν·
ἐκ δὲ καὶ αὐτοὶ βαῖνον ἐπὶ ῥηγμῖνι θαλάσσης·
ἐκ δ' ἑκατόμβην βῆσαν ἑκηβόλῳ Ἀπόλλωνι·
ἐκ δὲ Χρυσηῒς νηός βῆ ποντοπόροιο.

Write quantities and feet of the last three lines. Also write Attic forms for ἔῃσι, γνώσεαι, πολέμοιο.

COMPOSITION.

The king asked how many men, hoplites and horsemen, Proxenus brought with him. A thousand, seven hundred and fifty, was the answer, and if you treat them well, they will fight bravely in your behalf. I would not have persuaded them to march with me, said the King, if I did not intend to reward them well for their services. Have no fear that I shall give them over, or that we shall not conquer. To-morrow we shall march ninety parasangs to a large river, after crossing which we shall come to some villages full of provisions.

Show by a rough map the location of Attica, Athens, Euboea, Thermopylae, Delphi, Olympia, Byzantium, Hellespont, Delos, the Cyclades, Mytilene, Lydia, Crete.

LATIN.

State what Latin authors you have read and how much of each; what work you have done in writing Latin.

Use the right-hand pages only for your answers.

I.

1. Decline *meus, nox, dies, versus, quis, idem.*

2. Compare *superus, facilis, fortiter.*

3. Inflect *capio* in future indicative active and imperfect subjunctive passive. *Teneo* in imperative active and passive. *Nolo* in present indicative. *Eo* in infinitive.

4. Give examples of frequentative or intensive verbs; nouns of agency, and verbal adjectives with a passive significance.

5. Define a deponent, an impersonal, a preteritive verb, and give an example of each with its principal parts.

6. Show by examples four different uses of the ablative case, and two of the subjunctive mood.

II.

Write in Latin: —

1. It is the mark of a wise man to stand firm in adversity.

2. Labienus sent the fourth legion ahead to choose a place for the camp.

3. This I think, that friendship cannot exist except among the good.

4. Cicero was informed what Catiline was doing.

5. We hope to remain four years at Nassau Hall.[1]

[1] Aula Nassovica.

III.

1. Draw a map of Italy showing the divisions by their boundaries, five principal rivers, and eight cities.

2. Show by a diagram the seven hills of Rome, the Forum, Circus, and Campus Martius in their proper relative positions.

IV.

TRANSLATE:—

Sed *quid* ego longinqua commemoro? Fuit hoc quondam, fuit proprium populi Romani longe a domo bellare et propugnaculis imperii sociorum fortunas, non sua tecta *defendere:* sociis ego nostris *mare* per hos annos clausum fuisse dicam, cum exercitus vestri numquam a Brundisio nisi *hieme* summa transmiserint? Qui ad vos ab exteris nationibus venirent, captos *querar*, cum legati populi Romani redempti sint? *Mercatoribus* tutum mare non fuisse dicam cum duodecim secures in praedonum potestatem *pervenerint?*

Quid, mare, hieme, mercatoribus: explain the case of each.

Defendere, querar, pervenerint: explain mood and tense of each.

Or this:—

Atque haec omnia sic agentur, Quirites, ut maximae res minimo *motu*, pericula summa nullo tumultu, bellum intestinum ac domesticum post hominum memoriam crudelissimum et maximum me uno togato *duce* et imperatore *sedetur*. Quod ego sic administrabo, Quirites, ut, si ullo mode *fieri poterit*, ne improbus quidem quisquam in hac urbe poenam sui *sceleris* sufferat.

Motu, duce, sceleris: explain the case of each.

Sedetur, fieri, poterit: explain the mood and tense of each.

V.

TRANSLATE:—

His rebus ita actis, constituta nocte, qua proficiscerentur, Cicero per legatos cuncta edoctus, L. Valerio *Flacco*, et G. Pomptino praetoribus imperat, ut in ponte Mulvio per insidias Allobrogum comitatus *deprehendant;* rem omnem aperit, cujus *gratia* mittebantur, cetera, uti *facto* opus sit, ita agant, permittit. Illi, homines militares, sine tumultu praesidiis collocatis, sicuti praeceptum erat, occulte pontem obsidunt.

Flacco, gratia, facto: explain the case of each.

Deprehendant, sit, agant: explain mood and tense of each.

Or this:—

Haec atque alia hujusce *modi* saepe dicundo Memmius *populo* persuadet, uti L. Cassius, qui tum praetor erat, ad Jugurtham mitteretur cumque interposita fide publica *Romam* duceret, *quo* facilius indicio regis Scauri et reliquorum, quos pecuniae captae arcessebant, delicta patefierent. Dum haec Romae geruntur, qui in Numidia relicti a Bestia exercitui praeerant, secuti morem imperatoris sui plurima et flagitiosissima facinora fecere.

Modi, populo, Romam: explain the case of each.

Patefierent: why subjunctive? *Quo:* why not *ut?*

VI.

TRANSLATE:—

Quibus rebus cognitis, principes Britanniae, qui post proelium ad Caesarem convenerant, inter se collocuti, cum equites et naves et frumentum Romanis deesse intelligerent et paucitatem militum ex castrorum exiguitate cognoscerent, quae hoc erant etiam angustiora quod sine impedimentis Caesar legiones transportaverat, optimum factu esse duxerunt rebellione facta frumento commeatuque nostros prohibere et rem in hiemen producere, quod his superatis aut reditu interclusis neminem postea belli inferendi causa in Britanniam transiturum confidebant. Itaque rursus conjuratione facta paulatim ex castris discedere ac suos clam ex agris deducere coeperunt.

Quibus rebus cognitis: what relation is expressed by this ablative absolute?

Belli inferendi causa: is this gerund or gerundive? Change it from one to the other.

Postea: what kind of adverb?

Rursus: etymology?

VII.

TRANSLATE:—

At vero Aeneas aspectu obmutuit amens,
Arrectaeque horrore comae, et vox faucibus haesit.
Ardet abire fuga dulcesque relinquere terras.
Attonitus tanto montiu imperioque deorum.
Heu quid agat? quo nunc reginam ambire furentemd.
Audeat affatu? quae prima exordia sumat?
Atque animum nunc huc celerum, nunc dividit illuc.
Haec alternati portior sententia visa est:
Mnesthea Sergestumque vocat fortemque Serestum:
Classem aptent taciti, sociosque ad litora cogant,
Arma parent, et quae rebus sit causa novandis,
Dissimulent; sese interea, quando optima Dido
Nesciat, et tantos rumpi non speret amores,
Tentaturum aditus, et quae mollissima fandi
Tempora, quis rebus dexter modus. Ocius omnes
Imperio laeti parent ac jussa facessunt.

Mark the quantities, feet, and caesuras of any five of the foregoing lines.

ALGEBRA.

1. (a) Factor $x^2 - (a+b)x + ab$.
   (b) Factor $c^2 + d^2 - e^2 - f^2 + 2cd + 2ef$.
   (c) Find the greatest common divisor of
   $x^3 - 3x + 2$ and $x^3 + x^2 - 5x + 3$.

2. Divide $\dfrac{\dfrac{a}{c} + \dfrac{b}{d}}{\dfrac{a^2}{c^2} - \dfrac{b^2}{d^2}}$ by $\dfrac{cd}{e+f}$, reducing the quotient to the simplest form possible.

3. Simplify $\left(\dfrac{a^{\frac{1}{2}}b}{c^{-\frac{3}{4}}}\right)^{\frac{1}{3}} \times \left(\dfrac{\sqrt{c}}{e^{\frac{1}{3}}}\right)^{-\frac{1}{2}} \div \left(\dfrac{e}{b}\right)^{\frac{2}{3}}$.

4. Extract the square root of
   $a^2 + 2a^3 + a^4 - 4ba^2 - 4ba + 4b^2$.

5. Solve the equations
   (a) $\dfrac{2x-5}{x+2} = \dfrac{3}{5x}$;
   (b) $x^4 - 2x^3 + x - 2 = 0$; each for x.

6. Solve the equations $\left\{\begin{array}{r} 2x^2 + y^2 = 24 \\ xy = 8 \end{array}\right\}$; for x and y.

   Or, $\left\{\begin{array}{l} (x+1)(y-2) + (x+1)^2 = 2; \\ (y-2)^2 + 3(x+1)(y-2) = 4. \end{array}\right.$

7. A certain number of two digits is equal to twice the sum of its digits. The number got by interchanging the digits is equal to the square of the sum of the digits. Find the number.

ARITHMETIC.

1. Add $\frac{4}{5}$, $2\frac{5}{6}$, $\frac{7}{8}$, and $\frac{11}{12}$. Divide the sum by fifty-six thousandths.

2. $\dfrac{\frac{36}{51}}{\frac{3}{17}} + \dfrac{5.62}{33} - \dfrac{7\frac{1}{3}}{27} = ?$

3. What is the square root of 132.4801?

4. A put $780 in the bank, which was 15 per cent of all his money. He afterwards deposited 25 per cent of the remainder of his money. How much money has he then in the bank, and what per cent is this of all his money?

5. At what rate will $240 in 5 yrs. 4 mos. give $64 interest? What will be the interest on the same amount for the same time at 7 per cent?

6. How many cubic millimeters are in a cubic dekameter? How much will a cubic hektometer of water weigh in kilograms? Express the same quantity of water in liters.

GEOMETRY.

1. Give the construction for drawing a triangle when the three sides are given. When will it be scalene? When isosceles? What relation exists between the sides when it is right-angled?

2. If two triangles have two sides of the one equal to two sides of the other, each to each, but the angle contained by the two sides of the one greater than the angle contained by the two sides equal to them, of the other, the base of that which has the greater angle shall be greater than the base of the other.

3. Two triangles are equal in all respects when a side and two adjacent angles of the one are respectively equal to a side and two adjacent angles of the other. If two triangles have two sides and an angle of one respectively equal to two sides and the corresponding angle of the other, what theorem is true if the equal angles are the included angles? What if the equal angles are not the included angles?

4. Define parallelogram. Show that a quadrilateral is a parallelogram: (*a*) if its opposite sides are equal; (*b*) if its opposite angles are equal; (*c*) if one pair of its opposite sides are equal and parallel; (*d*) if its diagonals bisect each other.

5. Prove by use of a figure that if a straight line be divided into two equal and also into two unequal segments, the rectangle contained by the unequal segments, together with the square on the line between the points of section, is equal to the square on half the line.

[Equivalent statement: The rectangle of the sum and the difference of two lines is equal to the difference of the squares described on those straight lines.]

6. Give the construction for dividing a line into two parts, so that the rectangle contained by the whole and one of the parts may be equal to the square on the other part.

GREEK.

September, 1887.

[NOTE. — Write on first page (1) your name, (2) at what school prepared, (3) just what Greek you have studied and how long; and (4) if your examination is to be on a part of the Greek, state how much you offer.]

GREEK.

GRAMMAR

[For all candidates except those who have a certificate that they have passed Grammar in full.
Write with the accents.]

1. Decline in singular εἶδος, ἅμαξα, νύξ; in plural, ὄνομα, ἱππεύς, οὗτος.

2. Compare μάλα, καλός, πολύς. Form an adverb from the present participle of διαφέρω.

3. Give principal parts of στέλλω, τυγχάνω, δείκνυμι, ὁράω.
Give the infinitive and participle in the same tense and voice for each of these: ἤγαγον, μείναιμι, ἔστην, εἶμι, εἰμί, ἔλθω, ἐρράγην.
Inflect the aorist indicative middle of βάλλω, the perfect indicative passive of δοκέω, and the aorist optative passive of τάττω.

4. What case or cases follow πείθω, πείθομαι, ἄρχω, πίμπλημι, ἐλέγχω (convict)? ἄνευ, διά, περί, σύν, ὁμοῦ?

5. State how the verbal in -τέος is used. Give the rule for moods in fearing clauses. Explain when the optative is used for indirect discourse, and when its use would be wrong.

Put into Greek: —

This large river which flows by the wall runs through the middle of Lydia and empties into the sea. Cyrus once with four hundred of his bravest hoplites crossed the river in the night and attacked the city. They fought all day, but at nightfall Cyrus, fearing the coming of the enemy's cavalry, withdrew. Had he succeeded in taking the city, he would have destroyed it houses and all and put the inhabitants to the sword.

GEOGRAPHY. — Draw a rough map, and locate the following: Mt. Olympus, Thessaly, Messenia, Thebes, Corinth, Athens, Abydos, Ephesus, Rhodes, Corcyra.

For all candidates.

Ἔρχεται δὲ Μιθριδάτης σὺν ἱππεῦσιν ὡς τριάκοντα, καὶ καλεσάμενος τοὺς στρατηγοὺς εἰς ἐπήκοον λέγει ὧδε· Ἐγώ, ὦ ἄνδρες, καὶ Κύρῳ πιστὸς ἦν, ὡς ὑμεῖς ἐπίστασθε, καὶ νῦν ὑμῖν εὔνους· καὶ ἐνθάδε δ' εἰμὶ σὺν πολλῷ φόβῳ διάλων. εἰ οὖν ὁρῴην ὑμᾶς σωτήριόν τι βουλευομένους, ἔλθοιμι ἂν πρὸς ὑμᾶς καὶ τοὺς θεράποντας πάντας ἔχων. λέξατε οὖν πρός με, τί ἐν νῷ ἔχετε, ὡς φίλον τε καὶ εὔνουν καὶ βουλόμενον κοινῇ σὺν ὑμῖν τὸν στόλον ποιεῖσθαι. βουλευομένοις τοῖς στρατηγοῖς ἔδοξεν ἀποκρίνασθαι τάδε· καὶ ἔλεγε Χειρίσοφος· Ἡμῖν δοκεῖ, εἰ μέν τις ἐᾷ ἡμᾶς ἀπιέναι οἴκαδε, διαπορεύεσθαι τὴν χώραν ὡς ἂν δυνώμεθα ἀσινέστατα· ἢν δέ τις ἡμᾶς τῆς ὁδοῦ ἀποκωγύῃ, διαπολεμεῖν τούτῳ ὡς ἂν δυνώμεθα κράτιστα. ἐκ τούτου ἐπειρᾶτο Μιθριδάτης διδάσκειν ὡς ἄπορον εἴη βασιλέως ἄκοντος σωθῆναι. ἔνθα δὴ ἐγιγνώσκετο ὅτι ὑπόπεμπτος εἴη· καὶ γὰρ τῶν Τισσαφέρνους τις οἰκείων παρηκολούθει πίστεως ἕνεκα.

This passage is also for all except those taking a preliminary examination in three books only: —

Πορευομένων δὲ Χειρίσοφος μὲν ἀμφὶ κνέφας πρὸς κώμην ἀφικνεῖται καὶ ὑδροφορούσας ἐκ τῆς κώμης πρὸς τῇ κρήνῃ γυναῖκας καὶ κόρας καταλαμβάνει ἔμπροσθεν τοῦ ἐρύματος. αὗται ἠρώτων αὐτοὺς τίνες εἶεν. ὁ δ' ἑρμηνεὺς εἶπε περσιστὶ ὅτι παρὰ βασιλέως πορεύονται πρὸς τὸν σατράπην. αἱ δὲ ἀπεκρίναντο ὅτι οὐκ ἐνταῦθα εἴη, ἀλλ' ἀπέχοι ὅσον παρασάγγην. οἱ δ', ἐπεὶ ὀψὲ ἦν, πρὸς τὸν κωμάρχην συνεισέρχονται εἰς τὸ ἔρυμα σὺν ταῖς ὑδροφόδοις. Χειρίσοφος μὲν οὖν καὶ ὅσοι ἐδυνήθησαν τοῦ στρατεύματος ἐνταῦθα ἐστρατοπεδεύσοντο, τῶν δ᾽ ἄλλων στρατιωτῶν οἱ μὴ δυνάμενοι διατελέσαι τὴν ὁδὸν ἐνυκτέρευσαν ἄσιτοι καὶ ἄνευ πυρός· καὶ ἐνταῦθά τινες ἀπώλοντο τῶν στρατιωτῶν.

ILIAD.

Τὸν δ᾽ ἠμείβετ᾽ ἔπειτα Θέτις κατὰ δάκρυ χέουσα·
ὤ μοι, τέκνον ἐμόν, τί νύ σ᾽ ἔτρεφον, αἰνὰ τεκοῦσα;
αἴθ᾽ ὄφελες παρὰ νηυσὶν ἀδάκρυτος καὶ ἀπήμων
ἦσθαι· ἐπεί νύ τοι αἶσα μίνυνθά περ, οὔ τι μάλα δήν·
νῦν δ᾽ ἅμα τ᾽ ὠκύμορος καὶ ὀϊζυρὸς περὶ πάντων
ἔπλεο· τῷ σε κακῇ αἴσῃ τέκον ἐν μεγάροισιν.

Ἔνθα κεν Ἀργείοισιν ὑπέρμορα νόστος ἐτύχθη,
εἰ μὴ Ἀθηναίην Ἥρη πρὸς μῦθον ἔειπεν·
Ὦ πόποι, αἰγιόχοιο Διὸς τέκος, ἀτρυτώνη,
οὕτω δὴ οἰκόνδε, φίλην ἐς πατρίδα γαῖαν,
Ἀργεῖοι φεύξονται ἐφ᾽ εὐρέα νῶτα θαλάσσης;
κὰδ δέ κεν εὐχωλὴν Πριάμῳ καὶ Τρωσὶ λίποιεν
Ἀργείην Ἑλένην, ἧς εἵνεκα πολλοὶ Ἀχαιῶν
ἐν Τροίῃ ἀπόλοντο φίλης ἀπὸ πατρίδος αἴης;
ἀλλ᾽ ἴθι νῦν κατὰ λαὸν Ἀχαιῶν χαλκοχιτώνων·
σοῖς ἀγανοῖς ἐπέεσσιν ἐρήτυε φῶτα ἕκαστον.
μηδὲ ἔα νῆας ἅλαδ᾽ ἑλκέμεν ἀμφιελίσσας.

Mark the scanning of the last two lines.

September, 1887.

ARITHMETIC.

1. Add $\frac{\frac{4}{5}}{\frac{6}{7}}$ and $\frac{34}{60}$.

2. Simplify $\dfrac{0.005}{25} + \dfrac{0.6}{0.002}$, expressing the result in decimal form.

3. Extract the square root of 15227.56.

4. A railroad train makes a mile in 57 seconds. What is its rate per hour, and what per cent of the hour is occupied in its making a single mile?

5. What is the interest on $850 for 2 yrs. 5 mos. 20 dys. at 4 per cent? How long must $360 be at interest at 6 per cent to amount to $386.70?

6. Give the English equivalents of the meter and the gram. Required the weight in centigrams of water in a vessel $1^m\ 2^{cm}$ long, 6^{dm} broad, $5^{dm}\ 1^{mm}$ deep.

ALGEBRA.

1. (*a*) Factor $n^2 - n - 2$.
   (*b*) Factor $27a^3 + b^6$.
   (*c*) Find the least common multiple of
   $6x^2 + 13x - 28$ and $12x^2 - 31x + 20$.

2. From the sum of $\dfrac{a}{bc}$, $\dfrac{b}{ca}$, $\dfrac{c}{ab}$ subtract $2\left(\dfrac{1}{a} + \dfrac{1}{b} - \dfrac{1}{c}\right)$, reducing the result to its simplest form.

3. (a) Divide $\sqrt{\frac{1}{2}}$ by $\sqrt{\frac{1}{3}}$.

   (b) Simplify $(a^{z-3})^z \div \left(\dfrac{\sqrt[8]{b}}{a}\right)^{z+1}$.

4. Solve the following equations, each for x:

   (a) $\sqrt[3]{x^3 - 3x^2 + 1} = x$.

   (b) $\dfrac{x+3}{x+2} + \dfrac{x-1}{x+1} = \dfrac{2x-3}{x-1}$.

5. Solve the following for x and y:

   (a) $x^2 + xy - 2y^2 = 7$;
   $x^2 - 9y^2 = 27$.

   (b) $(x-2y)^2 + 3(x-2y) + 2 = 0$;
   $x^2 - 2xy - 3x + 6y = 1$.

6. Find three numbers of which the first is greater than the second by as many units as the second is greater than the third: the sum of the squares of the three being 66.

EUCLID.

1. Construct a triangle, having given

   (a) the three sides,
   (b) two angles and a side,
   (c) two sides and an angle.

2. If from the ends of a side of a triangle there be drawn straight lines to a point within the triangle, these shall be less than the other two sides of the triangle. Demonstrate this theorem and by its aid prove that three straight lines drawn to connect any point within a triangle with its angular points are together less than the sum of its sides.

3. The opposite sides and angles of a parallelogram are equal to one another. Furthermore, each diagonal bisects the parallelogram and the other diagonal.

4. Parallelograms on the same base and between the same parallels are equivalent. Demonstrate, and state the converse theorems.

5. Show how to construct a square which shall be equivalent to a given rectilineal figure.

6. In any triangle the square on the side opposite an acute angle is less the sum of the squares on the other two sides by twice the rectangle contained by either of those sides and the projection of the other upon it.

JOHN C. GREEN SCHOOL OF SCIENCE (PRINCETON).

June, 1887.

LATIN.

[The paper in English is the same as for admission to the Academic Department.]

I. GRAMMAR.

1. When is the ablative case used in Latin?

2. Give the perfect indicative, the infinite and the supine or participle of *sentio, teneo, audeo, augeo, capio, cupio, quaero, queror, nolo, peto.*

3. Parse the following sentence : Convocatis Aeduum principibus, graviter eos accusat quod ab iis non sublevetur.

II. RETRANSLATE INTO LATIN :—

1. Ambassadors came from the Aedui to Caesar.

2. He hastens to set out from the city and arrives at Geneva.

3. The Helvetii endeavor to make their march through the territories of the Sequani.

4. On the next day they move their camp from that place.

III. TRANSLATE INTO ENGLISH :—

1. Intelligere sese, tametsi pro veteribus Helvetiorum injuriis populi Romani ab his poenas bello repetisset, tamen eam rem non minus ex usu terrae Galliae quam populi Romani accidisse, propterea quod eo consilio florentissimis rebus

domos suas Helvetii reliquissent, uti toti Galliae bellum inferrent imperioque potirentur locumque domicilio ex magna copia deligerent, quem ex omni Gallia opportunissimum judicassent, reliquasque civitates stipendiarias haberent.

2. Adjuvabat etiam eorum consilium qui rem deferebant, quod Nervii antiquitus, quum equitatu nihil possent (neque enim ad hoc tempus ei rei student, sed quidquid possunt, pedestribus valent copiis) quo facilius finitimorum equitatum, si praedandi causa ad eos venissent impedirent, teneris arboribus incisis atque inflexis crebris in latitudinem ramis enatis et rubis sentibusque interjectis effecerant ut instar muri hae sepes munimentum praeberent, quo non modo intrari, sed ne perspici quidem possent.

3. Hac confirmata opinione timoris idoneum quendam hominem et callidum delegit Gallum ex his quos auxilii causa secum habebat. Huic magnis praemiis pollicitationibusque persuadet uti ad hostes transeat, et quid fieri velit edocet.

4. Quo loco qui celeriter arma capere potuerunt paulisper nostris restiterunt atque inter carros impedimentaque proelium commiserunt; at reliqua multitudo puerorum mulierumque, nam cum omnibus suis domo excesserant Rhenumque transierant, passim fugere coepit; ad quos consectandos Caesar equitatum misit.

5. Dum haec in his locis geruntur, Cassivellaunus ad Cantium, quod esse ad mare supra demonstravimus, quibus regionibus quatuor reges praeerant, nuncios mittit, atque his imperat uti coactis omnibus copiis castra navalia de improviso adoriantur atque oppugnent.

6. Quamquam quid loquor? Te ut ulla res frangat? Tu ut umquam te corrigas? Tu ut ullam fugam meditere? Tu ut exiliam cogites? Utinam tibi istam mentem di immortales dent.

ALGEBRA. 303

7. Sed si, omissis his rebus, quibus nos suppeditamur, eget ille, senatu, equitibus Romanis, urbe, aerario, vectigalibus, cuncta Italia, provinciis omnibus, exteris nationibus, si his rebus omissis causas ipsas, quae inter se confligunt, contendere velimus, ex eo ipso, quam valde illi jaceant, intelligere possumus.

8. Leguntur eadem ratione ad senatum Allobrogum populumque litterae; si quid de his rebus dicere vellet, feci potestatem: atque ille primo quidem negavit; post autem aliquanto, toto jam indicio exposito atque edito, surrexit.

9. Multo vero maxima pars eorum, qui in tabernis sunt, immo vero — id enim potius est dicendum — genus hoc universum amantissimum est otii.

ALGEBRA.

[N. B.—Give the work in full and number your answers to correspond with the questions. This paper may be reckoned as counting two-fifths of the whole Mathematical examination.]

1. State what text-book you have read.

2. Simplify $\dfrac{1}{x + \dfrac{1}{1 + \dfrac{x+1}{3-x}}}$.

3. Simplify $2\sqrt[3]{40} + 3\sqrt[3]{108} + \sqrt[3]{500} - \sqrt[3]{320} - 2\sqrt[3]{1372}$.

4. Solve the equation $4x - \dfrac{14-x}{x-1} = 14$.

5. Find the square root of

$$1 + 4y^{-\frac{1}{2}} - 2y^{-\frac{2}{3}} - 4y^{-1} + 25y^{-\frac{4}{3}} - 24y^{-\frac{5}{3}} + 16y^{-2}.$$

6. Solve the simultaneous equations

$$(a-b)x = (a+b)y;\ x+y=c.$$

7. Solve the simultaneous equations

$$x^2 + xy + y^2 = 52 \; ; \; xy - x^2 = 8.$$

Find all values and indicate which values of x and y belong together.

8. Find two numbers whose sum is 15, and the sum of whose squares is 113.

ARITHMETIC.

[N. B.—Give the work in full and number your answers to correspond with the questions. This paper may be reckoned as counting one-fifth of the whole Mathematical examination.]

1. Express 0.440 as a common fraction in its lowest terms.

2. Add $12\tfrac{1}{12}$, $13\tfrac{5}{16}$, $17\tfrac{2}{9}$, and $\tfrac{19}{144}$.

3. Find the value of $\dfrac{3}{\sqrt{19}-4}$, correct to four places of decimals.

4. In what time will $2275 amount to $2673.125 at 5 per cent simple interest?

5. Find the sum of 1871^{ccm}, 541^{l}, 4.51^{hl}, and give the answer in liters.

6. Find the number of liters in a vat 2^m by 75^{cm} by 50^{cm}. Also find the weight in kilograms of the sulphuric acid, specific gravity 1.84, required to fill it.

GEOMETRY.

[N. B.—Number your answers to correspond with the questions. This paper may be reckoned as counting two-fifths of the whole Mathematical examination.]

1. What text-book have you read?

2. Prove that if two angles have their sides respectively parallel and lying in the same direction they are equal. If two angles have their sides perpendicular each to each, what conclusion follows?

3. Prove that every point in the bisector of an angle is equally distant from the sides of the angle; and every point not in the bisector, but within the angle, is unequally distant from the sides of the angle.

4. Show how to draw a perpendicular to a given line from a given point of the line; also from a given point without the line.

5. Prove that if four quantities are in proportion, they will be in proportion by *division*. What is meant by *division?*

6. Prove that in any triangle, the bisector of an angle divides the opposite side into segments which are proportional to the adjacent sides.

7. State and prove what the area of a parallelogram is equal to. Define a parallelogram. Show how to construct a square equivalent to a given parallelogram.

8. Prove that the side of a regular hexagon is equal to the radius of the circumscribed circle.

9. Prove that of all triangles formed with the same two given sides, that one in which these sides are perpendicular to each other is a maximum.

FRENCH.

1. Put the definite article before *oncle, tante, neveu, homme, parents;* give the four forms for *of the* and *to the* respectively and translate, using the partitive article : *children, good children.*

2. Give the plural of *roi, chapeau, feu,* and the irregular plural forms of *ciel, œil, aïeul.*

3. The feminine form of *actif, blanc, discret, pareil, fou, frais, long, sot, roux, épais.*

4. The irregular comparative of *bon, mauvais, bien, mal;* with the translation of *as great as; greater than.*

5. The cardinal numerals from 10 to 20, and the equivalents of 30, 50, 60, 70, 72, 80, *the first, the third, the ninth;* with the translation of *Louis the Fourteenth; the third of April.*

6. The first person singular of the indicative imperfect, past definite and future of *avoir, être, donner, finir, recevoir, vendre;* the two participles of the same verbs; the complete conjugation of the present indicative and the present subjunctive of *avoir, être, recevoir, tenir.*

7. The two participles, the first person singular of the indicative present and past definite of *courir, croire, coudre, écrire, naître, mouvoir, tenir, savoir;* the first person singular of the future and subjunctive present of *acquérir, aller, faire, pouvoir, savoir, vouloir, venir;* the entire indicative present and subjunctive present of *aller, venir, valoir.*

8. Turn the following passages into English. Whenever you use a freer mode of expression, add the literal one in parenthesis: —

(*a*) Il avait toujours vécu sagement comme vivent les paysans laborieux. Marié à vingt ans, il n'avait aimé qu'une femme dans sa vie, et, depuis son veuvage, il n'avait ri avec aucune autre.

(*b*) Elle habitait une chaumière fort pauvre. Mais c'était une femme d'ordre et de volonté. Sa pauvre maison était propre et bien tenue, et ses vêtements annonçaient le respect de soi-même au milieu de la détresse.

(c) Les paysans ne mangent pas vite, et le petit Pierre avait si grand appétit qu'il se passa bien une heure avant que son père pût songer à se mettre en route.

9. Translate into French: —

(a) I have my brother and my little sister with me. Our parents are in France. We had a letter from our mother yesterday; she says that she likes Paris very much, that she has many good friends there, and that the weather has always been fine. They will return in the fall.

(b) Who is at the door? A beggar (*mendiant*). What does he want? Some money. Don't give him any money, but rather some bread and meat, and ask the cook (*cuisinière*) whether she has a cup of coffee for him. Here is also a pair of warm shoes; it is cold, and they will do him good.

GEOGRAPHY.

1. Name the capitals of the Atlantic border States.

2. What is meant by the water-shed of a continent? Give examples.

3. Show how the coast line of a continent depends upon the forms of relief.

4. Contrast the climate on the north side of the Himalayas with that on the south side.

5. Describe the course of the Kuro Sivo or Japanese current.

September, 1887.
ARITHMETIC.

[N. B. — Give the work in full and number your answers to correspond with the questions. This paper may be reckoned as counting one-fifth of the whole Mathematical examination.]

1. Find the least common multiple of 14, 36, 84, 108, 144.

2. Find the value of $5\frac{3}{4} - 4\frac{1}{7} + \frac{5}{28} - 1\frac{1}{2}$, and express the result in decimals.

3. Find the square root of 22.5 to two decimal places.

4. If 5 per cent be lost by selling an article for $2.47, find the per cent of gain or loss by selling it at $2.99.

5. Find the cube root of 405,224.

6. If a square field contain 10.24 hectares, find the length of its side in meters.

ALGEBRA.

[N. B. — Give the work in full and number your answers to correspond with the questions. This paper may be reckoned as counting two-fifths of the whole Mathematical examination.]

1. State what text-book you have read.

2. Find the prime factors of $(a^2 - b^2 - c^2)^2 - 4b^2c^2$.

3. Find the value of $(\sqrt[12]{32})^{-3}$.

4. Solve the equation $(x^2 - 5x)^2 - 8(x^2 - 5x) = 84$.

5. Find the square root of $x^{\frac{2}{3}} + 9x^2 - 4x + 10x^{\frac{4}{3}} - 12x^{\frac{5}{3}}$.

6. Solve the simultaneous equations

$$ax - by = 0; \quad mx - ny = p.$$

7. Solve the simultaneous equations
$$4x^2 + xy = 6; \quad 3xy + y^2 = 10.$$

8. Find two numbers whose product is 78, such that if one be divided by the other, the quotient is 2, and the remainder 1.

GEOMETRY.

[N. B. — Give the work in full and number your answers to correspond with the questions. This paper may be reckoned as counting two-fifths of the whole Mathematical examination.]

1. State what text-book you have read.

2. Prove that the diagonals of a parallelogram bisect each other.

3. Prove that two parallels intercept equal arcs on the circumference of a circle.

4. Give all the proportions which can be formed from the equation $ab = cd$.

5. Prove that if through a fixed point within a circle any chord is drawn, the product of its two segments has the same value, in whatever direction the chord is drawn (*i.e.* the segments are reciprocally proportional).

6. Show how, upon a given straight line, to construct a polygon similar to a given polygon.

7. Two triangles having an angle of the one equal to an angle of the other, are to each other as the products of the sides including the equal angles. Prove the above.

8. Prove that the circumference of a circle is the limit to which the perimeters of the regular inscribed and circumscribed polygons approach, when the number of their sides is increased indefinitely.

9. Prove that, of all triangles having the same base and equal perimeters, that which is isosceles is the maximum.

COLUMBIA SCHOOL OF MINES.

June, 1887

GEOMETRY.

1. Prove what the area of a rectangle is equal to.

2. Prove that if a straight line divides two sides of a triangle proportionally it is parallel to the third side.

3. Find the side and the altitude of an equilateral triangle in the terms of the radius of the inscribed circle.

4. Prove that if one of two parallels is perpendicular to a plane, the other one is also perpendicular to the same plane.

5. Prove that two rectangular parallelopipedons having a common lower base and incommensurable altitudes are to each other as their altitudes.

6. Find the volume of the frustum of a right triangular pyramid with each side of the lower base 6 feet, and each side of the upper base 4 feet, the altitude being 5 feet.

7. Prove that if a regular semi-polygon is revolved about its axis, the surface generated by the semi-perimeter is equal to the axis multiplied by the circumference of the inscribed circle.

8. The radius of a sphere is 5 feet; how many cubic feet in a spherical segment whose altitude is 7 feet, and the distance of whose lower base from the centre of the sphere is 3 feet?

9. Given the two supplemental spherical triangles ABC and DEF, show what the angle C is measured by.

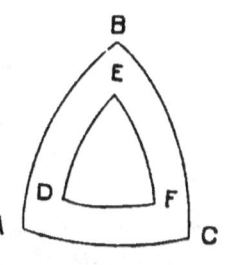

10. Find the volume of a spherical pyramid whose base is a regular spherical octagon, the sum of whose angles is 1140°, and the radius of the sphere is 12 feet.

ALGEBRA.

1. Given $10(x+\frac{1}{2}) - 6x(\frac{1}{x}-\frac{1}{3}) = 23$; find x.

2. Divide the number 1152 into three parts, such that 9 times the sum of the first and second shall be equal to 7 times the sum of the second and third; and if 8 times the first be subtracted from 8 times the second, the remainder shall be equal to the sum of the first and third.

3. $(a^2 + 1 + a^{-2})^3 = ?$ Develop by binomial formula.

4. What is the square root of
$$a^2b^{-2} - 10ab^{-1} - 10a^{-1}b + a^{-2}b^2 + 27?$$

5. Divide $(a^3 - b^4)$ by $(a^{\frac{1}{2}} - b^{\frac{2}{3}})$.

6. Given $x - \sqrt{9 + x\sqrt{x^2-3}} = 3$; find x.

7. Given $x^2 - 2x + 6\sqrt{x^2 - 2x + 5} = 11$; find x.

8. Given $\begin{cases} x^2 + y^2 - x - y = 78 \\ xy + x + y = 39 \end{cases}$; find x and y.

9. In an arithmetical progression $s = -\frac{55}{4}$, $n = 20$, and $a = \frac{1}{2}$; find d.

10. Resolve $\dfrac{2-x}{(x-2)^4}$ into partial fractions, using the principle of indeterminate coefficients.

ENGLISH GRAMMAR.

1. What is a noun?

2. What is a verb?

3. Write the grammatical subject, the logical subject, and the predicate of the sentence: *The black horse run down hill.*

4. Give the different parts of speech in the sentence: *The dogs barked loudly in the distant village.*

5. How many properties have verbs?

6. Name these properties.

Correct any errors found in the following sentences, giving the reason for the correction.

7. Did you suppose it was me?

8. Opportunities of gaining distinction do not now occur so frequent as they did in old times

9. The number of immigrants to this country have not diminished

10. Had your lawyer have looked into this case he would not have lost it.

COMPOSITION AND RHETORIC.

1. Punctuate the following sentence:—
Henry Jones Jr M D L L D came in What do you wish he said

2. Give an example of diæresis.

3. Give some of the principal figures of rhetoric.

4. Define each one given.

5. What is the difference between a simile and a metaphor.

6. What figure of rhetoric is used in the sentence: *The ship's flag shall not be struck.*

7. Define style.

8. Name some of the essential qualities of style.

9. Explain why each of the qualities named is essential.

10. Write in the form of a friendly letter some of the advantages anticipated from a course of study at the School of Mines.

AMERICAN HISTORY.

1. What land did Columbus first discover?

2. Who first discovered the mainland of America?

3. Where did the first English colony find a settlement?

4. Where was the second colony permanently settled?

5. What was the cause of the revolution of the colonies?

6. Why was the Confederation abandoned, and the Federal Constitution adopted?

7. What was the original number of the States, and what is the present number?

8. What caused the war of 1812?

9. Who was President when South Carolina seceded?

10. Give a brief statement of the cause of the war of rebellion, and its most prominent results.

ENGLISH HISTORY.

1. What people occupied England before the Roman Conquest?

2. When and why was the country called England?

3. What was the result of the battle of Hastings?

4. In whose reign was the great charter won?

5. What did the people gain by it?

6. At what period was the Papal power in England set aside?

7. Give a brief account of the Commonwealth.

8. What wars occurred during the reign of George III.?

9. When did Queen Victoria commence her reign?

10. Mention some of the most prominent events that have occurred during her reign.

BOOK-KEEPING.

1. What is book-keeping?

2. What is the distinction between single entry book-keeping and double entry book-keeping?

3. Explain how to record, by single entry, the business transactions of a farmer for a period of one month, such a variety of transactions to be assumed as will illustrate the accounts including the cash accounts.

4. Explain the general system of book-keeping by double entry.

PHYSICS.

1. State the general properties of matter.
2. What is meant by inertia?
3. What is a molecule? An atom?
4. What are the three states of matter?
5. Explain the principle of the artesian well.
6. Explain the term "specific gravity."
7. Give the formula of the pendulum.
8. What is the difference between the Fahrenheit and centigrade thermometers?
9. What is the difference between water at 0° C. and ice at 0° C.?
10. What is meant by "specific heat"?
11. What is the latent heat of water? Of steam?
12. How is sound propagated in air?
13. What is the velocity of sound in air?
14. Describe the properties of a magnet.
15. Give the laws of reflection of light.
16. Explain the action of a prism on light.
17. Describe the astronomical telescope.
18. Give the main facts of frictional electrical induction.
19. Describe some simple form of voltaic battery, and indicate plainly the direction of the positive current in all parts of the circuit.
20. Explain the principle and construction of the galvanometer.

CHEMISTRY.

1. Define matter, element, atom, molecule, mass, atomicity, monad, dyad, triad, allotropic, deliquescent, efflorescent.

2. Give the chemical names for —

H_2O_2 N_2O
O_2 N_2O_5
O_3 HNO_2
CO SO_2
CO_2 H_3PO_4

3. Write the symbols for the following compounds: —

Sodic Chloride,   Silica,
Potassic Chlorate,   Calcic Fluoride,
Ammonic Nitrate,   Potassic Nitrate,
Sulphuretted Hydrogen,   Ferrous Sulphate,
Hydriodic Acid,   Ferric Chloride.

4. Name the non-metallic elements and state where and in what forms each is found in nature.

5. Give the physical and chemical properties of each non-metallic element in the free state.

6. Name the common acids with their formulæ.

PHYSICAL GEOGRAPHY.

1. What is the difference between Geology and Physical Geography?

2. State the form and dimensions of the earth.

3. How are the land masses of the earth divided?

4. What has produced mountain chains?

5. Name the great divisions of the sea.

6. How are lakes formed?

7. Give the general law of climate.

8. Describe the animal and vegetable worlds of the different zones.

9. Where does man appear in his highest physical perfection?

10. What race is regarded as the normal race of the human family?

FRENCH.

I. TRANSLATE the following sentences:—

One is as old as the other.

One is older than the other.

This one is the oldest.

This boy is good, his brother is better, but these two are the best.

II. Give the third person singular (indicative mood), in the present, imperfect, past perfect, and first future tenses of the verb *finir*.

III. Decline (singular and plural):—

   Le cheval. *La table.*

IV. Write out the French cardinal numbers from one to twenty.

V. TRANSLATE the following:—

Peu de temps après les boutons paraissent, puis nous pouvons cueillir de belles fleurs. Les fleurs des arbres fruitiers perdent leurs pétales, nous apercevons de trés petits fruits qui peu à peu mûrissent. Enfin lorsque ces fruits sont mûrs nous les cueillons, comme nous avons cueilli les plus belles fleurs de nos jardins.

Quand l'automme arrive, la couleur des feuilles change encore. Elles étaient vertes au printemps et en été ; en automme elles deviennent jaunes, puis elles tombent et couvrent la terre.

Le mot employé en anglais pour indiquer l'automme, FALL, exprime cette chute des feuilles, qui commence en septembre, et continue jusqu'à l'hiver.

GERMAN.

[Answers may be written in German or in Roman characters.]

I. Decline (singular and plural) the following nouns : —

Der Bruder.   *Die Insel.*   *Das Mädchen.*

II. Name two prepositions which require respectively the gentive, the dative, the accusative case, and give examples.

III. Write out the present, the imperfect, and the first future tenses (indicative mood) of the auxiliary verb *haben*.

IV. Give the present, imperfect, perfect, and pluperfect (indicative mood), first person singular, of the verbs: *reisen, gehen, lachen.*

V. TRANSLATE the following : —

Der Flachs blühte. Er hat schöne, blaue Blumen, die so zart wie die Flügel einer Motte, und noch viel feiner sind ! — Die Sonne beschien den Flachs, und die Regenwolken begossen ihn und das thut ihm ebenso wohl, wie es kleinen Kindern thut, wenn sie gewaschen werden, sie werden ja viel schöner davon und das wurde der Flachs auch.

"Die Leute sagen, dass ich ausgezeichnet gut stehe," sagte der Flachs, "und dass ich schön lang werde, es wird ein prächtiges Stück Leinwand aus mir werden! Wie glücklich bin ich doch! Ich bin gewiss der Glücklichste von Allen! Ich habe es gut, und es wird etwas aus mir werden! Wie der Sonnenschein belebt und wie der Regen schmeckt und erfrischt! Ich bin ganz überglücklich, ich bin der Allerglücklichste!"

September, 1887.

ENGLISH HISTORY.

1. When did Cæsar land in Britain, and when did the Roman legions leave it?

2. Who founded the first English kingdom?

3. Who was the first of the Norman kings?

4. Who carried on the wars of the Roses, and why were they so called?

5. What was the cause of the dispute between Charles I. and Parliament?

6. What was the final result of the battle of Boyne?

7. Who was the first king of the House of Hanover?

8. Who were the Chartists, and what did they want?

9. What was the cause of the Crimean war?

10. Mention some of the events of the reign of Victoria which have been beneficial to the people of England.

AMERICAN HISTORY.

1. Who was the leader of the first settlers in Virginia, and what kind of people were they?

2. Describe the first settlers of Massachusetts.

3. What was the first Indian war the New England settlers engaged in?

4. What was the result in this country of the "Peace of Paris" in 1762?

5. What dispute afterwards arose between England and the American Colonies?

6. When was this dispute settled, and how?

7. What was the cause of the second quarrel with England?

8. In what year was this war begun, and when ended?

9. What caused the Mexican war?

10. At what period of American history could the war of the rebellion been prevented?

PHYSICAL GEOGRAPHY.

1. What forms the subject of geographical science?

2. Give the form and dimensions of the earth.

3. Describe the arrangement of the land masses upon the earth.

4. What contrast is observed in the positions of the Northern and Southern Continents?

5. Describe ocean currents and state their effect.

6. What is the cause, extent, and periods of tides?

7. What is the reason the average temperature is not the same in similar latitudes?

8. What is the mean annual temperature of the temperate zone?

9. What is the most valuable part of America?

10. What are the characteristics of its different sections?

ENGLISH GRAMMAR.

1. Write a simple sentence containing two words.

2. Change the grammatical subject of the above sentence into a logical subject.

3. Modify the principal parts of the sentence by the introduction of other words.

4. To what parts of speech do the modifying words belong?

5. How many parts of speech can be used in a sentence?

6. Name them.

7. Write a sentence containing a verb in the active voice.

8. Write an equivalent sentence with the verb in the passive voice.

9. Give the present tense of a verb in the indicative and subjunctive moods.

10. Correct the errors in the following sentence: —

As I was walking in the woods I met a black and white cow. I asked of the driver if they were both his, and he replied to me "one don't belong to me."

COMPOSITION AND RHETORIC.

1. Give a brief outline of the origin of the English language.

2. In what particular does it surpass other languages?

3. Punctuate this sentence: —
These are the three requirements that you must come every day that you must be punctual every morning and that you must be industrious during working hours

4. Give an illustration of figurative language.

5. Why are rhetorical figures used in composition?

6. Give an example of a simile that is to be avoided, and the objection to its use.

7. Give an illustration of Climax.

8. What is style?

9. What is the most essential property of style in a scientific work?

10. Write a short article on the course of study you intend to pursue.

GERMAN.

[Answers may be written in German or in Roman characters.]

I. Decline (singular and plural): —
    Der Garten.   *Die Herde.*   *Das Feuer.*

II. Translate into German: —
This mountain is high; it is the highest in this range.
The morning was cold, but the evening was colder.
This picture is beautiful, but that of my friend is more beautiful.

III. Decline (singular and plural) the relative pronoun *welcher, welche, welches.*

IV. Write out the present, the imperfect, and the first future (indicative) of the verbs *reisen* and *lesen.*

V. TRANSLATE INTO ENGLISH:—

Obgleich alle Wärme auf der Oberfläche der Erde nur von der Sonne kommt, so hat doch die Erde auch ihre eigenthümliche Wärme, wie aus der Temperaturzunahme folgt, welche man in grossen Tiefen beobachtet hat. Wenn die Wärme nach dem Mittel-punkte der Erde hin auch in grösserer Tiefe noch in dem Maasse zunimmt, welches uns diese Beobachtungen zeigen, so müsste schon in einer Tiefe von 10,000 Fuss die Temperatur des siedenden Wassers herrschen, im Mittel-punkte der Erde aber müssten alle Körper glühend sein und in geschmolzenem Zustande sich befinden.

FRENCH.

I. Write out the *Présent* and the *Imparfait* (*Indicatif*) of *avoir*, and the *Passé Défini* and *Futur* (*Indicatif*) of *être.*

II. How is the plural of adjectives formed in French? Give the plural of the following:—

> grand   heureux   beau   petite.

III. What ending is characteristic of the first, the second, the third, and the fourth conjugation? Name two verbs of each conjugation.

IV. Give the correct article to the following nouns:—

fils	fille	bois	plume	blé
cheval	eau	sel	viande	fourchette

V. TRANSLATE INTO ENGLISH:—

L'Académie Silencieuse. Il y avait à Amadan une célèbre académie, dont le premier statut était conçu en ces termes : *Les académiciens penseront beaucoup, écriront peu, et ne parleront que le moins possible.* On l'appelait *l'Académie silencieuse*, et il n'était point en Perse de vrai savant qui n'eût l'ambition d'y être admis. Le docteur Zeb, auteur d'un petit livre excellent, intitulé le *Bâillon*, apprit au fond de sa province, qu'il vaquait une place dans l'Academie silencieuse. Il part aussitôt ; il arrive à Amadan, et, se présentant à la porte de la salle où les académiciens sont assemblés, il prie l'huissier de remettre au président ce billet : Le docteur Zeb demande humblement la place vacante.

Greek Text-Books.

		Intro. Price.
Allen:	Medea of Euripides	$1.00
Flagg:	Hellenic Orations of Demosthenes	1.00
	Seven against Thebes	1.60
	Anacreontics	.35
Goodwin:	Greek Grammar	1.50
	Greek Reader	1.50
	Greek Moods and Tenses	1.50
	Selections from Xenophon and Herodotus	1.50
Goodwin & White:	Anabasis, with vocabulary	1.50
Harding:	Greek Inflection	.50
Keep:	Essential Uses of the Moods	.25
Leighton:	New Greek Lessons	1.20
Liddell & Scott:	Abridged Greek-English Lexicon	1.90
	Unabridged Greek-English Lexicon	9.40
Parsons:	Cebes' Tablet	.75
Seymour:	Selected Odes of Pindar	1.40
	Introd. to Language and Verse of Homer, Paper	.45
	Cloth	.60
Sidgwick:	Greek Prose Composition	1.50
Tarbell:	Philippics of Demosthenes	1.00
Tyler:	Selections from Greek Lyric Poets	1.00
White:	First Lessons in Greek	1.20
	Schmidt's Rhythmic and Metric	2.50
	Oedipus Tyrannus of Sophocles	1.12
	Stein's Dialect of Herodotus	.10
Whiton:	Orations of Lysias	1.00

College Series.

Beckwith: Euripides' Bacchantes.
  Text and Notes, Paper, .80; Cloth, $1.10; Text only, .20.
D'Ooge: Sophocles' Antigone.
  Text and Notes, Paper, .95; Cloth, $1.25; Text only, .20.
Dyer: Plato's Apology and Crito.
  Text and Notes, Paper, .95; Cloth, $1.25; Text only, .20.
Fowler: Thucydides, Book V.
  Text and Notes, Paper, .95; Cloth, $1.25; Text only, .20.
Humphreys: Aristophanes' Clouds.
  Text and Notes, Paper, .95; Cloth, $1.25; Text only, .20.
Manatt: Xenophon's Hellenica, Books I.-IV.
  Text and Notes, Paper, $1.20; Cloth, $1.50; Text only, .20.
Morris: Thucydides, Book I.
  Text and Notes, Paper, $1.20; Cloth, $1.50; Text only, .20.
Seymour: Homer's Iliad, Books I.-III.
  Text and Notes, Paper, .95; Cloth, $1.25; Text only, .20.
Smith: Thucydides, Book VII.
  Text and Notes, Paper, .95; Cloth, $1.25; Text only, .20.

Sanskrit.

Arrowsmith:	Kaegi's Rigveda, (*translation*)	$1.50
Elwell:	Nine Jatakas (*Pali*)	.60
Lanman:	Sanskrit Reader	1.80
Perry:	Sanskrit Primer	1.50
Whitney:	Sanskrit Grammar	2.50

Copies sent to Teachers for Examination, with a view to Introduction, on receipt of Introduction Price.

GINN & COMPANY, Publishers,
BOSTON, NEW YORK, AND CHICAGO.

Latin Text-Books.

		INTROD. PRICE.
ALLEN & GREENOUGH:	Latin Grammar	$1.12
	Cæsar (7 books, with vocabulary; illustrated)	1.25
	Cicero (13 orations, with vocabulary; illustrated)	1.25
	Sallust's Catiline	.60
	Cicero de Senectute	.50
	Ovid (with vocabulary)	1.40
	Preparatory Course of Latin Prose	1.40
	Latin Composition	1.12
ALLEN . . .	New Latin Method	.90
	Introduction to Latin Composition	.90
	Latin Primer	.90
	Latin Lexicon	.90
	Remnants of Early Latin	.75
	Germania and Agricola of Tacitus	1.00
BLACKBURN .	Essentials of Latin Grammar	.70
	Latin Exercises	.60
	Latin Grammar and Exercises (in one volume)	1.00
COLLAR & DANIELL:	Beginner's Latin Book	1.00
	Latine Reddenda (paper)	.20
	Latine Reddenda and Voc. (cloth)	.30
COLLEGE SERIES OF LATIN AUTHORS.		
	Greenough's Satires and Epistles of Horace (text edition) $0.20; (text and notes)	1.25
CROWELL . .	Selections from the Latin Poets	1.40
CROWELL & RICHARDSON:	Brief History of Roman Lit. (BENDER)	1.00
GREENOUGH .	Virgil:—	
	Bucolics and 6 Books of Æneid (with vocab.)	1.60
	Bucolics and 6 Books of Æneid (without vocab.)	1.12
	Last 6 Books of Æneid, and Georgics (with notes)	1.12
	Bucolics, Æneid, and Georgics (complete, with notes)	1.60
	Text of Virgil (complete)	.75
	Vocabulary to the whole of Virgil	1.00
GINN & CO. .	Classical Atlas and Geography (cloth)	2.00
HALSEY. . .	Etymology of Latin and Greek	1.12
KEEP . . .	Essential Uses of the Moods in Greek and Latin	.25
KING . . .	Latin Pronunciation	.25
LEIGHTON . .	Latin Lessons	1.12
	First Steps in Latin	1.12
MADVIG . .	Latin Grammar (by THACHER)	2.25
PARKER & PREBLE:	Handbook of Latin Writing	.50
PREBLE. . .	Terence's Adelphoe	.25
SHUMWAY . .	Latin Synonymes	.30
STICKNEY . .	Cicero de Natura Deorum	1.40
TETLOW . .	Inductive Latin Lessons	1.12
TOMLINSON .	Manual for the Study of Latin Grammar	.20
	Latin for Sight Reading	1.00
WHITE (J. W.)	Schmidt's Rhythmic and Metric	2.50
WHITE (J. T.)	Junior Students' Latin-English Lexicon (mor.)	1.75
	English-Latin Lexicon (sheep)	1.50
	Latin-English and English-Latin Lexicon (sheep)	3.00
WHITON . .	Auxilia Vergiliana; or, First Steps in Latin Prosody	.15
	Six Weeks' Preparation for Reading Cæsar	.40

Copies sent to Teachers for Examination, with a view to Introduction, on receipt of Introduction Price.

GINN & COMPANY, Publishers,
BOSTON, NEW YORK, AND CHICAGO.

Mathematics.[2]

		Introd. Prices.
Byerly	Differential Calculus	$2.00
	Integral Calculus	2.00
Ginn	Addition Manual	.15
Halsted	Mensuration	1.00
Hardy	Quaternions	2.00
Hill	Geometry for Beginners	1.00
Sprague	Rapid Addition	.10
Taylor	Elements of the Calculus	1.80
Wentworth	Grammar School Arithmetic	.75
	Shorter Course in Algebra	1.00
	Elements of Algebra	1.12
	Complete Algebra	1.40
	Plane Geometry	.75
	Plane and Solid Geometry	1.25
	Plane and Solid Geometry, and Trigonometry	1.40
	Plane Trigonometry and Tables. *Paper*	.60
	Pl. and Sph. Trig., Surv., and Navigation	1.12
	Pl. and Sph. Trig., Surv., and Tables	1.25
	Trigonometric Formulas	1.00
Wentworth & Hill:	Practical Arithmetic	1.00
	Abridged Practical Arithmetic	.75
	Exercises in Arithmetic	
	Part I. *Exercise Manual*	
	Part II. *Examination Manual*	.35
	Answers (to both Parts)	.25
	Exercises in Algebra	.70
	Part I. *Exercise Manual*	.35
	Part II. *Examination Manual*	.35
	Answers (to both Parts)	.25
	Exercises in Geometry	.70
	Five-place Log. and Trig. Tables (7 *Tables*)	.50
	Five-place Log. and Trig. Tables (*Comp. Ed.*)	1.00
Wentworth & Reed:	First Steps in Number, *Pupils' Edition*	.30
	Teachers' Edition, complete	.90
	Parts I., II., and III. (separate), each	.30
Wheeler	Plane and Spherical Trig. and Tables	1.00

Copies sent to Teachers for examination, with a view to Introduction, on receipt of Introduction Price.

GINN & COMPANY, Publishers.
BOSTON.   NEW YORK.   CHICAGO.

BOOKS ON ENGLISH LITERATURE.

Allen	Reader's Guide to English History	$ .25
Arnold . . .	English Literature	1.50
Bancroft . .	A Method of English Composition	.50
Browne . .	Shakespere Versification	.25
Fulton & Trueblood:	Choice Readings	1.50
	Chart Illustrating Principles of Vocal Expression,	2.00
Genung . .	Practical Elements of Rhetoric	1.25
Gilmore . .	Outlines of the Art of Expression	.60
Ginn	Scott's Lady of the Lake . . . *Bds.*, .35; *Cloth*,	.50
	Scott's Tales of a Grandfather . *Bds.*, .40; *Cloth*,	.50
Gummere .	Handbook of Poetics	1.00
Hudson . .	Harvard Edition of Shakespeare : —	
	20 Vol. Edition. *Cloth, retail*	25.00
	10 Vol. Edition. *Cloth, retail*	20.00
	Life, Art, and Character of Shakespeare. 2 vols.	
	Cloth, retail	4.00
	New School Shakespeare. *Cloth.* Each Play .	.45
	Old School Shakespeare, per play	.20
	Expurgated Family Shakespeare	10.00
	Essays on Education, English Studies, etc. . .	.25
	Three Volume Shakespeare, per vol.	1.25
	Text-Book of Poetry	1.25
	Text-Book of Prose	1.25
	Pamphlet Selections, Prose and Poetry . . .	.15
	Classical English Reader	1.00
Johnson . .	Rasselas . . . . *Bds.*, .30; *Cloth*,	.40
Lee	Graphic Chart of English Literature	.25
Martineau .	The Peasant and the Prince . . *Bds.*, .35; *Cloth*,	.50
Minto . . .	Manual of English Prose Literature	1.50
	Characteristics of English Poets	2.00
Rolfe	Craik's English of Shakespeare	.90
Scott	Guy Mannering . . . . . . *Bds.*, .60; *Cloth*,	.75
	Ivanhoe . . . . *Bds.*, .60; *Cloth*,	.75
	Talisman . . . . *Bds.*, .50; *Cloth*,	.60
	Rob Roy . . . . *Bds.*, .60; *Cloth*,	.75
Sprague . .	Milton's Paradise Lost, and Lycidas	.45
	Six Selections from Irving's Sketch-Book	
	Bds., .25; *Cloth*,	.35
Swift	Gulliver's Travels . . . . . . *Bds.*, .30; *Cloth*,	.40
Thom	Shakespeare and Chaucer Examinations . . .	.00

Copies sent to Teachers for Examination, with a view to Introduction,
on receipt of the Introduction Price given above.

GINN & COMPANY, Publishers,
Boston. New York, and Chicago.

www.ingramcontent.com/pod-product-compliance
Lightning Source LLC
Chambersburg PA
CBHW021202230426
43667CB00006B/522